Yorkshire Dales Trigpointing Walks

Hill walking with a point to it!

Keith Stevens

SIGMA

Published by Sigma Leisure – an imprint of
Sigma Press, Stobart House, Pontyclerc, Penybanc Road
Ammanford, Carmarthenshire SA18 3HP

British Library Cataloguing in Publication Data

A CIP record for this book is available from the British Library

ISBN: 978-1-85058-924-2

Typesetting and Design by: Sigma Press, Ammanford, Carmarthenshire

Maps and Photographs: © Keith Stevens

Cover photograph: The Weets pillar – looking west © Keith Stevens

Printed by: TJ International, Padstow, Cornwall

Disclaimer: The information in this book is given in good faith and is believed to be correct at the time of publication. Care should always be taken when walking in hill country. Where appropriate, attention has been drawn to matters of safety. The author and publisher cannot take responsibility for any accidents or injury incurred whilst following these walks. Only you can judge your own fitness, competence and experience. Do not rely solely on sketch maps for navigation: we strongly recommend the use of appropriate Ordnance Survey (or equivalent) maps.

Preface

The western and southern Dales with a difference! Find all the 41 Ordnance Survey triangulation pillars and you'll see the Yorkshire Dales from a completely new angle, including the famous 'Three Peaks' – Pen-y-ghent, Whernside and Ingleborough. The best walks, the most spectacular viewpoints, superb walking areas that you'd never have thought of; they're all part of the new rambler's pastime of 'Trigpointing'. Fresh challenges, new terrain, navigation, searching and exploring, getting to know the geography and geology; it's the complete walking experience.

You'll catch the bug. Once you've done the Western and Southern Dales, where else can you explore? Can you find 1000 pillars before you hang up your boots? You'll enjoy trying, and you'll seldom do the same walk twice. There are over 5000 of them still standing nationwide, so you have plenty to choose from, not least in the great British National Parks such as The Peaks, The Lakes and Snowdonia.

This book contains everything you need to be a Trigpointer, including information on the location co-ordinates of the pillars, their history and their triangulation. Their original purpose was to survey and map the country, and I show you how to spot all those surrounding pillars that are in sight from the one you've reached. Dally a while at the pillar, scan the landscape around you, get to know all the names and geographical features.

Whilst the pillars are the prime objectives, these walks also provide a complete experience, with historical landmarks and geological features included, supported by fascinating background information, history and folklore. Often, I throw in an additional challenge – to find some of the lower order OS marks and wall-brackets that litter the country.

There's a fascinating introduction; a concise summary of the Ordnance Survey history and how the triangulation and mapping was achieved, backed by an explanation of Global Positioning Satellite navigation, the British Grid co-ordinate system, longitude and latitude, compass bearings, and finding your way by the sun. You just can't go wrong!

There are 25 superb walks in this book, assembled in groups around four Yorkshire Dales towns – Skipton, Settle, Ingleton and Sedbergh – with the easy ones coming early to help you get in the swing. Go on, enjoy a week's trigpointing holiday at each centre, and then come back again and again until you've bagged all the pillars. Then it's onwards to the rest of the country!

Aknowledgement
I'd like to thank my friend and walking colleague Peter Whittaker for making such an excellent job of drawing all the route maps

Contents

Introduction

This book introduces the pastime of trigpointing, with 25 challenging walks in the Yorkshire Dales, each aimed at finding Ordnance Survey pillars. They're just pyramids of stone, nothing to right home about, but they're part of our heritage and worthy of our patronage. It's an excuse to get out in the fresh air and try out some new ground, with the objective of reaching the pillars adding a new dimension to the walking experience. And back home your can amuse yourself with a walker's log, recording the visits and assembling your photographs.

Fig 1. Ingleborough pillar – Yorkshire Dales

Nationwide there are over 6000 pillars, on average about 8km apart, so there are always plenty to visit in your area. Once you've bagged the local trigs you'll find yourself dreaming about travelling further a field and perhaps logging 1000 visits before hanging up your boots. Incredibly, there are walkers with more than 5000 visits under their belt.

The walks are for all ramblers, experienced or otherwise, some easy and others more challenging. A Global Positioning Satellite receiver (GPS) is helpful, both for navigation and to enhance the walking experience – programming in an objective and homing in on the target makes for great walking.

Each walk visits at least one triangulation pillar, but usually more, as well as taking in features of geological and historical interest. To help, there is a section on navigation, an important aspect of some of the walks.

The Ordnance Survey pillars

The network of 1.5m (4 ft) pillars was created between 1935 and 1962, each one topped by a 'spider' on which could be mounted a theodolite, an accurate compass and telescope. With each pillar built on a prominent point, and line-of-sight to nearby pillars, the shape of the country could be determined by measuring the angle from one pillar to another.

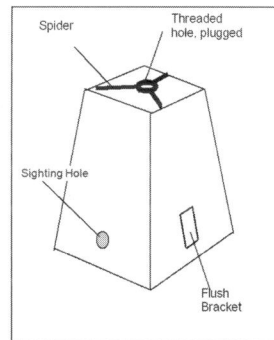

Fig 2 – Schematic of a pillar

As well as the spider, the top of the pillar has a threaded hole to accommodate a light. When not in use, that hole is plugged, so that most pillars today contain a screwed insert, usually with OS lettering. On the side of the pillar there is a metal plate called a flush-bracket, showing the OS number, and with a horizontal line and arrow that marks an accurately known height above sea level. Finally, under the pillar is a concrete platform bedded securely to the bedrock.

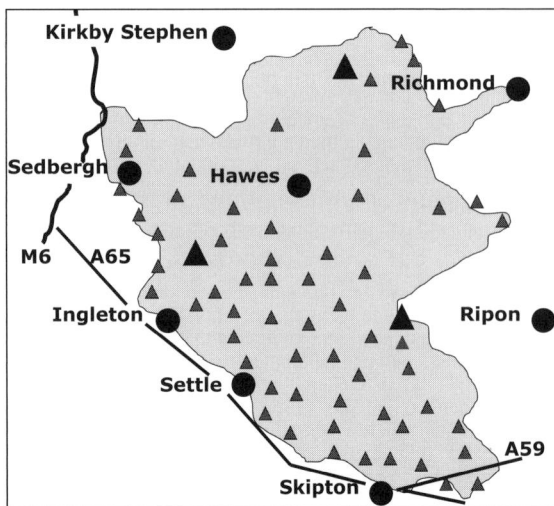

Fig 3. Pillars around the Yorkshire Dales – The three larger ones are primaries

The process of survey-ing is called 'triangulation', and it has created a network of accurate reference positions throughout the country, enabling the creation of the excellent OS maps that we enjoy today. They are the basis of the British National Grid system that is so easy to use.

The first 300 pillars were called 'primaries', covering the country from the most visible locations. There are three in the Yorkshire Dales – Whernside (west Dales), Great Whernside (east Dales) and Water Crag (NE Dales), as shown in Figure 3. The spaces between the primaries were afterwards filled with thousands of 'secondary' pillars to provide ever more comprehensive triangulation.

Who built them?

The Ordnance Survey gave the task of mapping the country to Captain Martin Hotine, head of the Trigonometrical and Levelling Division. His first decision was that all surveys should be from rigid platforms, so he commissioned the construction of the now famous pillars. He was determined to reduce uncertainty by ensuring that any survey from one point was always carried out under exactly the same conditions. The pillars provided a repeatable location, with a fixed height, and ensured that the theodolite could always be precisely levelled.

Starting in the south, he worked his teams of men, spreading his pillars across the country, building them on the spot. There were no helicopters to airlift them into position; men and mules had to haul large amounts of material across the most inhospitable terrain, the exact weight of cement, sand and chippings being laid down in the handbook. Hotine was certainly a hard taskmaster. It took 12 days in appalling weather to construct the pillar on Cadair Idris, and men shivered in the snow for 20 days on Ben Nevis before they could complete their edifice. However, there were some compromises. If there was good quality local stone at the site, pillars were occasionally put together as a cemented structure.

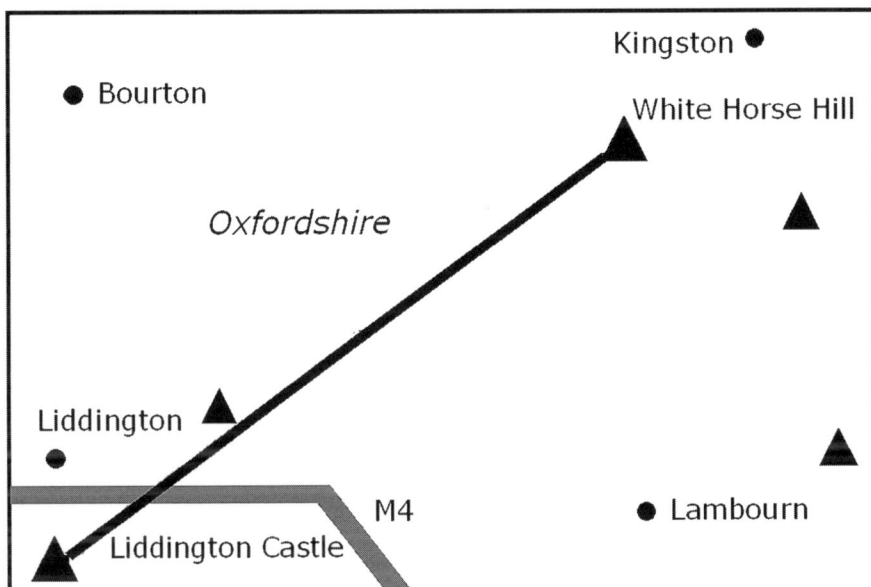

Fig 4. The Liddington Baseline

Hotine established his baseline on the Ridgeway path, creating two pillars, one at Liddington Castle and one to the NE on White Horse Hill. He called this the 'Liddington Baseline' (Figure 4), and accurately measured its length (11.256km) by using a long tape and a series of careful steps between the two pillars.

From that line he created his first triangle to a third pillar. Using night-time observations to avoid the distortions of the daytime heat-haze, he mounted lights on the pillars and focussed his theodolite on those from the other positions. His handbook was very clear; each compass bearing had to be measured 32 times and then averaged, regardless of the labour involved. And woe-betide any man caught fiddling the results to get home early!

Considering Figure 5, having measured side 'a' very precisely, and taken bearings from 'L' to 'W' and to the new pillar at 'X', angle 'B' is established. Repeating the steps from 'W', taking bearings to 'L' and 'X' gives angle 'C'.

After that, angle 'A' is known (180 – A – B). Now sides 'b' and 'c' can be computed by the ratios:

$$^a/_A = {}^b/_B = {}^c/_C$$

If the position of any one of the pillars (i.e. its longitude/latitude) is accurately determined by taking readings from the stars, then the positions of the other two can be computed. After that, sides 'b' and 'c' can each form a baseline for two new triangles, a principle that was repeated until the whole country had been covered.

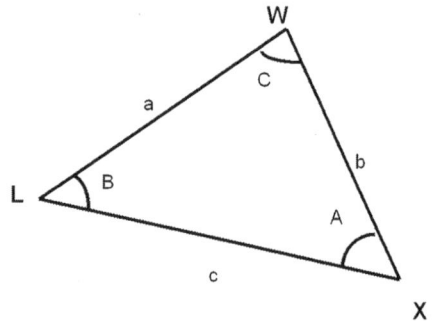

Fig 5. Triangulation

There were critics who said that errors would multiply and that distant positions would be inaccurate. To prove them wrong Hotine repeated an accurate tape measurement between two pillars in NE Scotland, as far from the baseline as he could get. Using a 30m tape it took his team 800 steps and 54 days to determine the true distance between the two Scottish pillars (about 25km apart), finding that his computed distance after all the successive triangulations was only 43cm different, less than a 0.002 per cent error.

By 1962 all the triangulations had been completed and the familiar maps that we use today were created. Whilst we are used to seeing the pillars on prominent peaks, the majority occupy less distinguished sites, and in some cases a pillar can be difficult to find, even when your GPS is telling you that you should be standing on it! Some are buried in hedges, others are in the middle of forests, the plantation having post-dated the pillar and grown around it. Fortunately, most of the Yorkshire Dales pillars are in clear view, but some, for instance 'Langcliffe' in Figure 6, are nearly buried.

So how many are left? Probably well over 5000. Some have fallen victim to road or housing developments, others to expanding

Fig 6. Langcliffe pillar – nearly buried

quarries, some to farmers' tractors and others to wanton vandalism. And many of the remaining pillars are showing the ravages of time, with frost and weather erosion chipping away at the fabric. But there are plenty to visit and to log, and we owe it to Captain Hotine to look after them as best we can.

Other Ordnance Survey relics

The pillars are only one aspect of the UK's Ordnance Survey history. Before them came a whole host of benchmarks, all aimed at determining the height above sea-level of fixed points around the country, enabling the drawing of contour maps and the accurate surveying for local engineering projects. The principle uses the technique of levelling, again employing a theodolite, determining the height difference between two close-by fixed points, and then repeating the measurements to other fixed points until the whole network

Fig 7. Cut-mark – a low-order benchmark

can be referred to one absolute 'zero' level, the mean sea level around our island. For that, the location chosen is Newlyn, where a bolt in the floor of the Tidal Observatory marks an exact measurement of 4.751 metres above mean sea-level.

The requirement is to have a permanent benchmark, one that can be visited again and be recorded as a known point on the ground. So the marks were made on structures that were not likely to be disturbed. Be it a horizontal engraved line, as in Figure 7, on the stonework of a church, or a bolt or rivet sunk into a rock, they were fixed points that could be detailed in the records.

The historical sequence of surveys

The motivation for the surveys was military, because good maps were needed for the successful defence of the country.

1840 - 1860	'First Geodetic Levelling', using engraved marks, bolts and rivets. ('Geodetic' means that the surveying took account of the Earth's curvature.)
1912 - 1921	'Second Geodetic Levelling', using numbered flush-brackets supported by more engraved marks.

1950 - 1968	'Third Geodetic Levelling', using flush-brackets and bolts, with more engraved marks and rivets.
1935 - 1962	Triangulation pillars, establishing accurate locations as well as heights.
1989 to now	GPS era, making most of the foregoing redundant. However, some pillars and bolts are used as 'passive stations', surveyed by GPS on a five-yearly basis.

The legacy of these surveys is that the country is littered with benchmarks, flush-brackets and pillars. It's not easy to translate them on to a map, but Figure 8 gives an example, around Hawes in the centre of the Dales, of just how many there are. The three triangles are the nearby triangulation pillars. The squares are bronze flush-brackets (Figure 9), following the main roads and generally attached to buildings. Finally, the circles are some of the cut-marks, rivets and bolts on buildings, posts, water-troughs, walls and bridges.

The second and third levelling exercises employed another type of pillar,

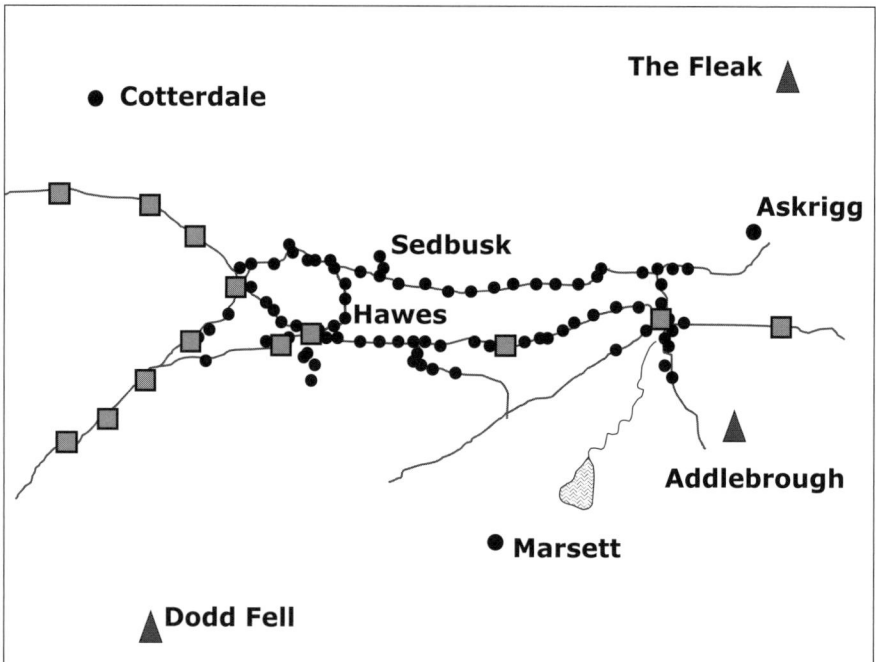

Fig 8. Benchmarks around Hawes

called 'Fundamental Benchmarks' (FBM – Figure 10). They were made in granite, and anchored on the most stable bedrock at 190 locations across the country. The height of a bolt in the top was determined very accurately, so that the pillars formed a precise network from which all the other benchmarks could be referenced. They were the nodes for a web of flush-brackets crisscrossing the country, comprising a series of 'primary lines'. Then the areas in between were surveyed with scores of 'secondary lines'.

The Yorkshire Dales area is crossed by a primary line of flush-brackets joining the FBMs at Kirkby Stephen, Ribblesdale and Skipton, with a secondary line branching off at Hawes. As shown in Figure 11, there are others around the perimeter. Some brackets have been lost, but there are still plenty to

Fig 9. Flush-bracket

Fig 10. Fundamental Benchmark

look for. (In Figure 11, the seven black squares are the local FBMs.)

Many of those FBMs still survive, but are usually in poor condition. The one at Skipton (Figure 12) is typical, looking neglected in its rusting cage enclosure behind a dilapidated wall down an undistinguished lane.

It is not clear what determined the choice of a particular benchmark, but it might simply have been that people objected to the engraving, perhaps on a church, and that a small bolt or rivet was considered less intrusive. Whatever the mark, it is clear from the most well preserved ones that a great deal of pride was invested in the engraving. The workmanship is exquisite, even on very porous materials like household brick.

So there are plenty of OS relics around the country, many difficult to find, and a determined Trigpointer can keep himself amused for years whilst

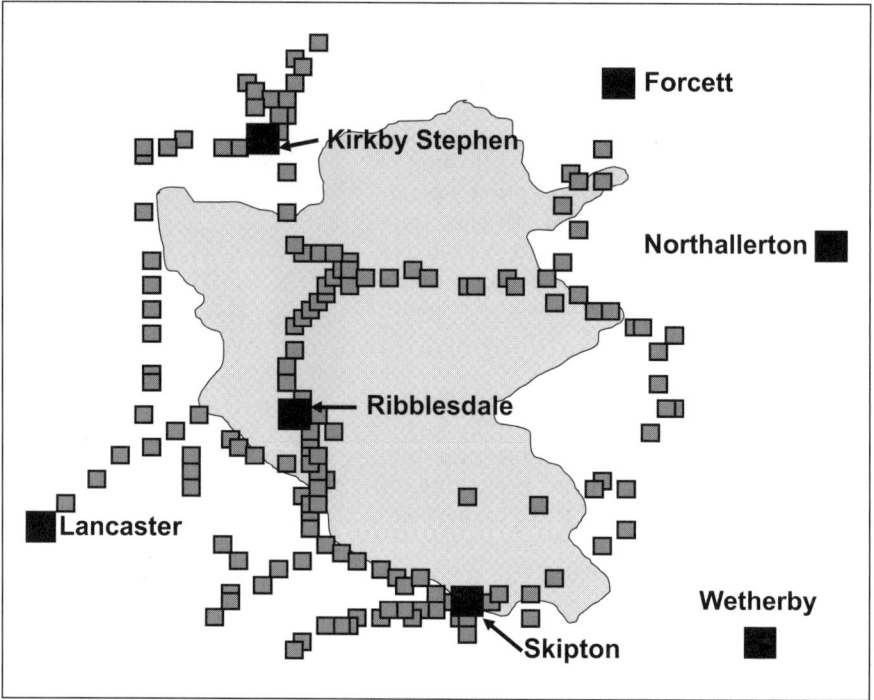

Fig 11. FBMs and flush-brackets around the Dales

enjoying hundreds of miles of splendid walking.

Navigation

Globally, navigation systems make use of longitude (circles all passing through the poles, with 'zero degrees' through Greenwich in London) and latitude (parallel circles around the globe, with 'zero degrees' at the equator and '90 degrees' at the poles). For walkers in the UK, the easier method is the familiar 'British Grid', a system that underpins our OS maps by breaking the country down into simple 100km squares.

Fig 12. Skipton FBM –
buried and forgotten

For the walks described in this book, there are two requirements for good navigation. One is out on the moors, crossing open-access land, targeting a distant point, and the other relates to unearthing the various benchmarks. For instance, the OS records relating to finding an old 'cut-mark' might read:

Methodist church, NW side of lane, E angle, NE face, 0.6m H, SE 0605 5935

That gives the British Grid position (in square 'SE') to within 10 metres or so, and says that the mark is engraved on the corner of the Methodist church stonework, the building being on the NW side of the lane. The mark is 0.6m from the ground, on the corner of the building that points east, and on the northeast face of that corner. So you need to know your northeast from your southwest, and you need to know how the British Grid system works.

The British Grid system

The system is centred on a line that that runs down the spine of the UK – the longitude line that is exactly two degrees west of the Greenwich zero, called the 'Central Meridian' – and on a base that follows the 49 degrees north latitude line. Technically, the true origin of the grid is 100km south of the intersection of those lines (Figure 13), but that would lead to confusing negative and positive co-ordinates for positions in the UK. So

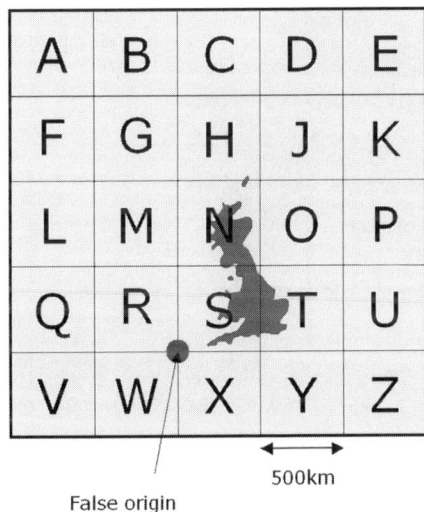

Fig 13. Setting the zero point for the grid

the origin (the 'false origin') is taken at a point 100km north and 400km west of the true origin, off the SW of the UK. From there, any point on the UK land has a unique positive east/north co-ordinate.

For instance, the church in Hubberholme in the centre of the Yorkshire Dales has the co-ordinates:

East 492560, North 478310 (metres)

That is 492.56km east and 478.310km north of the false origin, to within 100 metres.

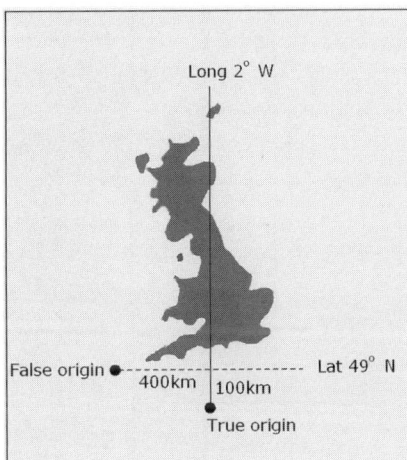

False origin

Fig 14. The matrix of 500km squares

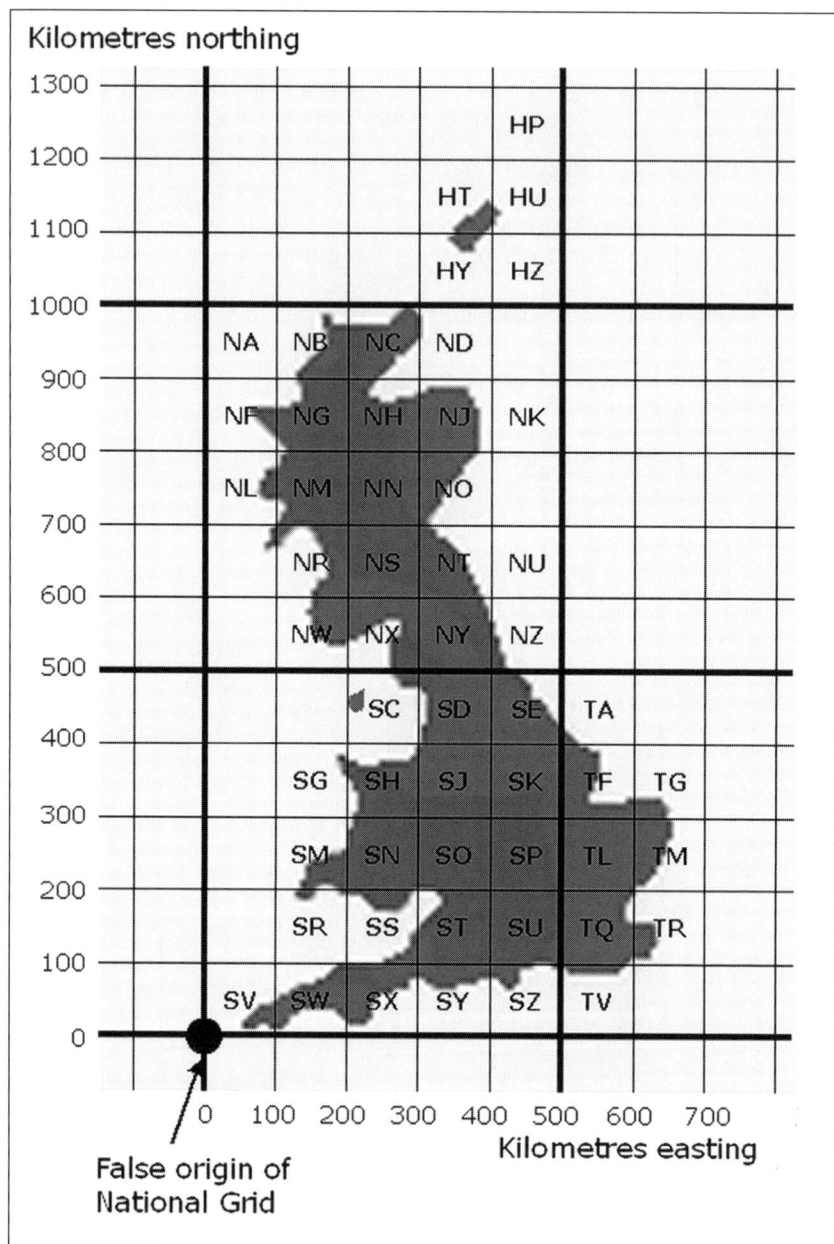

Fig 15. The system of 100km squares

However, they are big numbers, and the system can be further simplified by first subdividing the area into a matrix of 500km squares. Here, the principle is based on an old military grid square, following the letters of the alphabet (no 'I') as in Figure 14. On land we are interested in only the H, N, O, S and T squares, and those are then divided into the familiar 100km grid squares we see on the OS maps, as in Figure 15. So there are 25 smaller squares in each bigger one, again lettered from A to Z (again, no 'I') from top left to bottom right. In the Yorkshire Dales we are concerned mostly with the east side of square 'SD' and the west side of square 'SE', that is the 100km 'D' and 'E' squares within the bigger, 500km, 'S' square.

Now the co-ordinates are measured from the southwest corner of the square in which you are in, so that the church in Hubberholme becomes:

SD 92560 78310

where the convention is always to quote the easting first.

The four corners of the SD square are:

SW – SD 00000, 00000   NE – SD 99999, 99999
NW – SD 00000, 99999   SE – SD 99999, 00000

And, for instance, the northeast corner of square SD will be coincident with the southwest corner of square NZ, at NZ 00000, 00000.

Five numbers means, theoretically, that you're defining the position down to one metre. In practice, that's a false precision, since even GPS gives an uncertainty of more like 20 or 30 metres. Therefore, in this book, positions are quoted to only four figures (10 metres). Talking of GPS, here's an explanation of how it all works.

Global Position Satellite (GPS) system

A hand-held GPS comes as a huge revelation. It brings so much more than does a traditional compass, and can greatly add to the enjoyment of a walk. It receives signals from the orbiting satellites, and when it has locked on to sufficient numbers (three is a minimum), it can display your position and height. Then, by defining a 'waypoint' with specific co-ordinates, you can select that as a 'go-to' target and the receiver will display the direction to follow and the distance to your objective.

The equipment also allows you to plot a 'route', that is a sequence of waypoints, so that you can pre-programme the walk, the receiver automatically moving on to point to

Fig 16. Hand-held GPS receiver

the next waypoint as you progress. So the real enthusiast could load in all the co-ordinates beforehand, ready to lead his party around the walk in style.

The GPS will also compute your distance walked, your average speed, your time actually moving, your total time out, and allow you to 'mark' a spot as you walk. This last facility is useful for recording the exact co-ordinates of interesting features and, not least, the starting point of your walk. This then provides a ready answer to the most common question from your walking colleagues; "How far is it back to the car?"

Compass bearings

It is easy to take the old compass for granted, but a reminder of the principles will not go amiss. Starting with North, the direction you take, i.e. the 'bearing', is measured in degrees, rotating clockwise. So north is zero, east is 90 deg, south is 180 deg and west is 270 deg. It is a simpler concept, once you get to know it, than the compass point system. That relies on successively halving the angle between two directions to describe a new direction.

Direction	Bearing (deg)	Direction	Bearing (deg)
N	0/360	S	180
NNE	23	SSW	203
NE	45	SW	225
ENE	68	WSW	248
E	90	W	270
ESE	113	WNW	293
SE	135	NW	315
SSE	158	NNW	338

For instance, half way between north (N) and east (E) is 'northeast' (NE). Half way between N and NE is NNE (meaning north of northeast). And half way between N and NNE is NNNE (meaning north of north northeast). But half way between NNE and NE is ENNE (meaning east of north northeast). And so on, until your brain hurts! So, to help, the table summarises the main compass bearings in degrees.

Finding the direction by your watch

As a final string to your bow, you can easily navigate by the sun, provided that you can see it. Simply point the hour hand of your watch at the sun, and then south is halfway between the hour hand and the '12' on your dial. That's assuming it's Greenwich Mean Time (GMT). If it's British Summer Time (BST), then south is half way between the hour hand and the '1' on your dial.

Time		Direction of sun
GMT	**BST**	
6am	7am	E
9am	10am	SE
12 noon	1pm	S
3pm	4pm	SW
6pm	7pm	W

An easy table to remember

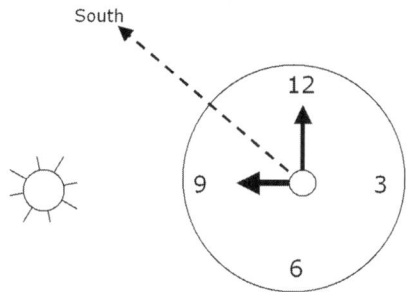

Fig 17. Finding your way by the sun

For instance, at 6am GMT the sun will be due east. If you point the hour hand at that, the '12' will be opposite, due west. And halfway is obviously due south. The example in Figure 16 is for 9am GMT.

The Yorkshire Dales pillars
A full and accurate list of UK pillars is not easy to come by, with some of the OS records being incomplete or lost in the mists of time. But, in this book, we are interested only in the 41 pillars in the western and southern Dales, as listed in the table below.

Nearly all the pillars are intact, even if some of them are damaged or eroded, and the only two that are missing are indicated as 'Mis'. The passive station (PS) and primary pillar (PRIM) is also indicated. The majority are in British Grid square SD, with the rest in SE. Not many are on private property, and those on the moors are accessible via open-access land under the 'Countryside and Rights of Way' Act (CROW), but sometimes with certain restrictions.

Name	Grid Ref	Height (m)	Name	Grid Ref	Height (m)
Aye Gill Pike	SD 72067 88613	557	Low Green Field Lings	SD 83834 80881	501
Beamsley Beacon	SE 09888 52434	393	Parson's Pulpit (Mis)	SD 91839 68748	538
Blea Moor	SD 77264 82584	536	Newton Moor	SD 85835 58744	292
Calf Top	SD 66447 85634	610	New Pasture Edge	SD 01383 66375	396
Calton	SD 91717 59837	275	North Nab	SE 08471 56428	319
Cave Hill	SD 80378 77850	285	Park Fell	SD 76447 76965	564
Cow Close	SD 88453 72795	624	Pen-y-ghent	SD 83853 73383	695
Crag Hill	SD 69212 83319	683	Sharp Law	SD 95948 55270	357
Crookrise	SD 98749 55883	415	Rye Loaf	SD 86421 63313	547
Gragareth Fell	SD 67891 79306	627	Langerton Hill	SD 04172 62205	278
Great Knout berry Hill	SD 78860 87157	672	Simon's Seat	SE 07891 59808	485
Halton Height	SE 03091 55262	357	Smearsett Scar	SD 80248 67805	363
Haw Crag	SD 91336 56471	207	Sulber	SD 78749 73879	349
Holme Knott	SD 64601 89530	350	Swinden (Mis)	SD 97636 61153	291
Hunter Bark	SD 82638 61045	315	The Calf	SD 66733 97055	677
Ingleborough	SD 74119 74559	724	The Weets	SD 92568 63202	414
Kilnsey Moor	SD 95174 66060	450	Thorpe Fell	SE 00850 59689	506
Knowe Fell	SD 86629 68551	593	Tow Scar	SD 68469 76003	383
Langcliffe	SD 83372 64226	440	Whernside (Prim & PS)	SD 73849 81414	736
East Baugh Fell	SD 73133 91938	676	Winder Hill	SD 65393 93272	474
Moughton	SD 78683 71185	428			

Pillars in the western and southern Dales

The Walks

For each walk I've indicated the start and parking facilities, the route and its degree of difficulty, including the distance, total ascent, climbing gradients and estimated walking time. Those are based on an average speed of about 2.5 km/hour (1.7 miles/hour) and allow for extra time at the pillars. The 41 pillars are discussed in terms of their history and condition, as well as the line-of-sight to each of the nearby pillars. Where possible, I describe interesting geographical and historical features to make the day a complete experience. The walks are divided into groups, with a specific town nominated as a base for each area, and I've tried to avoid driving long distances on single-track roads to reach the start points. Ideally, you would do the walks in order so that the changing viewpoints unfold in a logical sequence.

In the Dales, the pillars are quite widely spaced, and it has not always been possible to fit two pillars into a sensible circular walk. So some walks are shorter, to one pillar, with a suggestion that two such visits might be undertaken either side of lunch, with a brief car journey to the second starting point.

I suggest the use of a GPS, and provide the important waypoints that define the route. And for those walkers who prefer a compass I give the accurate bearings needed to negotiate the more difficult sections of the walks. This particularly applies when moving off established paths across open-access land. A compass is also useful when reaching each pillar, so that all the nearby pillars can be identified. However, for every pillar there is information about the direction of an easily identifiable landmark to help you. There is also a 'star' drawing showing the distance and bearing of all the nearby pillar sites that are in view (up to about 10km), with an added description of the landscape around you. It's suggested that you place the book on top of the pillar and orientate the page so that the star map lines up with the surrounding features. A pair of binoculars will help pick them out, and an OS map will provide you with hill names and positions to cross-reference with my description. As always, clear visibility makes all the difference to your enjoyment, but it particularly applies to these walks where one objective is to scan right round the horizon and to get to know the topography. A digital camera, zooming in and looking for the pillars, is also useful.

All the walks are on established rights of way, open-access areas or unmarked routes that are well used and accepted concessionary paths. For the few pillars that are on private land I've provided information on how to approach them, asking permission if necessary. There is some road walking, mostly on quiet lanes. If an area is open-access, but with some restrictions, I provide the relevant information in the walk description. Usually, on grouse moor, those restrictions will forbid dogs at any time of the year.

A useful website to consult about access rights and restrictions is:
http://www.naturalengland.org.uk/

Route sketches

Each walk has a hand-drawn route sketch and height profile, produced by observations on the ground and by using a GPS to record a sequence of waypoints and elevations. Whilst every effort has been made to ensure that the sketches are a good representation of the walks, they cannot be used as your sole walking guide. It is important that you take a good quality Ordnance Survey map, preferably with a 25 000 to 1 scale, and that time is spent before the walk matching the route to the official map. If you have the facility, it can also be useful to view the area on Google Earth™ before you leave home.

Where relevant, I've added key grid-references for critical points on the route, and included a summary table of waypoints and compass bearings at the end of each walk description. Ideally, you would program that sequence of waypoints into a GPS as a 'route'. The walks can be followed without a GPS, but a quality OS map and good map-reading skills would then be doubly important.

Many of the walks pass by old OS benchmarks, and an additional challenge to find them is thrown in. They are indicated on the route sketches as open triangles. In the walk text there is just enough information to guide your search, so that their discovery is not made too easy. Should you get stuck, there is a table of more detailed directions provided at the end of each walk.

Units of distance

The walks are described in kilometres (km) and metres (m), with some conversions to miles and feet where it is helpful. OS maps are laid out in 1km squares, and the British Grid system is based on metres, so for walks that make use of a GPS and British Grid co-ordinates it is best to employ the metric system. When judging walking distances, one yard and one metre can be regarded as equivalent, and 1.6km = 1 mile. So a 10 mile walk is 16km.

Safety

Any walk can bring hazards, even on established paths, and some of the routes are across open moor, with challenging terrain. Be extra cautious, don't rush, and carefully judge the ground in front. Peat or grass moor presents some particular hazards, as streams can undercut the surface, leaving fragile overhangs or bridges. Heather moor is hard walking, with a risk of unseen bog holes or gullies beneath the undergrowth. They might not be deep, but they come as a nasty surprise.

Do not walk alone. On some of the walks, particularly in less than ideal weather, you may not meet any other ramblers, so an accident could leave you in difficulty. In an emergency, use your mobile phone to dial 999, asking for 'mountain rescue'. But remember that it is for emergencies only, not to help find your way if you are lost. Finally, make sure you have enough daylight to complete the walk, with a bit to spare for unforeseen delays.

Country code
Respect the country code at all times; take your litter home, close gates, don't abuse fences or walls, keep to the path wherever possible and do not alarm grazing stock or free-range birds, especially with dogs. If you do find yourself on private land, and you are challenged, be polite and apologetic, and comply gracefully with any requests to move on.

Be cautious of farming stock. On established paths, farmers have certain obligations, for instance not to endanger walkers with unpredictable animals such as a lone bull. But if walking on private land (even with permission), be aware that those same obligations will not apply. Some of the walks are across long stretches of open moor. In very dry weather the risk of fire is serious; be extra vigilant, don't smoke.

Finally, on open-access land you can climb a gate or a wall to reach a new area, but you must cause no damage. Ideally, you will always look for a stile or gate that opens.

Equipment
I suggest the following equipment is essential.

- Good sized rucksack
- Good quality walking boots, with spare socks. Also, take spats and waterproof over-trousers for wet conditions
- Waterproof and windproof jacket, and a fleece for winter conditions
- In hot summer conditions, a hat for head protection
- In winter conditions, a balaclava to protect your face. Also, gloves and at least one walking pole
- Spare clothing, such as shirt and underwear
- Adequate food, and particularly water. Beware of dehydration during hot summer conditions
- First-aid kit, and survival bag for emergency use
- Good maps, a clear route plan, your GPS, fully charged, a compass and a mobile phone
- Whistle and torch.

Finally, inform friends or family where you are planning to walk and your likely return time.

Distribution of the walks

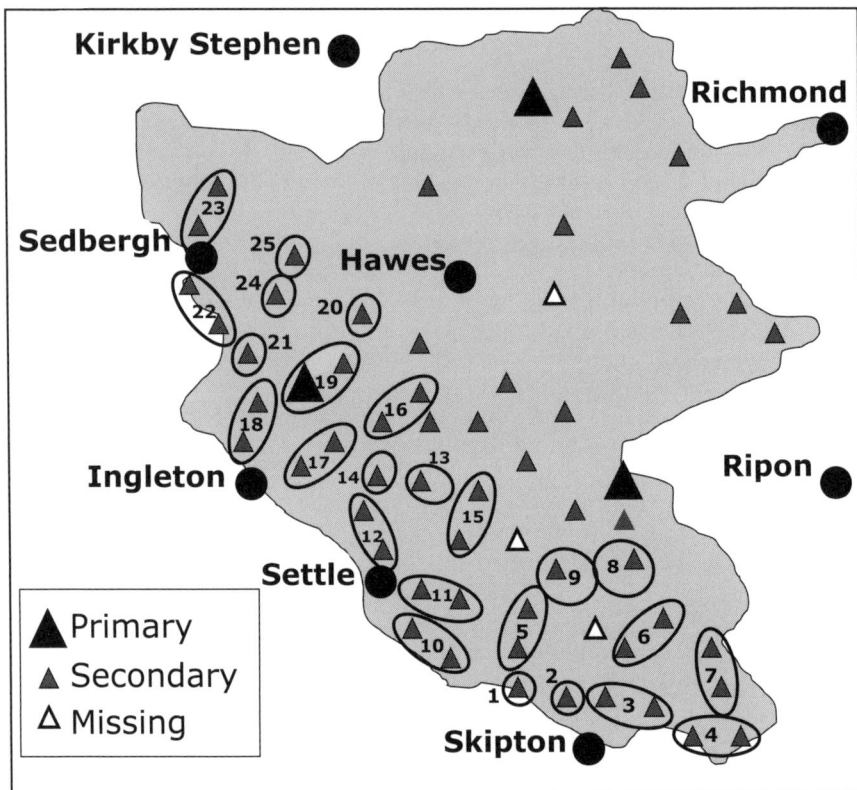

No	Pillars visisted	No	Pillars visited
1	Haw Crag	14	Sulber
2	Sharp Haw	15	Knowe Fell and Cow Close Fell
3	Crookrise and Halton Height	16	Cave Hill and Low Green Field Lings
4	Beamsley Beacon	17	Park Fell and Ingleborough
5	Calton and Weets	18	Gragareth Fell and Tow Scar
6	Thorpe Fell and Langerton Hill	19	Blea Moor and Whernside
7	North Nab and Simon's Seat	20	Great Knoutberry Hill
8	NewPasture Edge	21	Crag Hill
9	Kilnsey Moor	22	Holme Knott and Calf Top
10	Newton Moor and Hunter Bark	23	Winder and The Calf
11	Langcliffe and Rye Loaf	24	Aye Gill Pike
12	Smearsett Scar and Moughton	25	East Baugh Fell
13	Pen-y-ghent		

Walk Grading

These walks are graded as follows:

Easy: On established paths, with a relatively short distance and modest total ascent.

Moderate: On established paths, around 14km distance and up to a 500m total ascent.

Strenuous: Generally longer than 16km, and/or with greater than a 500m total ascent, but mostly using established paths.

Difficult: Involving off-path walking across difficult terrain, such as peat bog, wet grass moor or deep heather moor. Distance and ascent may be in the 'moderate' category, but a 'difficult' walk will also be 'strenuous'.

Key to Walks

〰〰〰	Route on road or track	🌲🌲	Deciduous woodland
– – ➤	Route over moor or pasture		
··········	Other paths	🌲 🌲	Evergreen woodland
::::::::::	Other tracks		
▭▭▭	A Road	⣿⣿⣿	Limestone pavement
▬▬▬	B Road		
• • • • •	Tunnel	⏤⏥⏤	Hill or summit
╬╬╬●╬╬╬	Railway and station		
═ ═ ═	Disused railway	▒▒▒	Steep edge, with scree
▬▮▬	Canal and lock		Wet or marshy area
⌐Ⱶ⌐	River, with bridge	▬▬	Rocky outcrops
⠿⠿⠿	Wall		
— · — · — ·	Fence	▰▰	Major rock formation
▪	Building	▲	Triangulation pillar
★	Cairn	△	OS benchmark
▯	Point of interest	■	Fundamental Benchmark
⦂⦂	Bell Pit or Sink Hole		

Part B. Walks based around Skipton

Skipton (meaning 'sheep town') is described as 'The gateway to the Dales'. It's a reasonable claim, with easy access via the A65 and A59 trunk roads, and with the B6265 and B6160 (from Bolton Bridge, east along the A59), providing good routes into the heart of the southern fells. For accommodation and camping consult the town web site at www.skiptonweb.co.uk. It's comprehensive and informative.

The centrepiece in the town is undoubtedly the castle, with 900 years of history, superbly preserved and with instructive guided tours. There is also a museum (Skipton High Street), exhibiting artefacts that reflect the local history and geology. It's well worth a visit. And for an enjoyable day out, a short trip to Embsay allows you to ride on the Embsay and Bolton Abbey Steam Railway, with a pleasant walk to the Abbey at the far end.

There are nine walks centred on Skipton, visiting 13 pillars:

1 Haw Crag	6 Thorpe Fell and Langerton Hill
2 Sharp Haw	7 North Nab and Simon's Seat
3 Crookrise and Halton Height	8 New Pasture Edge
4 Beamsley Beacon	9 Kilnsey Moor
5 Calton and Weets	

Since Walks 1 and 2 can be managed in one day, as can Walks 8 and 9, a week in Skipton should provide enough time for all the visits, as well as some sightseeing. On the way from Skipton to Walk 6 you might also stop off near Cracoe on the B6265 to visit the area of the pillar called 'Swinden' (SD 97636 61153) that was lost to the quarrying in 1985. Park off-road at SD 9854 6236 and use the track north of the quarry to get near to the old site.

Two of the walks use the B6160 from Bolton Abbey, east of Skipton, so there's an opportunity to visit the ruined priory. It offers a pleasant few hours of relaxed entertainment, with history and folk-law to absorb. And closer to Barden Bridge (Walk 7), there is the Barden Tower and the Priest House to explore.

Skipton is overflowing with OS Benchmarks – too many to go searching for. From the second and third geodetic levelling exercises, the three lines of flush-brackets joining Skipton with Greetland, Ribblesdale, and Wetherby all come through the town. So, within 1km of the town centre, there are five you could look for, as well as the end-point of all the lines, the Skipton Fundamental Benchmark.

Name of flush-bracket	Number	Location	Grid reference
Town Hall	989	SW face of Town Hall. (I couldn't find this one.)	SD 9904 5180
The Bailey	1466	SE face of wall, opposite SE end of Skipton Church, NW side of The Bailey	SD 9908 5189
Drill Hall	2289	NE angle of Drill Hall (ex Armoury House), junction of Otleystreet, North side of street, east face.	SD 9925 5172
Wilderness Beck	2290	NW parapet of bridge over Wilderness Beck, NE end of Otley Road. (I couldn't find this one either.)	SD 9988 5206
Railway Bridge	988	West face of abutment of north side of railway bridge, east side of Keithley Road	SD 9883 5091
Skipton Fundamental Benchmark	None	Skipton Road (a lane) 320m north off The Bailey, west side of lane, behind a wall, after a tree-lined bend.	SD 9960 5250

The FBM is listed as a Passive Station (part of the GPS fixed reference network), but the OS records show only that it was last visited in September 1999 and that no position or height measurements were recorded. Certainly, the pillar looks neglected and forlorn, so the OS may have written it off.

As you explore the town, there are more than 100 lower-order benchmarks that you could stumble across. Look at banks, pubs, churches and public buildings, as well as shops; you're bound to notice some, especially the cut-marks. Perhaps the most interesting one is on the Old Toll House (SD 9975 5144 – 250m SE of the railway bridge) on Shortbank Road (SE off Newmarket Street). Notice how the building has windows all round, so the toll-keeper could see the carriages coming from both directions.

Shortbank Road is part of the old Turnpike road between Ilkley and Skipton, opened in 1755. If you walk SE up the hill it changes into a steeply rising walled track. (You could follow it if you like, and visit the pillar on Skipton Moor – called 'Vicars Allotment' – SE 01405 50911.)

The Old Toll House

The word 'Turnpike' refers to pikes embedded in the embankments either side of the road, so that it was impossible for the coachman to turn round or go cross-country to avoid the toll. And imagine the coaches careering down the steep hill, with the tollgate barring their way at the bottom. Apparently, many a traveller emerged from the coach ashen-faced, only too willing to take the air and pay the money.

Walk 1. Haw Crag

Start:	Car park, North Street, Gargrave
Map reference:	SD 9322 5434
Distance:	9.7km (6.1 miles)
Total ascent:	155m (510 ft) – average climbing gradient 1 in 16
Estimated time:	3.5 hours
Walk grading:	Easy
OS map:	Landranger 103

Walk summary

The route follows an easy circuit from Gargrave, using quiet lanes, a meadow path by the river and a canal towpath. It's suitable for any weather and it could be fitted either side of lunch with Walk 2. There are nine benchmarks to find.

Parking and access

Take the A65 from Skipton into the centre of Gargrave (meaning 'The copse in a triangular piece of land'), turning right into North Street at the point where the main road turns sharp left. The free car park is then 200m on the right.

The walk

Walk north along West Street, to cross over the canal. See if you can find the cut-mark (BM No 1) somewhere on the bridge – it's dangerously close to the water. (In all the walk write-ups, the BMs are indicated as open triangles on the route map, and there's a table of accurate directions at the end if you have problems.)

After the bridge it's easy, quiet walking NW along Mark House Lane, part of the Pennine Way, tarmac at first and eventually a stony bridleway. After 2.4km there is the first view of the Haw Crag hill to the NW, and after another 400m the track turns sharp left, with the Crag Laithe farm buildings to the fore (meaning 'Barn by the rocky outcrop'). Turn right there, through the gate, following the grass path to the SE of the pillar summit and round the back for the easiest approach.

It looks like an old quarry. But, because of the ancient name 'Haw Crag' (meaning 'view from the rocky outcrop'), it is more likely to be natural, perhaps a collapsed cavern in the limestone rock. The geology here is on the boundary between the Carboniferous Limestone that characterises the central and western Dales and the coarse Millstone Grit of the southeast area.

The pillar is sound, with an original plug, and the flush-bracket faces NE, towards the quarry (with its missing pillar) at Swindon. With binoculars, you

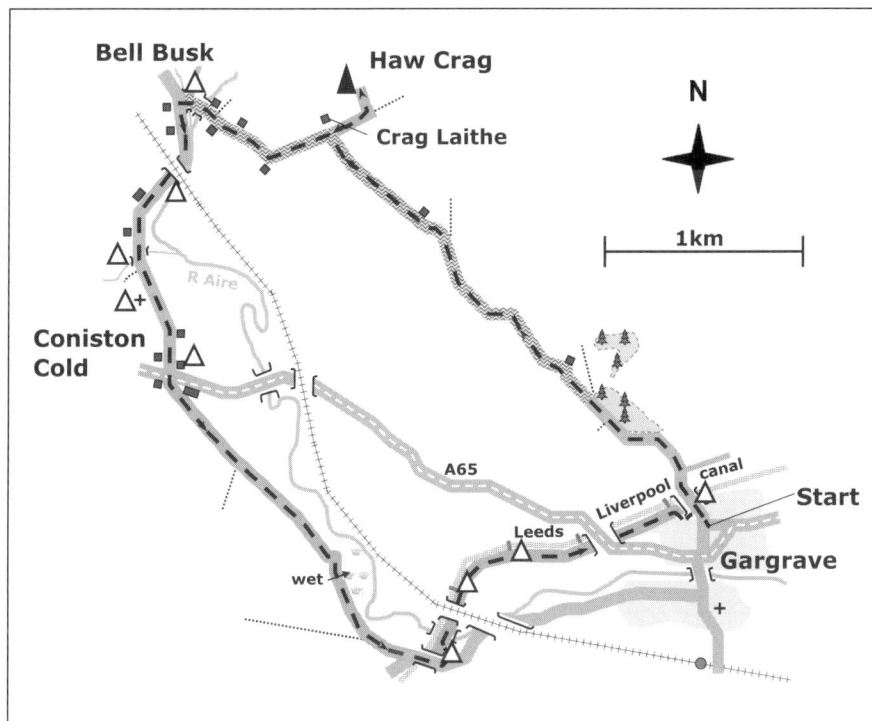

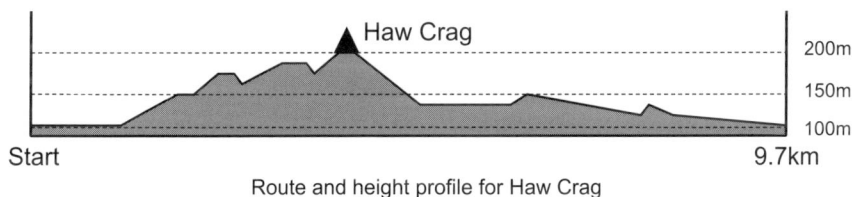

Route and height profile for Haw Crag

can just see the green, un-quarried side of the hill. ENE, the obelisk on Watt Crag (Cracoe Fell) is clear, and east, Sharp Haw (with its pillar) is close, with Rough Haw left of it. Then the tree-covered Crookrise is left again and behind Rough Haw, its pillar close to a bush. (As always, place the open book on the pillar and line up the star map, and have your OS map to hand to help spot the various features.)

SSE, looking over the rocky hole immediately by your feet, Elslack Moor is the gentle hill on the horizon. It's too far to spot the pillar. Then Mickleber Hill is the close-by green hill, crossed by a wall, more or less on the same bearing, but low, so that the pillar is hard to spot. (It's there – I visited it.)

Pillar details for Haw Crag	
Name:	Haw Crag
Position:	SD 91336 56471
Flush-Bracket No:	S5308
Height:	207m (679 ft)
Built:	March 1949
Historic use:	Secondary
Current use:	None
Condition:	Good

Haw Crag pillar – from the south

SW, 19km distant, the profile of Pendle Hill (of witches fame) is unmistakeable. Left of that line, SSW, Thornton is a low green hill, with a mast close by. I could see the mast, but not the pillar. Then SW, in line with the west edge of Pendle, Flambers Hill, with its pillar against a wall, is another low green hill. I could just make it out.

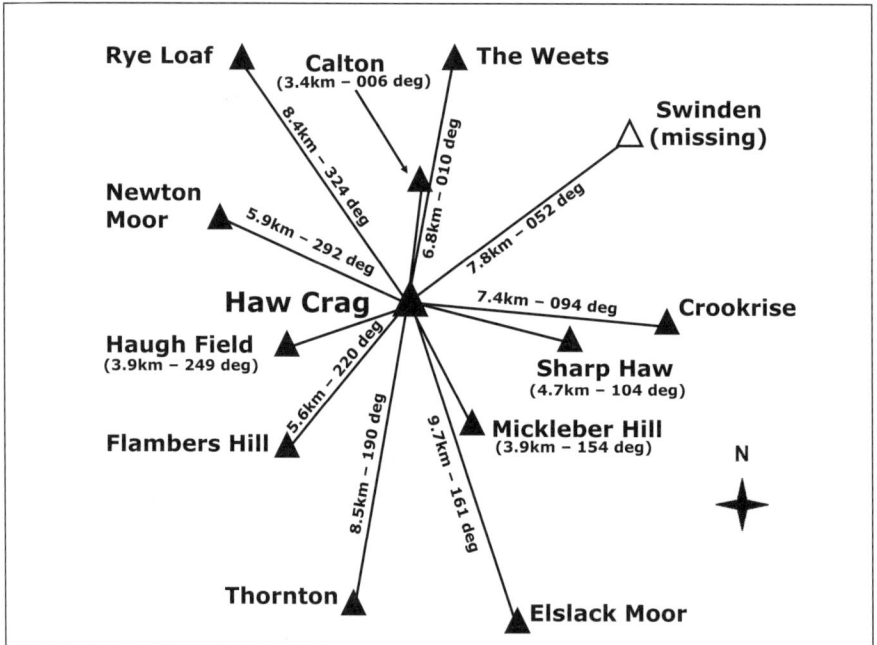

Nearby pillars in view from Haw Crag

WSW, the pillar on Haugh Field is unmistakeable. It's a green hill with a wide swathe of trees to the fore. WNW, Newton Moor is the brown-coloured hill left of a large area of trees (pillar just visible) and NW, Rye Loaf (with a cairn, and pillar behind) is the central peak of the range forming the horizon. Finally, just east of north, The Weets is on the left hand of the two brown hills, the one with a 'nick' in the middle and with a path going up to it. Its pillar is against a wall, right of the 'nick'. Then, just west of that bearing, Calton (a straw-coloured grass moor hill) is closer and lower, but very difficult to make out.

From the pillar, retrace your steps to the track and continue WSW and then NW, eventually passing an ancient boundary marker stone opposite the 'Airebridge' property. Soon after, the track becomes a tarmac lane as it approaches the bridge itself, over the River Aire. Then it is the second bridge, near the lane junction, over Otterburn Beck, where you can look for another cut-mark (BM No 2).

Go left (south) down the Airton lane, towards Coniston Cold ('The king's farm, exposed to the cold'), following the river. It's quiet, pleasant walking and you can look for BM No 3 somewhere on the railway viaduct as you pass beneath it. Then BM No 4 is on the bridge parapet crossing a small stream (Syke Gill) that joins the Aire. That one could be difficult – I had to remove a lot of moss to find it. BM No 5 is on the church at the top of the hill, and then,

Expectant sheep? – I had nothing to offer (Pendle Hill behind)

as you arrive at the main road in Coniston Cold, the very faint BM No 6 is somewhere on the building at the NE corner of the junction.

Cross the A65 and follow the tarmac drive on the opposite side. After 250m, as it veers sharp right, leave the lane to squeeze through the impossibly narrow kissing gate and then follow the field path alongside the dilapidated wall. It eventually leads to open pasture, with the footpath arrows always clearly pointing the way. There is a wall stile, then two wooden stiles either side of a very boggy area around a pond by the river. After that the path follows the river, seldom more than 100m from the bank, goes through a gate, crosses a gully and follows a fence up to the lane bridge over the canal.

The gate leading down to the towpath is at the SE corner of the bridge. Once below, spot BM No 7 on the bridge. Then as you walk on along the canal, look for the cut-mark (BM No 8) on bridge No 169 by Stegneck Lock (Lock No 35). It's unusual on these walks to follow a canal, and this one, the 'Leeds and Liverpool', has a distinguished history. Built during the period 1773 to 1816, it is England's longest, and in its heyday was used to move coal and stone in huge quantities. Unlike many canals it fought hard against

There's always a pair waiting to be feed

the railways, and it was the coal-carrying lorries that finally relegated it to the leisure use that we see today, evident all along the walk back to Gargrave.

500m on from BM No 8, BM No 9 is on Scarland Lock (Lock No 34). It's a rivet, right on the edge after the most easterly of the gates, with a dangerous drop into the lock. Why put it there? How many OS stonemasons drowned trying to hammer rivets into places like that, I wonder?

The next lock is 350m on. Before it, you'll see a stack of boards, and you'll also see the slot in the edging stonework just before the gates where they are dropped in to make a dam. But after they've drained, cleaned and repaired a section, how do they get the boards out again, with all that water leaning on them? That's what I want to know. Anyway, from there it's another 800m along the towpath and back to the car, with a chance to feed the ducks on the way.

Route summary for Walk 1

Your present location	Your next objective	Waypoint at next objective	Directions and distance
Car park, North Street SD 9322 5434	Lane goes left by Crag Laithe. Go right on path	SD 9121 5627	NNW along West Street (one BM to find), then NW on Mark House Lane – 2.9km
SD 9121 5627	Haw Crag pillar	SD 9134 5647	NE and NW around the crag – 350m
SD 9134 5647	Crag Laithe	SD 9121 5627	Retrace your steps to Crag Laithe – 350m
SD 9121 5627	Tee-junction Bell Busk	SD 9045 4648	WSW and NW on Mark House Lane, one BM to find – 900m
SD 9045 5648	Main road at Coniston Cold	SD 9037 5509	Generally south on the Airton lane, four BMs to find – 1.5km
SD 9037 5509	Canal bridge on Marton Road	SD 9176 5376	SE on posted meadow path, close to river – 2km
SD 9176 5376	Canal bridge on West Street	SD 9313 5440	Generally NE along the canal, three BMs to find – 1.6km
SD 9313 5440	Car park, North Street	SD 9322 5434	SSE on North Street – 100m

Benchmark summary for Walk 1

BM No	Type of Benchmark and location	Grid reference
1	Bolt – NE face of base of Higher Land Bridge, SE side of canal. (At water's edge, on the arch – cut-mark is there, but the bolt – normally at the point of the arrow – is not clear.)	SD 9312 5439
2	Cut-mark – Parapet of Red Bridge, 5.9m east of road junction, north side of road, centre of bridge	SD 9042 5642
3	Cut-mark – SW end face of Bell Busk viaduct, SE side of road – may be overgrown	SD 9040 5605
4	Cut-mark – Post at end of parapet of Gill Syke Bridge, 3.4m south of stream centre, west side of road	SD 9019 5564
5	Cut-mark – St Peters Church, centre of east face, below the stained glass window	SD 9029 5537
6	Cut-mark – Church Close Farm, SW angle, south face	SD 9036 5504
7	Cut-mark – NE face of bridge arch, SE side of canal, near water's edge	SD 9176 5372
8	Cut-mark – Stegneck Bridge, NE face of arch, SE side of canal, near water's edge	SD 9185 5397
9	Rivet – South side of Scarland Lock, 0.9m east of easterly lock gates, south face, right on the edge	SD 9216 5415

Walk 2. Sharp Haw

Start:	Roadside pull-off on Bog Lane
Map reference:	SD 9752 5393
Distance:	6.3km (3.9 miles)
Total ascent:	240m (790 ft) – average climbing gradient 1 in 12
Estimated time:	2.5 hours
Walk grading:	Easy
OS map:	Landranger 103

Walk summary

The route follows a track from Bog Lane into Crag Wood, before turning back on a path though the trees to reach the open-access area around the pillar. Return is via a grass track across rough pasture. There are no benchmarks, and the walk could be fitted either side of lunch with Walk 1.

Parking and access

From the A59 west of Skipton, take the A65 NW from the roundabout. Turn right after 200m and follow Bog Lane through Stirton and past a hotel and caravan complex. The lane then turns sharp left, sharp right, left again and finally right. There is roadside parking on that second right-hand bend.

The walk

Go though the gate and follow the limestone drive, keeping left after the first cattle grid. The drive goes first NW, then west and finally SW into Crag Wood, part of the Flasby Estate. On the way, 350m on from the car, after the second cattle grid, you'll pass a bridleway fingerpost on the right. It's to there that you will return after visiting the pillar.

The track through the forest is pleasant walking, with good views into the Aire valley, with the river and the Leeds-Liverpool canal, and SW to Pendle Hill (with its flat top, 22km away). The area is not open-access, but is well walked, with stiles and notices that confirm the concession. Most of the time the trees are sparse, having been extensively harvested, and there is also a good view north to the Skyrakes crag.

At SD 9617 5421 the track divides into three. Keep right, going uphill, with a denser area of trees to the fore. After 1.7km the track turns sharp left (SD 9523 5545), with a wide path leaving SW just after the apex of the bend. Follow that for only 30m, then turn NW uphill, amongst the bushes, to reach a clearing (SD 9529 5554) after another 70m, where there is a fingerpost to Flasby and Stirton.

From the clearing cut back SE (not signposted to anywhere on the fingerpost) and follow the path as it zigzags up through the undergrowth. For

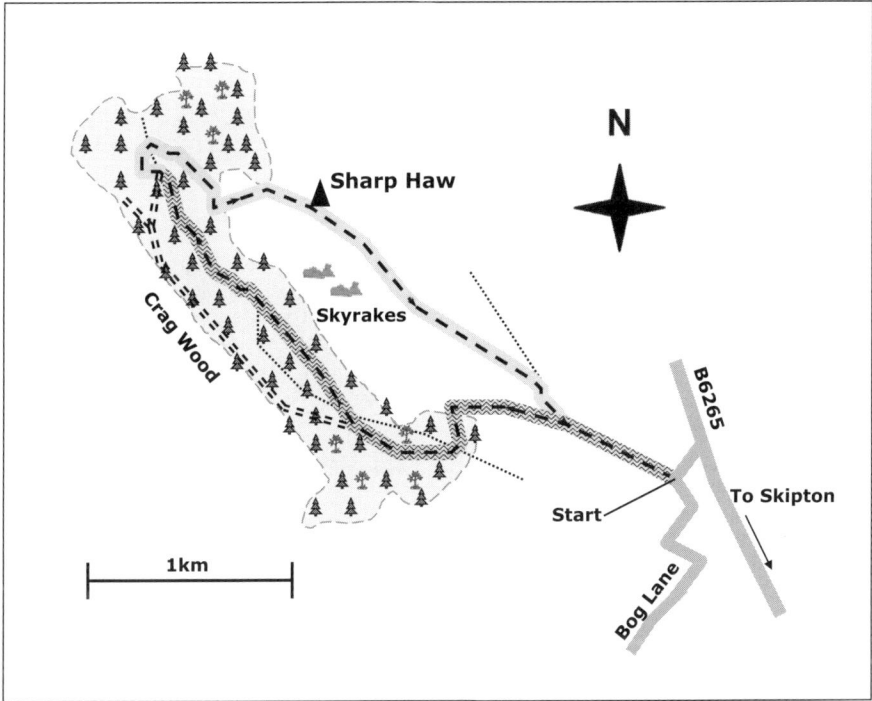

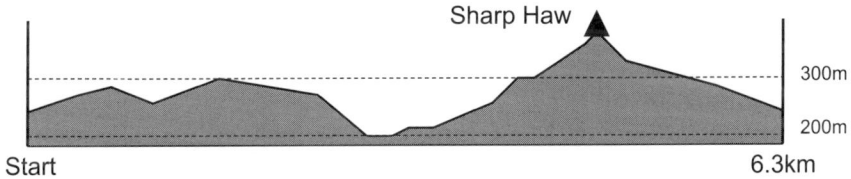

Route and height profile for Sharp Haw

some time you are walking under a low canopy of bushes, so it's quite unusual. After 350m you emerge into the light and reach a gate (at SD 9553 5536), marking the boundary of open-access land. On the other side go left on the path for 300m, by the ferns and heather, to reach the path that leaves to the SSE, rising up to the Sharp Haw summit. ('Haw' means 'view', and the hill is clearly pointed.) The local name for the hill is Sharpah, and that is the name in the OS records. Likewise, the nearby Rough Haw is called Roughah by the locals.

The pillar is in reasonable condition, with some damage around the base, and with a plastic plug. The flush-bracket faces NW, and on the SE side, about

80cm from the base, there is a round plate fixed in the ground. It looks like a buried benchmark, but I could find no record of such for that location. It remains a mystery.

Pillar details for Sharp Haw	
Name:	Sharp Haw
Position:	SD 95948 55270
Flush-Bracket No:	S5498
Height:	357m (1171 ft)
Built:	May 1949
Historic use:	Secondary
Current use:	None
Condition:	Slightly damaged

Sharp Haw pillar – Watt Crag behind (NE)

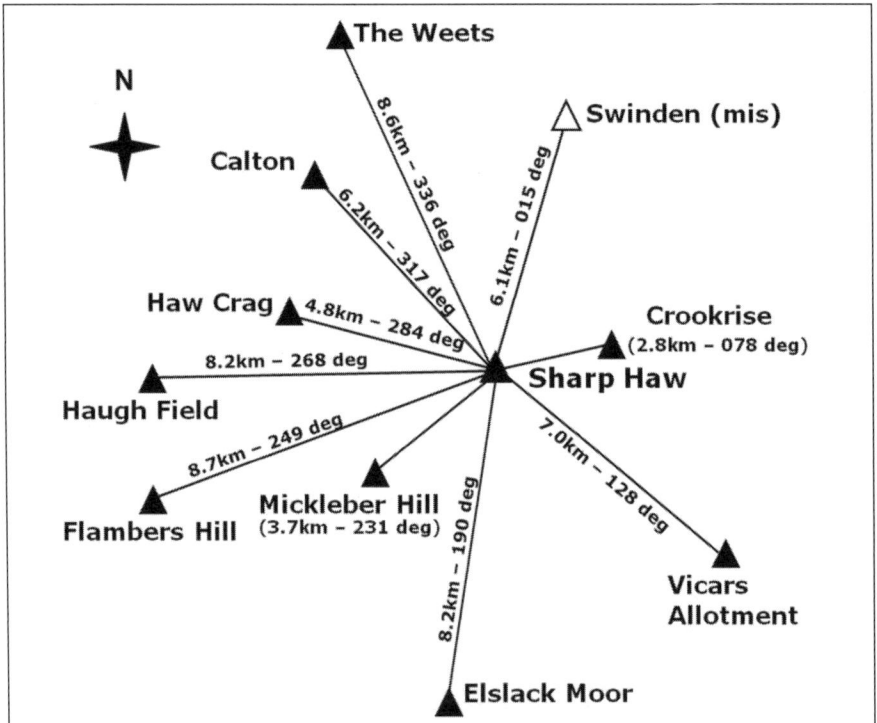

Nearby pillars in view from Sharp Haw

Begin your observations NE, as in the picture, towards the obelisk at Watt Crag. Just to the left, looking over the left side of Rough Haw (immediately to your fore), the low green hill is the un-quarried side of Swinden, where the pillar is missing. Beyond it, forming the horizon 19km away, is Great Whernside (a Primary pillar site, not to be confused with Whernside, which is to the west, and visited in Walk 19). Behind Watt Crag, and only just obscured, is Thorpe Fell. Turning east, the Crookrise pillar is right of a bush on the tree-covered hill immediately across the valley.

Looking SE, over the stile by which you will eventually leave the pillar, the rounded hill on the other side of Skipton is Skipton Moor, with the pillar (called 'Vicars Allotment') on the central high point. Just west of south, over Skyrakes, the distant rounded hill across the valley is Elslack Moor, the pillar clear enough with binoculars. Mickleber Hill is near SW; the low grassy hill with a lane in front of it, and directly in line with the right-hand hump of Pendle Hill.

WSW and west, Flambers Hill and Haugh Field are too indistinct to make out, but WNW and closer, Haw Crag is just behind a finger of trees that points NE. Finally, NW, Calton pillar is low and directly in line with the path on which you came up, with The Weets NNW at the top of the long straw-coloured slope with a wall going up to it. The pillar is by a wall, so it's impossible to resolve.

For your way back, go SE over the wall-stile, with the grassy path visible to the fore. It's easy to follow, but may be wet. After the gate that marks the open-access boundary head past the manhole cover to keep to the path – it gets a bit vague. Finally, after a few more potentially muddy areas, the path regains the limestone track at the bridleway marker and then it's just 400m to the car.

Route summary for Walk 2

Your present location	Your next objective	Waypoint at next objective	Directions and distance
Verge parking, Bog Lane SD 9752 5393	Forest track divides, keep right	SD 9617 5421	NW on track, veering SW into Crag Wood, then NW again – 1.8km
SD 9617 5421	Path to right off bend in track	SD 9523 5545	NW along forest track – 1.7km
SD 9523 5545	Clearing with signpost	SD 9529 5554	NW and NE on rough path though bushes – 200m
SD 9529 5554	Emerge on to open-access land at gate	SD 9553 5536	Generally SE on zigzag path under canopy of bushes – 350m
SD 9553 5536	Sharp Haw pillar	SD 9595 5527	ENE (left) after gate, by ferns and heather – 300m. Then SSE (right) on open path to summit – 200m
SD 9595 5527	Regain track	SD 9716 5420	SE on moor path – 1.7km
SD 9716 5420	Car, Bog Lane	SD 9752 5393	SE on track – 400m

Walk 3. Crookrise and Halton Height

Start:	Car park, Main Street, Embsay
Map reference:	SE 0098 5385
Distance:	13.9km (8.7 miles)
Total ascent:	410m (1340 ft) – average climbing gradient 1 in 10
Estimated time:	5 hours
Walk grading:	Difficult
OS maps:	Landranger 103 and Landranger 104

Walk summary

The route rises steeply out of Embsay, past the reservoir and up to the Crookrise pillar, before crossing Embsay Moor to Brown Bank and following a track to Halton Height. Return is along the lane via Eastby. There are OS benchmarks to find at the start and end of the walk, 12 in total. The walk is difficult in parts, crossing open-access heather moorland. So walking in shorts or when there is snow would not be appropriate, and it's important to observe any local restriction notices during critical periods of the grouse season.

Parking and access

From the centre of Skipton, go NE along 'The Bailey' (A6131) and then left into Skipton Road, directed to Embsay. Keep straight on to Elm Tree Square and turn right along Main Street, where the car park is on the left after 100m.

The walk

Walk west from the car park to Elm Tree Square. The Elm has long gone, succumbing to the beetle, and the present undistinguished tree is the second attempt at a replacement. Only the sign outside the Elm Tree pub hints at what the original might have looked like. As you walk into Pasture Road, see if you can spot the benchmark on house No 6 Elm Tree Square (BM No 1), and further on look for the one on the school (BM No 2). Obviously, during term time, dawdling and photographing would be inappropriate.

From the school, follow Pasture Lane west and then WNW, past an old chimney and the impressive 'Manor House' property, with the hugely populated duck-pond opposite. On from the water, the lane drops down over a stream, rising on the other side. See if you can find a cut-mark (BM No 3) somewhere at the top of the hill before the lane bends right to the NNW. Finally, look for the last benchmark (BM No 4) on the outward leg, near the large spreading tree after you've rounded that bend. It's faint.

After the tree, the lane turns left and the walk follows the bridleway alongside Embsay Reservoir, with Embsay Crag dominating the skyline to the

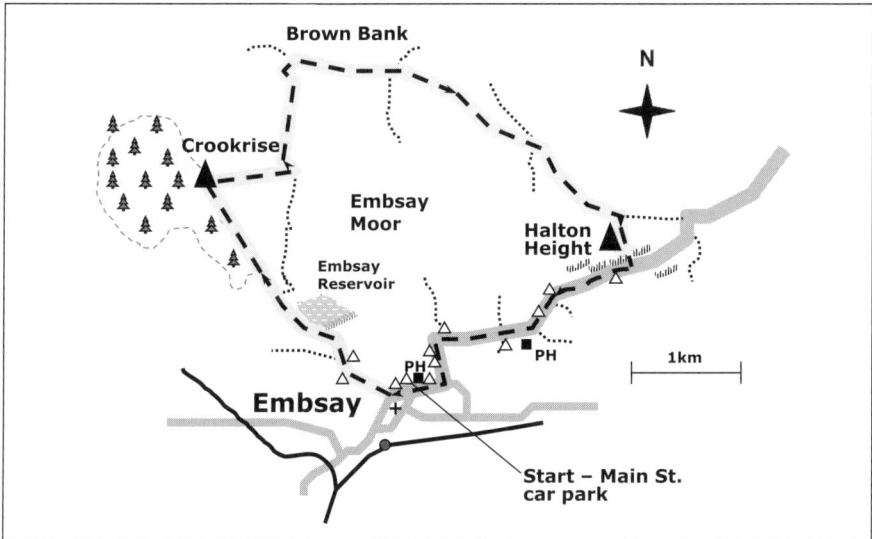

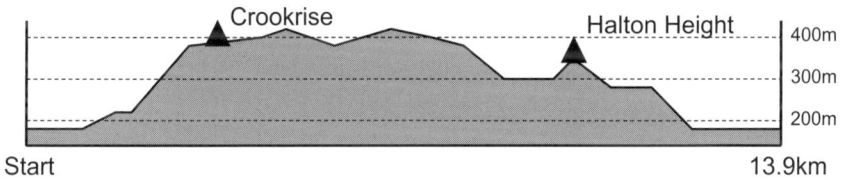

Route and height profile for Crookrise and Halton Height

NE. The reservoir is unremarkable, but you might be lucky enough to witness some sailing. At the far end, as the bridleway veers left to Crag Nook, take the stile to the open-access moor (SD 9955 5481). It's here that you'll find any restriction notices.

From the stile, one path leaves to the right. But the walk route keeps west, eventually alongside the wall that you'll see over towards Crag Nook. The path is not marked on most OS maps, and the first bit through the reeds is vague. A useful waypoint is SD 9953 5484, where the path becomes clear. Thereafter, it zigzags west across a stream and rises steeply close to the wall.

It's 1.2km of uphill walking to reach the Crookrise pillar, never far from the wall and with occasional excursions around rocky outcrops. The vegetation changes from ferns to heather, and the path is alternately grassy and stony. Occasionally there is a ladder stile bridging the wall, providing access to the open moor. The last of the stiles is important, since it provides access to the pillar to the west of the wall.

Pillar details for Crookrise	
Name:	Crookrise
Position:	SD 98749 55883
Flush-Bracket No:	S5781
Height:	415m (1362 ft)
Built:	September 1949
Historic use:	Secondary
Current use:	None
Condition:	Good

Crookrise pillar – looking west

It's in good condition, nicely painted, with its original OS plug, spider and flush-bracket all intact. To help with establishing your bearings, the nearby wall runs SE-NW and the obelisk 3km away at Watt Crag is just slightly east of north. Allegedly, 'Crookrise' means 'The brushwood by the bend in the valley'. The valley does bend, and there is (and presumably was, in Nordic times) a wood, so it could well be true.

To look for nearby pillars, start in the NNE, where Thorpe Fell is the rounded moorland hill to the right and behind the obelisk. (I couldn't find its pillar – it may be too far back.) The other pillar on this walk, at Halton Height, is not

Looking back at Crookrise from Vicars Allotment

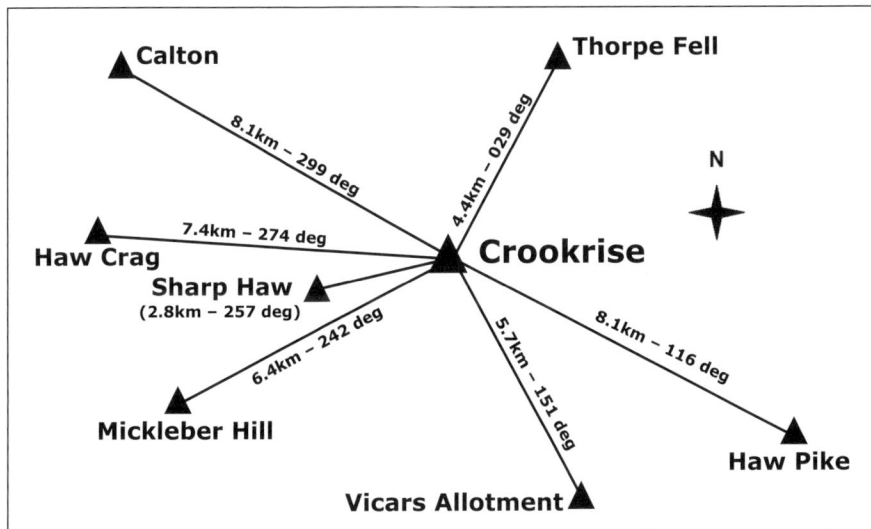

Nearby pillars in view from Crookrise

visible (ESE); it's obscured by the Deer Gallows Plain moor. SE, looking over
Embsay Crag in the foreground, the low, narrow ridge of Haw Pike is just left
of the Chelker reservoir. You should also be able to make out the wind
turbines nearby (if they haven't been dismantled).

SSE, the Vicars Allotment pillar is on Skipton Moor, the rounded hill across
the valley, looking along the wall you followed on the way up. In the SW, on
the distant horizon, is the distinctive flat top of Pendle Hill. Theoretically,
Mickleber Hill should be visible, just right of the line-of-sight to Pendle, behind
the Crag Wood ridge, but I couldn't make it out. Easier, to the WSW and closer,
is the Sharp Haw grassy summit, with the rounded Rough Haw (due west) to
its right and in front. Finally, Haw Crag (behind Rough Haw) and Calton (WNW)
are both low hills, under the horizon, so are difficult to make out.

From the pillar, retake the stile and set a course due east across the heather
moor. The target waypoint is SD 9964 5588, which is on the moorland
bridleway. It's 900m of hard work, with water-filled bog holes ready to catch
the unwary, and it's a part of the walk that will be prohibited at certain times
of the year, including august. It's in huge contrast to the grassy, well drained
limestone that typifies much of the Dales, the unyielding millstone grit
holding the surface water and supporting the peat and heather. As you trudge
through that heather, the grouse leave it to the very last moment before
getting up from under your feet in a flurry of squawking and feathers,
frightening the life out of you.

Once on the bridleway it's easy going, turning generally north. It's a well-
made limestone track – nothing but the best for the grouse shooting

fraternity in their four-by-fours – with 1.5km of walking up to Brown Bank (SD 9970 5717), where the track turns east. On the way you'll pass a posh shooting hut, but other than that it's unrelenting heather moor. After another 1km the track turns SE (SE 0076 5710), where a side track leaves down to the Upper Barden Reservoir. There is then another 2.5km on the track, with the two Barden reservoirs coming into view, the route eventually crossing two small streams. As you approach them, the Halton Height hill comes into view to the fore.

Pillar details for Halton Height	
Name:	Halton Height
Position:	SE 03091 55262
Flush-Bracket No:	S5313
Height:	357m (1171 ft)
Built:	April 1949
Historic use:	Secondary
Current use:	None
Condition:	Good

200m on from the second stream, at SE 0290 5569, leave the track and turn SSE up through the heather, towards a small stone visible against the horizon, about 50m distant. It's 500m of hard slog to the pillar, not for the faint-hearted. But there appears to be no easy route to the top, so this trek is as good as any. The small stone amongst the heather turns out to be something of

Halton Height pillar – Simon's Seat behind

an oddity, deliberately cut with two crosses. An ancient memorial? A boundary marker? Who knows? It's the only point of interest on the way to the pillar, keeping on a SSE heading and looking for burnt areas of heather to ease the way.

The pillar is sound, still with its OS plug, spider and flush-bracket, with a large cairn alongside. Helpfully, that pile of rocks is exactly due east of the pillar, so that the Simon's Seat outcrop, with its pillar very clear through binoculars, is unmistakeable to the NE. North Nab is closer, just north of east and lower, in the foreground. Behind it, a track winds its way up the moor beyond. Turning SE, the Beamsley Beacon ridge is clear on the skyline, with two prominences. The one to the right is the pillar, masked by a huge cairn, and to the left is 'The Old Pike' rocks.

In the SSE, Haw Pike is in the foreground, with the wind turbines behind and to the right. It's not easy to make out the pillar against the background. To the SSW, Vicars Allotment (Skipton Moor) is the rounded hill, sloping down to the right, with a very distant peak on the horizon behind it. (It's Combe Hill, nearly 20km away, with a pillar.) Turning to the WSW, Mickleber Hill should just be in view, but the nearby plantation has grown up to obscure the line-of-sight. Finally, round to the NNW, Thorpe Fell is the rounded moorland hill forming the highpoint on the skyline, with the Watt Crag obelisk to the left. Again, as from Crookrise, I couldn't spot the Thorpe Fell pillar.

'Halton' means 'farm', one tucked away in a valley. So this 'height' overlooks the one at Halton East to the SE. (Halton West is west of Gargrave.) From the top, look for a narrow path that leaves SSE from the cairn, directly towards the escarpment to the south of the pillar. (There is also a narrow path that leaves due east from the cairn. Ignore that; it becomes vague.) As you

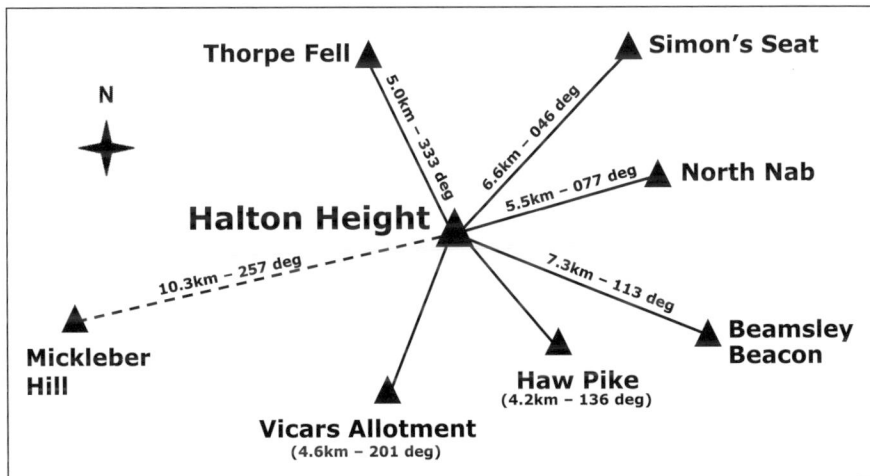

Nearby pillars in view from Halton Height

approach the escarpment, the Barden Road Lane comes into view, and you'll be able to see the continuation of the path below you, where it reaches the road (at SE 0344 5520). To pick your way along the short route as it zigzags down amongst the rocks is easy enough.

Once on the lane, it is 3.5km of pleasant walking back to the car, following Barden Road through Eastby (meaning 'The farm to the east of the parish'), where it becomes Kirk Lane. It passes the church (the 'Kirk', with a history going back to 1120, built on the site of an old monastery) before reaching Main Street in Embsay ('Embe's enclosure', Embe being a person's name). The road is quiet, and you can amuse yourself by trying to find eight more benchmarks on the way. (As always, the table at the end gives more precise directions if you get stuck.)

The first (BM No 5) is a rivet, with an engraved arrow pointing to it. Look for a rock on the south verge of the lane, about 100m SW from where you reached the road at the bottom of the escarpment. BM No 6 is somewhere near a footpath sign for Eastby Crag. It comes not far after the lane has turned sharp left and right, downhill. For BM No 7, search around the bus turning point that is just after a left-hand bend, with the 'Eastby' sign in view down the hill. Then BM No 8 is somewhere on house No 32, Kirk Lane. It's small and faint. It's off the lane a few metres, so access is somewhat intrusive. Be ready with an explanation if the householder asks your business, and use the book to blame the author.

200m on from No 32 look for an old stone water-trough. The records say it should have a cut-mark on its SW angle. I couldn't make it out. Perhaps the overflowing water has worn it away, or maybe one of the readers has better eyesight than the author. BM No 9 is somewhere near the old gate entrance to No 13 Kirk Lane, and BM No 10 is on a stone wall, after the lane turns left and before the church. To help, look for a road drain, a telegraph pole and a lamppost, which are all nearby. (The wall base might be overgrown.) Finally, BM No 11 is somewhere on the church and BM No 12 is on No 47 Main Street (called 'Salt Pie Cottage'), with then just 150m to go to the car.

Route summary for Walk 3

Your present location	Your next objective	Waypoint at next objective	Directions and distance
Car park, Main Street, Embsay SE 0098 5385	Stile to moor path leaving Pasture Road to the north	SD 9955 5481	West on Main St, then follow Pasture Rd past the reservoir – 2.1km, passing four BMs
SD 9955 5481	Point on path	SD 9953 5484	Vague path, keep NW for 40m through the reeds
SD 9953 5484	Crookrise pillar	SD 9875 5588	Stony path, NW, close to wall – 1.5km
SD 9875 5588	Moor path running N-S	SD 9964 5588	Due east across the heather moor – 900m
SD 9964 5588	Path along Brown Bank	SD 9970 5717	North along the moor path – 1.4km
SD 9970 5717	Fork in path	SE 0076 5710	East on track; keep right (SE) at the fork – 1.1km
SE 0076 5710	Leave path	SE 0290 5569	SE along the track – 2.5Km
SE 0290 5569	Halton Height pillar	SE 0309 5526	SE across moor, via an engraved stone – 600m
SE 0309 5526	Barden Road	SE 0344 5520	Narrow path, ESE down the escarpment – 400m
SE 0344 5520	Car park, Embsay	SE 0098 5385	SW along Barden Road, Kirk Lane and Main Street – 3.5km, passing eight BMs

Benchmark summary for Walk 3

BM No	Type of benchmark and location	Grid reference
Start 1	Cut-mark – House, No 6 Elm Tree Sq, south face, SW angle	SE 0088 5380
2	Cut-mark – School, N side Pasture Rd, south face, SW angle	SE 0076 5379
3	Cut-mark – Gatepost, SW Side Pasture Rd, 39.6m east of the corner	SE 0023 5394
4	Cut-mark – West face of gatepost, 3.4m north of wall junction on east side of road	SE 0016 5408
Return 5	Rivet – Rock, south side of Barden Rd, 79.7m SW of path/road junction on north side of road	SE 0335 5511
6	Cut-mark – Gatepost, 8.5m south of wall junction, near a footpath fingerpost	SE 0229 5467
7	Cut-mark – Gatepost, 15.2m north of Barden Rd, at the back of the bus turning area	SE 0215 5454
8	Cut-mark – House, SE angle of No 32 Kirk Lane. Side of house, first SE angle, base stone	SE 0184 5441
9	Cut-mark – Gatepost, entrance to No 13 Kirk Lane	SE 0130 5435
10	Cut-mark – Wall, west side of Kirk Lane	SE 0117 5423
11	Cut-mark – Buttress on the SE angle of St Mary's church	SE 0117 5409
12	Cut-mark – House, No 47 Main St, south face, SE angle	SE 0113 5388

Walk 4. Beamsley Beacon

Start:	Small car park, Bolton Bridge
Map reference:	SE 0705 5300
Distance:	11.5km (7.2 miles)
Total ascent:	360m (1180 ft) – average climbing gradient 1 in 11
Estimated time:	4.5 hours
Walk grading:	Easy to moderate
OS map:	Landranger 104

Walk summary

The route uses lanes and a track to reach Beamsley Beacon, before returning via Langbar and the Dales Way along the River Wharfe. Weather should not be an issue, and there are seven benchmarks to spot.

Parking and access

Take the A59 east from Skipton, driving 10km (6 miles) to Bolton Bridge. Go left off the roundabout (B6160) for only 150m, where there are some designated parking spaces on the right, off the lane that goes back over the Bolton bridge.

The walk

Follow the lane SE over the Bolton bridge, looking for the arrowed bolt (BM No 1) as you pass over the river. Immediately after the bridge, use the gate on the right marked 'Public Bridleway to Beamsley Lane'. It leads you under the road bridge and then along a sheltered path going east by the A59, eventually emerging on to the pavement. After a further 100m take the lane to the right, signposted to Beamsley. It's quiet walking, and after 400m there's another bridge to examine for BM No 2. It's faint.

200m on from that bridge, at SE 0786 5235, go left on the lane signposted to Langbar ('The long barley field' is my best guess). It's even quieter walking, going first NE, and then SE, rising steadily towards the Beamsley Beacon ridge. On the way, for BM No 3 (a rivet on a rock), search the base of the wall about 10m left of the gate to the 'Resphill' property. It was the only one of five rivets along this lane that I could find, but BM No 4, a cut-mark, is easy, on the 'Barn Bowers' property on the left, after a cattle grid. (A 'bower' is like a barn, so that name seems something of a tautology.)

One of the elusive rivets was close to the 'Gibbeter' property, just before a steeper section of the lane, on the right. It most likely refers to the man who dangled the corpses on the gibbet after they'd been hanged – a stark visual warning for other would-be criminals. A mock gibbet is at the entrance to the

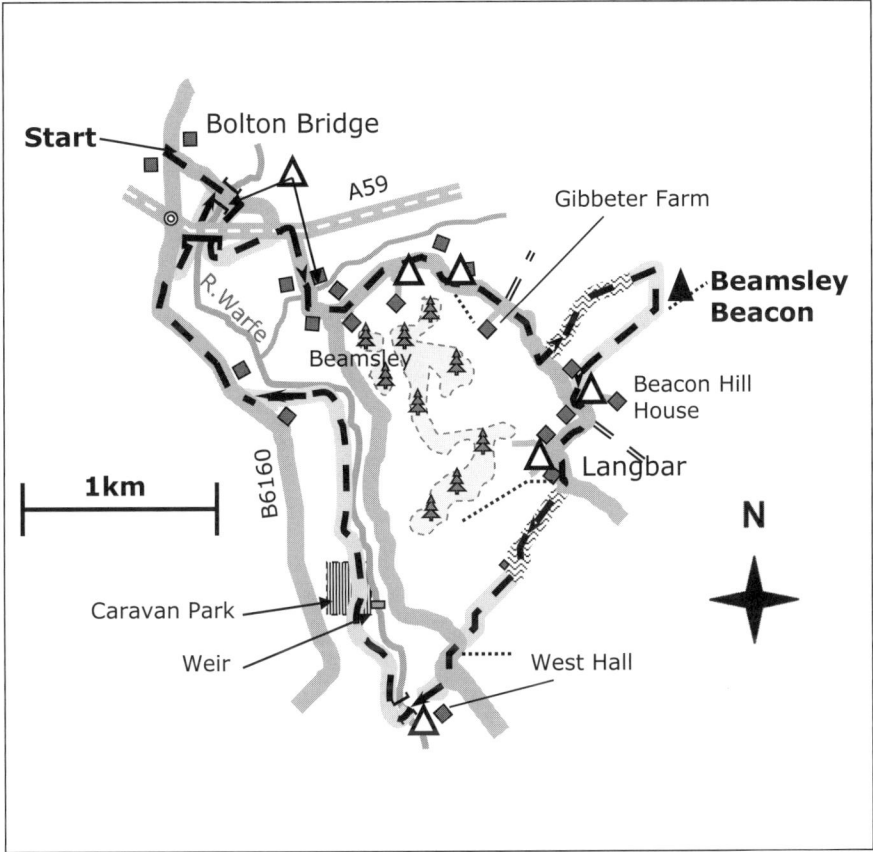

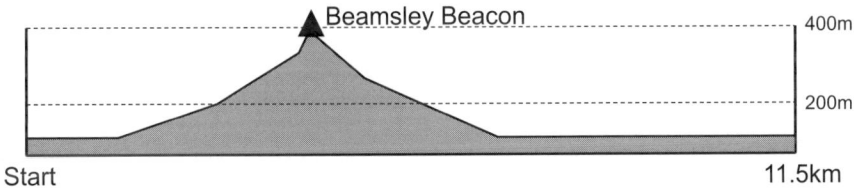

Route and height profile for Beamsley Beacon

farm drive, and it set me wondering if it would work today. Obviously not, since we've abolished the death penalty, but perhaps a milder version, like the village stocks? I guess not – health and safety requirements alone would mean that onlookers would need to complete a dozen EU forms before they could throw anything at the unfortunate miscreant.

Pillar details for Beamsley Beacon	
Name:	Beamsley Beacon
Position:	SE 09888 52434
Flush-Bracket No:	S5299
Height:	393m (1289 ft)
Built:	April 1949
Historic use:	Secondary
Current use:	None
Condition:	Slightly damaged

Beamsley Beacon pillar – looking NNW

400m on from the gibbet take the track to the left (SE 0919 5213), signposted as a footpath to Beamsley Beacon (all open-access). It runs below the ridge, with a splendid view into the Kex valley and to the Little Crag escarpment to the fore. Eventually, the track becomes a path and then follows the left side of a shallow gully. You can choose your point to cross the gully and struggle up the heather-clad slope to the pillar, but I waited until I was due north (SE 0991 5260, 900m on from the lane) and then came back on a diagonal.

The pillar is poor shape, badly eroded, with a stone plug. The flush-bracket faces NW, and to the NE the view is obscured by the huge cairn. A local told me it wasn't there when they erected the pillar in 1949, so I worked out that, on average, one person has added one stone every other day for 60 years to build it.

As it happens, no close-by pillars were in sight around the NE, but across the valley to the NNW, North Nab (second green hill away, track on its right flank) and Simon's Seat (rock formation on the horizon, with the 'Lord's Seat' rocks to its right) are both clear. Due east you can see Fewston Reservoir, so that Askwith Moor is just right of that and the same distance out. But I couldn't find it. (The distant tower, just north of east, is a BT mast.)

SSE, the two masts on the horizon are at Whetstone Gate, with the Rombalds Moor pillar on the high point to the left, actually Ilkley Moor. I think I could see the pillar. Just left of that bearing, close and low, Ling Park is hidden inside the line of trees with the track entering the centre. Looking SSW, Overgate Croft Farm is near the end of the long ridge, but the trees at the back make the pillar difficult to find. Likewise, Delph Farm in the SW is low and elusive, on a bearing looking down the Beamsley ridge.

In contrast, near due west, Skipton Moor ('Vicars Allotment' pillar) is easy, on the highest peak of the hills behind the wind turbines (if they haven't demolished them) and Chelker Reservoir. Then Haw Pike is closer, on the modest low green hill just right of the reservoir. Finally, WNW, Halton Height

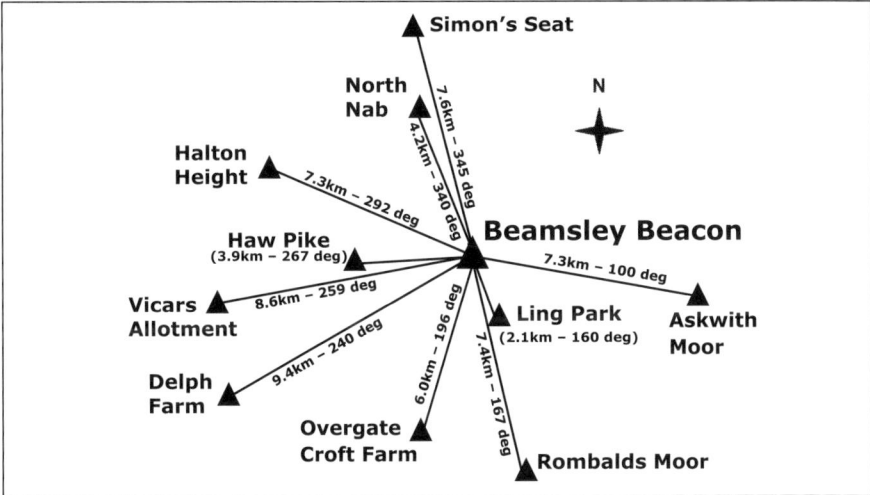

Nearby pillars in view from Beamsley Beacon

is the dark, heather-clad ridge with the long sweep of Rylstone Fell and Thorpe Fell behind it. The pillar blends into the undergrowth.

'Beamsley'? I'd guess it means 'a clearing', one belonging to someone from the long distant past with a name since corrupted to 'Beams'. And the 'Beacon'? Part of a wide network of hills, each in sight from the next, where fires could be lit to spread the word of a pending threat, not least the feared arrival of the Spanish during Elizabethan times. If you look on the OS maps you'll find lots more beacons in the Dales.

To begin the return leg, walk SW down the ridge path, all gritstone and sand, turning south at the bottom towards the walled plantation and emerging again on to the lane (SE 0935 5187). Go left (SE), past the Beacon Hill property (where you can search for BM No 5, a cut-mark), then follow the lane as it veers SW downhill (signposted 'Ilkley 4 miles'). In Langbar, the lane turns back SE, and after 200m it passes Beach House Farm (SE 0936 5132) on the right. BM No 6 (a cut-mark) is there, but on the house, not the garage. So it's intrusive. Go to the south of that property on the lane, then back west across the cattle-grid and around the back (a right of way, but with no fingerpost) to pick up the pleasant walled track that leaves SW.

After 500m that track ends at a gate, with the path then routed around a property. It's narrow, in a gully, with nettles maybe threatening from both sides, eventually taking you into open pasture and downhill to a lane (SE 0865 5036). Go left on that lane, and then straight on from the next bend, down the track signposted to Addingham. Before you reach the farm take the gate on the right, cross the little stream and then follow the field path along that stream to the impressive footbridge over the River Wharfe ('The winding river').

Before crossing the bridge see if you can spot the rivet (BM No 7) on the top of one of the bridge supports. It's small, painted green, with the faint remains of an arrow. From the bridge you can look north along the river to the weir – it makes a good picture. On the other side, as the path divides, go right and follow the edge of the river along the Dales Way. When the path divides again, keep right near the water, so that you pass the old mill and the weir before entering a caravan park. Half way through that look out for the routing sign that takes you back to the riverside, and note the landowner's request that you then keep to the edge of the fields, by the river.

It's delightful walking, with the river heaving and boiling when I was there, after heavy rain. The sheep and lambs were oblivious to my passing, clearly well used to walkers, and the path eventually leads out on to the B6160. It's a shame that the Dales Way has to take to the road at this point, and some care is needed. My tactic is to deploy something intimidating in my roadside hand (a walking pole for instance), forcing the traffic to give me a wide berth.

Destined for the pot – they were far too trusting

After 1km, 50m before the roundabout, take the gate to the right (Dales Way), over the narrow bridge back to the edge of the river. Then you pass under the main road, with the pigeons roosting above you, to emerge by the Bolton bridge and the lane back to the car.

Route summary for Walk 4

Your present location	Your next objective	Waypoint at next objective	Directions and distance
Bolton Bridge SE 0705 5300	Left along Lanshaw Bank Lane	SE 0786 5235	SE to Bolton Bridge, south under A59, east to Beamsley Lane, then south – 1.5km, passing two BMs
SE 0786 5235	Track to left	SE 0919 5213	NE, turning SE, on lane – 1.7km, passing two BMS
SE 0919 5213	Start climb to pillar	SE 0991 5260	NE, turning east, on track and path – 900m
SE 0991 5260	Beamsley Beacon pillar	SE 0989 5243	South up the steep heather-clad slope – 200m
SE 0989 5243	Lanshaw Bank Lane	SE 0935 5187	SW along the ridge – 800m
SE 0935 5187	Beach House Farm, track leaves at back	SE 0936 5132	SE, SW and again SE on lane, and round the back of the farm – 750m, passing two BMs
SE 0936 5132	Gate to lane	SE 0865 5036	SW on track, path and pasture – 1.2km
SE 0865 5036	Footbridge	SE 0839 4995	SW on lane, track and field path – 500m (with one BM)
SE 0839 4995	Lane	SE 0764 5185	North along the river – 2.4km
SE 0764 5185	Gate to right – Dales Way	SE 0709 5265	NNE on the lane – 1km
SE 0709 5265	Bolton Bridge	SE 0705 5300	Across the footbridge, NNE along the river, NW on the lane – 300m

Benchmark summary for Walk 4

BM No	Type of benchmark and location	Grid reference
Start 1	Bolt – Bolton Bridge, SW side of lane, parapet centre	SE 0720 5287
2	Cut-mark – North end of parapet, Beamsley Bridge, east side of lane	SE 0775 5248
3	Rivet – Wall base-stone, 10m north of gate entrance to Resphill, SE side of lane	SE 0819 5261
4	Cut-mark – Gatepost, SW angle of Barn Bowers, NE side of lane	SE 0866 5254
Return 5	Cut-mark – Gatepost, south side of entrance to Beacon Hill House, NE side of lane	SE 0939 5183
6	Cut-mark – Beach House Farm, NE angle, north face, west side of lane	SE 0934 5136
7	Rivet – North angle of buttress, SE side of footbridge, NE side of River Wharfe	SE 0836 4993

Walk 5. Calton and The Weets

Start:	Calton village
Map reference:	SD 9087 5922
Distance:	11.5km (7.2 miles)
Total ascent:	340m (1120 ft) – average climbing gradient 1 in 15
Estimated time:	4.5 hours
Walk grading:	Easy to moderate
OS maps:	Landranger 103 and Landranger 98

Walk Summary

The route begins NE from Calton village, following Foss Gill. After an excursion to visit the Calton pillar, the outward leg then crosses Calton Moor to the Weets pillar. The return is across Hanlith Moor to Hanlith village, and then uses the Pennine Way along the River Aire back to Calton. It can be very muddy, so this walk is best enjoyed after a dry spell. There are no OS benchmarks to find.

Parking and access

Take the A65 NW from Skipton, through Gargrave. At Coniston Cold, turn right down the narrow lane signposted to Airton and follow it north to the village (4.5km, 3 miles). In Airton, go right alongside the village square, following the signpost to Calton and Winterburn. The lane crosses a bridge, then goes steeply uphill. When the lane turns right for Winterburn keep straight on ('Calton village only' signpost) and park on the right by the wall.

Since the walk is around 4 hours, you could consider a visit to Malham to round off your day. Malham Cove, with its dramatic limestone crag and fissured 'pavement' is alone worth the trip. (I discuss limestone pavements in later walks.)

The walk

Before you start the walk look over the wall to the SE, into the field. There are five ancient standing stones in a rough circle. My enquiries established that they date back as far as 2006! They were put there by a local resident to host an annual display of new

Ancient standing stones!

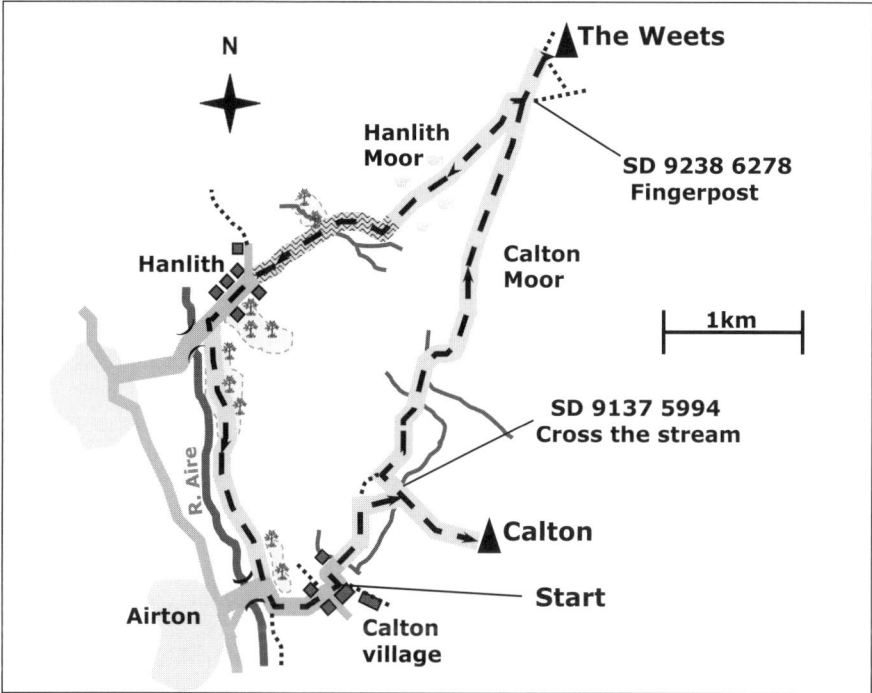

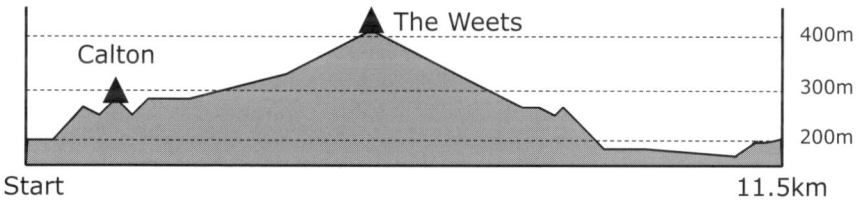

Route and height profile for Calton and The Weets

sculptures, only to find dozens of gullible people like me asking if they were thousands of years old. They must get several laughs a week on that basis.

From the parking spot in Calton (meaning, 'The farm where calves were reared') walk NE along the limestone drive that leaves from the corner of the lane. It goes downhill and fords Foss Gill ('Foss' meaning 'Waterfall') at the bottom. You can either wade it or use the dodgy wooden bridge. I wasn't keen on either – the water was in full spate and the bridge was slippery.

After the stream, the track reaches a gate (with a signpost to 'Weets Top') and leads on to a field path. Follow it uphill as it winds alongside the tree-lined stream, to a point where the valley is well below and you can see the

Pillar details for Calton	
Name:	Calton
Position:	SE 91717 59837
Flush-Bracket No:	S5560
Height:	275m (902 ft)
Built:	June 1949
Historic use:	Secondary
Current use:	None
Condition:	Good

Look for this

wall that marks the edge of the field. Walk diagonally down to the bottom, looking for a spot where the stream comes through the wall, with a low gate protecting the breach (SD 9137 5994). You can jump the stream there and then climb the gate on the other side. That is allowed (without damage) since the area on the far side is open-access land.

There's a brief, steep climb on the other side, going east, and then a 400m walk across the grass moor to the Calton pillar. It's in fine condition; even retaining its original OS plug. The flush-bracket faces SW, but it's best to begin your observations just east of north, towards the second pillar on this walk,

Calton pillar – looking NW

The Weets. It's the left hand of the two close-by rounded moorland summits, with a wall going up to the top. The pillar is up against a wall running west to east, so it's difficult to see.

Turning east, the gentle sweep of Thorpe Fell is unmistakeable (The small, rounded hill at its north end is Elbolton Hill – see Walk 6.) I could not see the pillar on Thorpe; the rounded top means the heather is just high enough to hide it. ESE, Crookrise is the high point before the south end of the ridge, the pillar just right of a bush. SE, the pillar on the pronounced Sharp Haw peak is very clear. South, Mickleber Hill is low and indistinct, beyond Gargrave, but the close-by Haw Crag is visible, low, on a grassy point just beyond a square of trees. SSW, the distant skyline is dominated by Pendle Hill, 22km away. To the SW, low and in the foreground, the Haugh Field pillar on its green pasture hill is surprisingly obvious.

Just south of west, Newton Moor is the straw-coloured hill just behind the right-hand edge of the large plantation on Otterburn Moor, but I couldn't resolve the pillar amongst the long grass. Finally, to the NW, Rye Loaf is unmistakeable, high on the skyline with a fairly steep southern flank. On the top you can see a cairn and the pillar. (The rounded peak to its right, and slightly closer, is Kirby Fell.)

From the pillar, retrace your steps westwards to the stream and make the jump again. Then climb the grassy slope and regain the field path, turning NE

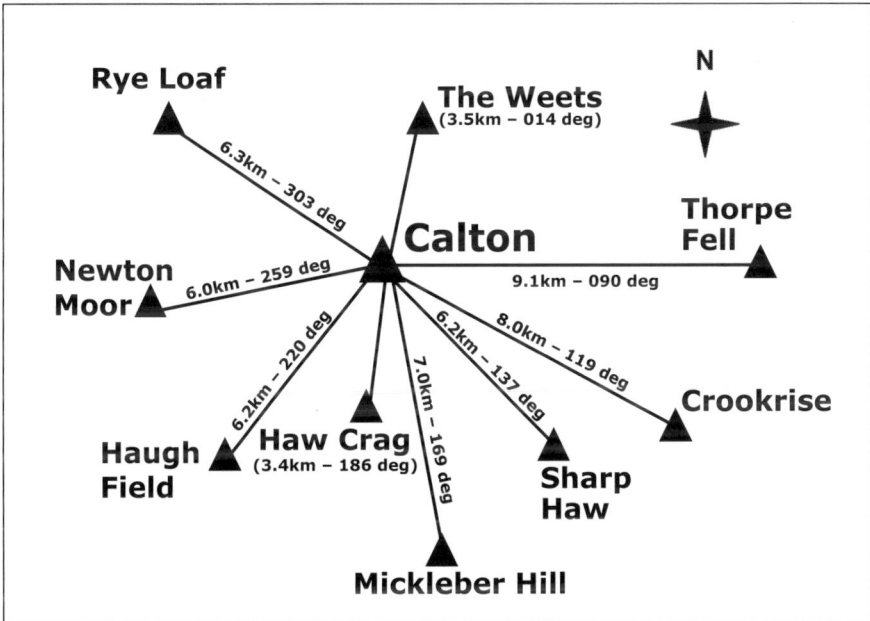

Nearby pillars in view from Calton

Pillar details for The Weets	
Name:	The Weets
Position:	SE 92568 63202
Flush-Bracket No:	S5563
Height:	414m (1358 ft)
Built:	June 1949
Historic use:	Secondary
Current use:	None
Condition:	Good

The Weets pillar – looking west

and making for the Weets pillar. It's 3.5km, first on a likely wet grass path (at one point, fording a stream), and joining a wall on the left. After a gate and stile, bordering open-access land, the walking improves, with a gravel path through the moor grass. 400m before the pillar you pass a fingerpost indicating left to Hanlith - it's the point you'll return to after visiting the pillar.

The Weets is also in good condition, but missing its plug. It's by the wall, which is not that unusual. With a tripod and theodolite, the surveyor will have

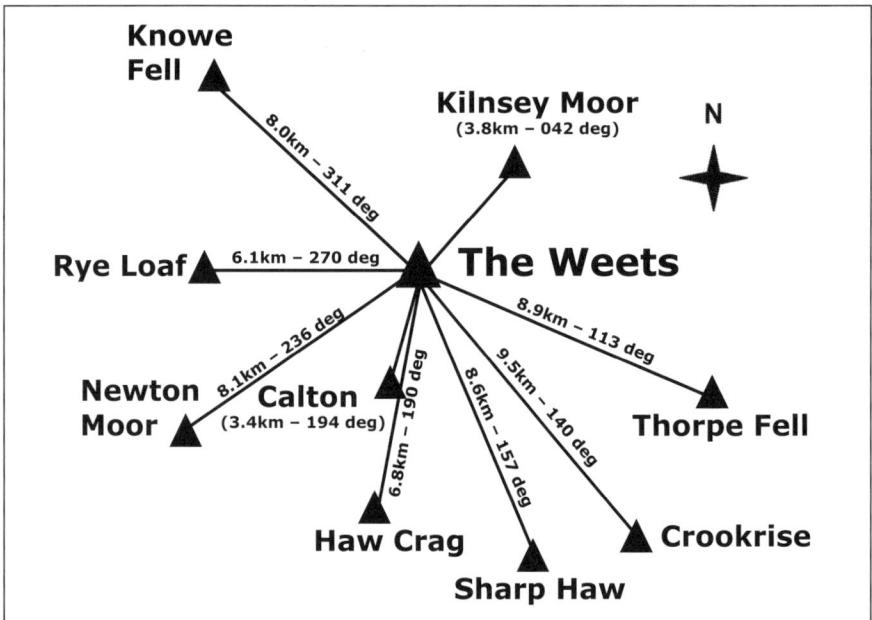
Nearby pillars in view from The Weets

been able to get a line-of-sight over the top. The flush-bracket faces south so it's easy to establish your directions. NE, Kilnsey Moor is clear, on the close-by limestone hill across the valley that has the hamlet of Bordley in the bottom. ESE, because Weets is higher than Calton, the pillar on Thorpe Fell is now visible, no longer submerged by the heather. And to the left of Thorpe, 16km back on the horizon, the distinctive crags of Simon's Seat have come into view.

To the SE, Crookrise and Sharp Haw are clear, with Sharp Haw just above the line of the moor immediately in front of you. (The round hill to the left of Sharp Haw is Rough Haw.) SSW, left of Pendle Hill on the horizon, Calton and Haw Crag are on the same bearing, but very difficult to spot as they blend into the low background. SW, Newton Moor is still hidden by the grass on its straw-coloured hill, whereas due west, Rye Loaf is clear, and WNW, 21km away on the horizon, the sloping flat top of Ingleborough is now showing. Finally, Knowe Fell (NW) is the right-hand summit of the long hill that forms the horizon, in line with the deep gorge of Gordale Scar in the foreground. I couldn't make out the pillar.

The meaning of 'Weets'? Possibly an Old English personal name related to 'Wit', a person of humour, who may have owned the area back in the Middle Ages. It also means 'To know', so the owner may equally have been a 'Wise man'.

Before you leave The Weets look over the gate by the wall. There is an ancient standing stone, greatly weathered and set in a rock base. Such single stones are difficult to date, and most have no history. It could be 500 years old, or even 5000 years old (unlike the ones at Calton!); it's impossible to say without digging underneath it to see if there are any artefacts (pottery, tools or weapons) that could be reliably dated. Of all the possible functions – maybe a place to meet, for any sort of ceremony, a grave, a memorial, a parish boundary marker or a declaration of land ownership – I'd say it was most likely a signpost to mark the summit of the track, visible from afar.

From The Weets retrace your steps SSW to the fingerpost for Hanlith (SD 9238 6278) and walk down to the gate. The other side is Hanlith Moor and was one of the wettest areas I've ever walked. The route is straight, aiming just right of Pendle Hill (SW, on the horizon), and mostly clear on the ground. At first, keep close to the wall so you skirt east of the tributaries. On the way there is a series of boggy dykes to negotiate, as well as the natural moor bogs. Looking on Google Earth™, the dykes are clearly man-made, in a regular network. I'm not sure they help. In consolation, the splendid views over Malham and the surrounding scenery steady unfold – it's classic Yorkshire Dales.

After 1.2km of bog-hopping you come to a walled limestone track, the gate (SD 9146 6197) marking the edge of open-access moorland. Then it's 1.8km SW, eventually on a tarmac lane, down to the bridge at Hanlith, passing Hanlith Hall, with its turrets, on the way. 'Hanlith' means 'Hagne's hill slope', Hagne being a Norse personal name, and the original hall dates back to 1668.

From the bridge take the wall stile south and follow the River Aire for 2.2km along the Pennine Way to Airton Bridge. 'Aire' means 'The strong river', and it was churning and boiling when I walked it. If you check the OS map you'll see that it starts from Malham Tarn, but then disappears underground through 'Sink-Holes' (a common feature of limestone geology, discussed in later walks), before rising again at Malham Cove. Surprisingly, the ground along the river is not too wet and the path is generally clear and never too far from the water. After 1.2km the river makes a meander to the west – avoid straying too far east at that point, uphill (a mistake I made). Just after that is a fingerpost, with a small bridge over the stream going left, indicated to Airton Bridge. Follow that.

Finally, from the bridge at Airton ('The farm by the River Aire'), follow the lane SE up the steep hill and round east back to Calton village.

Route Summary for Walk 5

Your present location	Your next objective	Waypoint at next objective	Directions and distance
Lane side, Calton village SD 9087 5922	Point to cross Foss Gill	SD 9137 5994	NE on track and field path, following the stream – 900m
SD 9137 5994	Calton pillar	SD 9172 5984	East across grassy moor – 400m
SD 9172 5984	Point to re-cross Foss Gill	SD 9137 5994	Retrace your steps west and cross back over the stream – 400m
SD 9137 5994	The Weets pillar	SD 9257 6320	Regain the grass path and follow it NNE – 3.5km
SD 9257 6320	Fingerpost to Hanlith	SD 9238 6278	Retrace your steps SSW – 50m
SD 9238 6278	Gate to track	SD 9146 6197	SW across Hanlith Moor – 1.3km
SD 9146 6197	Hanlith Bridge	SD 8999 6117	Generally SW on track, then lane – 1.3km
SD 8999 6117	Airton Bridge	SD 9044 5925	South on Pennine Way, along the river – 2.1km
SD 9044 5925	Calton village and car	SD 9087 5922	South and then east along the lane – 700m

Walk 6. Thorpe Fell and Langerton Hill

Start:	Car park, B6160, Burnsall
Map reference:	SD 0317 6100
Distance:	14.5km (9.1 miles)
Total ascent:	550m (1800 ft) – average climbing gradient 1 in 11
Estimated time:	5 hours
Walk grading:	Difficult
OS maps:	Landranger 98 and Landranger 104

Walk summary

The route follows the B6160 to the Intake Plantation before crossing the Folly Top moor on to Thorpe Fell. The inward leg is via Thorpe, across the River Wharfe and along the lane to Hartlington. After an excursion to Langerton Hill the return is via the bridge into Burnsall. There are 11 benchmarks to find. Lying snow would make the walk difficult, and shorts would not be appropriate. Grouse shooting restrictions will apply.

Parking and access

Take the A6265 north out of Skipton, via Cracoe, to Linton (13km, 8 miles), perhaps stopping off on the way to look at the site of the missing pillar at Swinden quarry (see the introduction to Part A).

Turn right (east) at Linton and drive 3km (2 miles) to Burnsall along the B6160. Parking is in a pay-and-display facility on the B6160 near the bridge.

The walk

From the parking area, walk SSE up the steeply rising lane, with the River Wharfe meandering below and the rounded top of Kail Hill to the fore, Simon's Seat behind it. 'Kail' means 'cabbage', and there is another such hill later in the walk, suggesting that the Ancient Britains of that area had something of a monotonous diet. After 700m turn right through the wood (SE 0344 6044), past the information board. Before that, on the way along the lane, look for a cut-mark (BM No 1) on a gatepost. And across the lane from the turning into

Burnsall Bridge from the car park

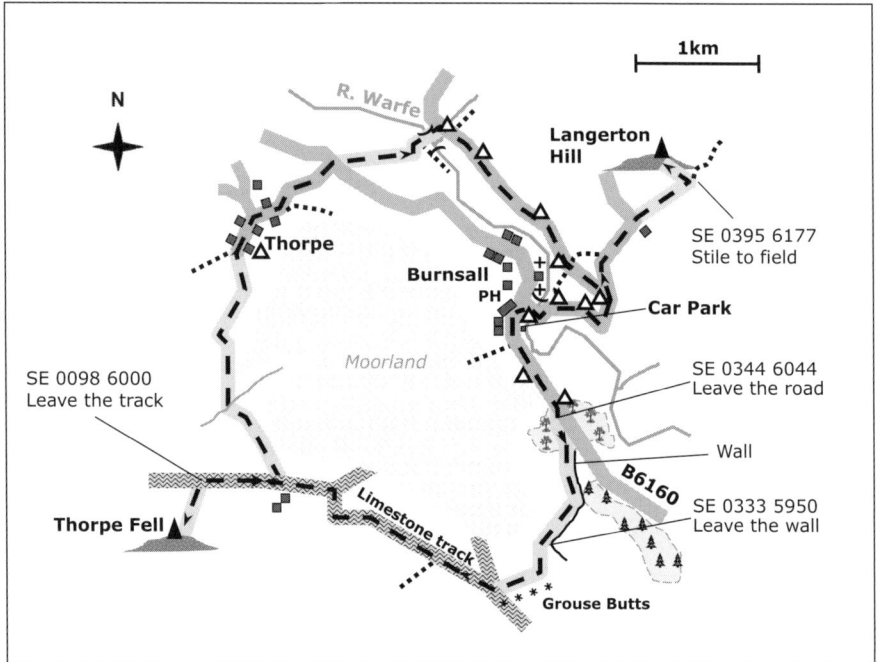

1km

N

R. Warfe

Langerton
Hill

SE 0395 6177
Stile to field

Thorpe

Burnsall

PH

Car Park

SE 0098 6000
Leave the track

Moorland

SE 0344 6044
Leave the road

Wall

B6160

SE 0333 5950
Leave the wall

Thorpe Fell

Limestone track

Grouse Butts

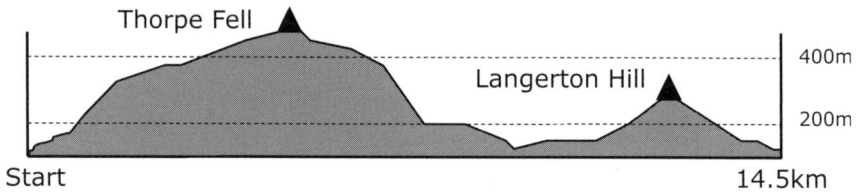

Thorpe Fell

Langerton Hill

400m

200m

Start

14.5km

Route and height profile for Thorpe Fell and Langerton Hill

the wood, see if you can find one on the wall (BM No 2). It's difficult.

The path rises steeply through the wood, to run by a wall along the SW perimeter, emerging over a stile in the SE corner. It's then 700m south and SSW through the ferns and heather, keeping a wall on your left. You'll pass a post with an inscription – something like 'C:R II', but it's not clear. It doesn't look very old – probably a boundary marker.

At SE 0333 5950 the wall turns away SW. Leave it there and head towards a grouse butt (SE 0331 5935) 250m due south across Folly Top. There's a faint path through the heather. The grouse butt is 'No 4', and as you turn west along a more definite path there are several more, up to 'No 9' before you join a track that goes WNW (SE 0299 5925). On the OS map you will see two such tracks running parallel; keep to the southerly one.

Clearly, these tracks serve the grouse shooting fraternity. So what is it about grouse? Is it that good to eat? A bit rich for me – very lean, and usually roasted with bacon to add some fat. There's not much on the bird; give me a plumped-up, water-injected, intensively reared corn-fed chicken any day! The real point is the sport, bringing in the money. The birds fly at up to 80mph, so they present a challenge.

As you walk the track, if the weather is good, the next objective – a large stone dwelling – is clear on the horizon, 1.7km distant. On the way, apart from the relentless moor, there's a small pool and dam to the south, and later, the remains of a building, with its robust chimney stack still standing. With a chimney like that it must have been more than a simple house – my bet is something to do with lead smelting.

The large stone dwelling turns out to have a smaller shelter nearby, an excellent spot to take refreshment. That spot (SE 0154 5998) is also the point you'll return to later, to take the path down to Thorpe. From the shelter, continue west for 600m along the track. Your objective is SE 0098 6000, which is as close as you can get to the pillar before having to cross the moor. The spot is marked to the right (north) by a pair of stones, one leaning on the other.

Pillar details for Thorpe Fell	
Name:	Thorpe Fell
Position:	SE 00850 59689
Flush-Bracket No:	S5312
Height:	506m (1660 ft)
Built:	May 1949
Historic use:	Secondary
Current use:	None
Condition:	Damaged

Thorpe Fell pillar – looking SW

The trek to the pillar is a 350m slog SSW through the heather – hard work. Watch out of hidden bog holes and take time to look back to establish a landmark so you can retrace your steps later. The pillar is in poor condition, standing on a rock outcrop, with the top badly eroded, so that the spider is nearly detached. It has a plastic plug, and the flush-bracket faces just west of south.

The obelisk at Watt Crag is 2km away to the SW, so that is a good start for your observations. Turning west, Calton should just be visible, but when looking the other way (from Calton), the Thorpe Fell pillar is below the heather line, so Calton may be in sight only for tall people. The Weets, to the WNW, is higher – it's the straw coloured hill with a wall below you, with the moors

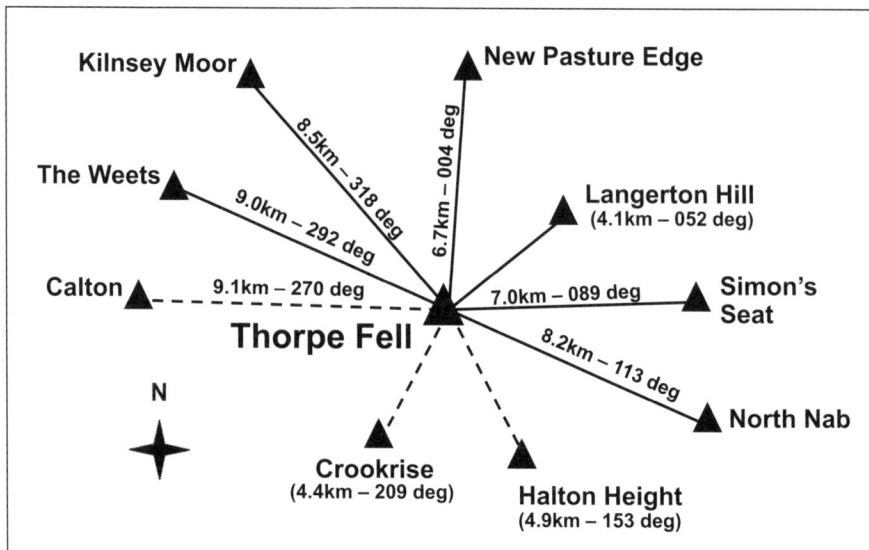

Nearby pillars in view from Thorpe Fell

behind Mallam forming the horizon. NW, Kilnsey Moor is the green hill just beyond a wood, with a white rocky area to its fore.

North, New Pasture Edge is low, with the higher moors behind. It's difficult to pinpoint. But the second pillar on this walk, Langerton Hill, is easier to spot in the NE. Find the right-hand edge of Grimwith Reservoir and then come forward to the low green hill in the foreground, with a wall going NW-SE across it. The pillar is behind the wall.

Due east, the rocky outcrop of Simon's Seat (pillar left) is easy to see, but right of that (SE), North Nab is more difficult. It's left of the Barden Valley, but I'd been enveloped by a shower by that time and lost all visibility. That meant that I couldn't look for Halton Height and Crookrise, both of which are theoretically visible. But the wide sweep of the Thorpe Fell heather top could well get in the way, and when looking back from those two hills, I could not find the Thorpe Fell pillar. So overall, it's not a very good pillar site.

From the top, retrace your steps to the track, NNE. It's important to get this right or you can end up with a long, hard slog through the heather. Once on the track, return to the stone shelter and take the grassy path that descends to the NW. It's an easy walk down, with the path well marked by small cairns and with the two pleasing round hills in view to the fore. The one to the right (NE) is the second Kail Hill, now devoid of cabbages, but the direction of the route (NW) is generally towards Elbolton Hill, which is allegedly 'The hill of the fairies' – a magical place. It's part of the so-called 'Barden Triangle', with its legends of supernatural undertones.

The path crosses a stream at SE 0115 6051, before dividing into a number of alternative trails. They all make for one spot, a gate that leads on to a grassy track flanked by two walls. At first, as you walk down, Elbolton Hill is directly to the fore. In fact, it is one of several old coral reefs in the area, built in ancient seas millions of years ago. It has a modest cave, the entrance no more than a hole, but it boasts a few Neolithic finds – bones and pottery.

Follow the track as it veers right, eventually reaching a tarmac road at the entrance to Thorpe Village (the name meaning 'The outlying farm'). At the point where a track joins from the left there is a stone barn behind the wall on the right of the road (SE 0124 6159). The records show it has a cut-mark (BM No 3), but I was defeated by a sea of nettles and a hidden stream, one that is easy to fall into. It must be there, so maybe you'll have better luck.

Follow the lane north through Thorpe, keeping right at the village centre, eventually reaching the B6160 (at SE 0185 6216). Cross the road and take the grassy path that goes east, indicated to Hebden. It follows a wall downhill before crossing a meadow to the top of the river embankment. Then, as you descend diagonally, you'll see the unusual suspension footbridge below, which was the whole point of bringing you this way. I have to admit that I found it unnerving, with the river churning below. Not too many people at once is the maxim, lest it shake too much.

A wobbly bridge

Pillar details for Langerton Hill	
Name:	Langerton Hill
Position:	SE 04172 62205
Flush-Bracket No:	S5305
Height:	278m (912 ft)
Built:	May 1949
Historic use:	Secondary
Current use:	None
Condition:	Good

Langerton Hill pillar – Simon's Seat behind to the SE

On the other side, the path emerges on to Mill Lane, and you then have 1.7km of quiet lane walking with five benchmarks to find. In order, first look on the bridge parapet (BM No 4), then on a gatepost for a rusty gate, just before the entrance to Ranelands Farm (BM No 5). That one is easy to miss. The next (BM No 6) is on a wall, where there is a marker post inscribed 'WO'. I had to scrape away years of ivy and moss to find it. BM No 7 is near a footpath post for Burnsall Bridge, where there is a splendid view over the river and village. Finally, near the end of the lane, BM No 8 is on a gatepost.

At the Tee-junction go left along Hartlington Raikes Lane, up the hill to Raikes Farm and the Walker Fold Guest House (excellent accommodation, by the way). At the corner, near the bench, take the stile (SE 0395 6177) into the field and

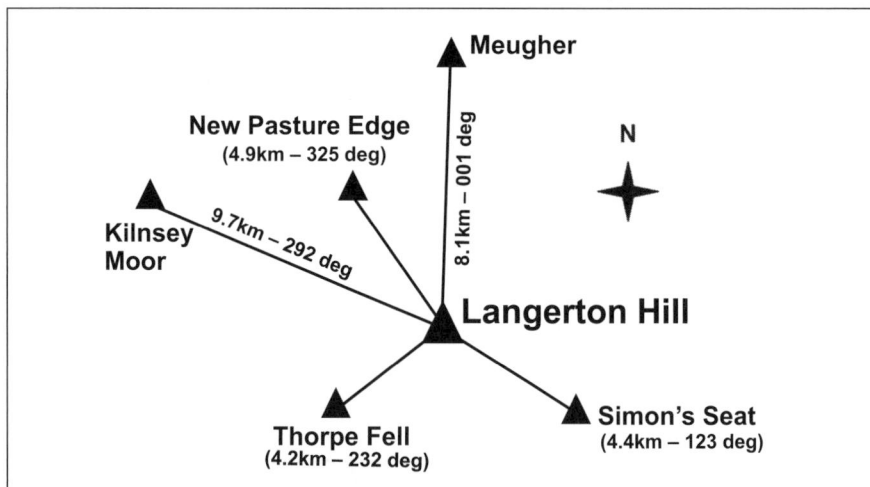

Nearby pillars in view from Langerton Hill

follow the path uphill along the wall, going left to the pillar after two more stiles. It's private land, but the landowner at Raikes Farm has no objection to responsible walkers making the visit, without the need to ask permission. The meaning of 'Raikes'? It is referenced only as a rare surname as far as I could determine. And my best guess for 'Langerton' is 'The long farmstead'.

The pillar is fine condition, with its original OS plug. The flush-bracket faces NNE, but the best direction to start looking is ESE, towards the distinctive Simon's Seat. The pillar is on the left side of the rocky outcrops. SW, the Thorpe Fell pillar is on the high point of the moorland top; then west there are the two rounded hills (Kail and Elbolton) that you looked at during the descent from Thorpe.

The fence going down Langerton Hill points WSW at Kilnsey Moor, but it's a long way off and indistinct. NW, towards New Pasture Edge, is just right of the left hand farm of the two that you'll see below you. Immediately behind the farm is the western slope of Scar Top, then New Pasture Edge is behind that, and behind again and a bit left, just visible, is (I think) Firth Fell (17km distant).

NNW is easier, with the unmistakeable profile of Great Whernside forming the horizon 12km away. Finally, to find Meugher, first look NNE for the green front face of the dam creating Grimwith Reservoir. Then Meugher (just east of due north) is somewhere on the moorland horizon left of the reservoir. I couldn't find that pillar, or the two in the NW sector, so Langerton was not a very interesting viewpoint.

From the pillar, retrace your steps to Raikes Farm and then follow Hartlington Raikes Lane down to the Tee-junction. Turn right there and follow the road into Burnsall, over the bridge and back to the car. Between the Tee-junction and Burnsall there are three more BMs to find, the first on a farm building (BM No 9), the second on a gatepost (BM No 10) and the third on Burnsall Bridge (BM No 11).

Route summary for Walk 6

Your present location	Your next objective	Waypoint at next objective	Directions and distance
Car park, Burnsall SE 0317 6100	Turn left into wood	SE 0344 6044	SSE up the lane – 700m (Two BMs to find)
SE 0344 6044	Leave the wall	SE 0333 5950	South through wood to stile, then south and SSW along a wall – 1.0km
SE 0333 5950	Grouse butt No 4	SE 0331 5935	South, narrow path through heather – 250m
SE 0331 5935	Join limestone track	SE 0299 5925	WSW along the line of grouse butts – 350m
SE 0299 5925	Stone shelter	SE 0154 5998	NW on limestone track – 1.7km
SE 0154 5998	Spot to cross the moor	SE 0098 6000	West on limestone track, to leaning stones – 600m
SE 0098 6000	Thorpe Fell pillar	SE 0085 5969	SSW through heather – 350m
SE 0085 5969	Back to the track	SE 0098 6000	NNE through the heather, retracing steps – 350m
SE 0098 6000	Back to shelter	SE 0154 5998	East on track – 600m
SE 0154 5998	Stream crossing	SE 0115 6051	NW on grass path – 650m
SE 0115 6051	Lane, B6160	SE 0185 6216	North to track, then via Thorpe – 2.1km (One BM to find)
SE 0185 6216	Lane, B6265	SE 0264 6242	ENE, field path and river bridge – 900m
SE 0264 6242	Stile to field	SE 0395 6177	SW to Hartlington, then left (NNE) to lane corner – 2.3km (Five BMs to find)
SE 0395 6177	Langerton Hill pillar	SE 0417 6220	NE along the wall over two stiles, then NW – 750m
SE 0417 6220	Stile to lane	SE 0395 6177	Return SE and SW to stile
SE 0395 6177	Lane junction	SE 0376 6170	SSW down lane – 750m
SE 0376 6170	Car park, Burnsall	SE 0317 6100	West on lane – 600m (Three BMs to find)

Benchmark summary for Walk 6

BM No	Type of benchmark and location	Grid reference
Start 1	Cut-mark – NW face of gatepost, 65.1m NW of wall junction, SW side of lane	SE 0327 6074
2	Cut-mark – SW face of wall, 1.8m NW of stream centre, NE side of lane	SE 0345 6045
Inward 3	Cut-mark – West side of barn, east side of road	SE 0124 6159
4	Cut-mark – Parapet, Mill Bridge, NE side lane	SE 0269 6239
5	Cut-mark – Gatepost, NE side of lane, 16m NW of entrance to Ranelands Farm	SE 0288 6217
6	Cut-mark – SW face of wall end, 2.1m NW centre of Skuff Beck, NE side of lane	SE 0333 6176
7	Cut-mark – Stile, NE face of wall, west side of road	SE 0352 6144
8	Cut-mark – North face gatepost, 1.8m west of wall angle, SW side of road	SE 0378 6127
9	Cut-mark – SW face farm building, NE side of road	SE 0370 6111
10	Cut-mark – South face of gatepost, north side of road, opposite footpath to south	SE 0339 6115
11	Cut-mark – NE face of SW parapet, NW end of Burnsall Bridge	SE 0324 6118

Walk 7. North Nab and Simon's Seat

Start:	Car park, Stangs Lane, Barden Bridge
Map reference:	SD 0527 5744
Distance:	14.8km (9.3 miles)
Total ascent:	520m (1705 ft) – average climbing gradient 1 in 11
Estimated time:	6 hours
Walk grading:	Moderate
OS map:	Landranger 104

Walk summary

The route follows the River Wharfe SE before turning NE up the Valley of Desolation and then east to North Nab. From there to Simon's Seat is by moorland track, with no walking off path over open-access land. However, the moor is an active grouse shooting area, so dogs are forbidden and walking around 12th August should be avoided. The return is via the Lower Fell Plantation and Howgill Lane. There are three benchmarks to find and the weather should not be a problem.

Parking and access

From the A59 east of Skipton, take the B6160 at Bolton Abbey and drive 6km (4 miles) to the lane that forks right and crosses the river at Barden Bridge, with car parking on the north side.

The walk

From the parking area walk SE through the gate and take the grassy path that follows the river. Before you do, make a brief excursion on to the bridge to find the cut-mark (BM No 1) on one of the parapets.

The route follows the River Wharfe for 3km, winding through open pasture into Strid Wood (meaning 'the striding place', which implies it's a nice a place to walk). The river is renown for its fly-fishing, with trout and grayling to tempt the enthusiasts. As the path takes the higher ground there are dramatic glimpses of the churning water below, as well as seats for an early rest and contemplation. Look out for the curious log embedded with pennies. It appears to be a wooden equivalent of a wishing well, but you need a hammer as well as a coin to make your wish come true!

After a footbridge (3km from the start, at SE 0744 5584), with the Posforth road-bridge alongside, step across to the lane and follow it 200m to the top of the hill, up to the drive that leaves NE (left) to Waterfall Cottage. It's then a pleasant walk, the track rising gently through the meadows, with the South Nab hill on the right. The area is called the 'Valley of Desolation', and 400m along the track from the lane there is an information sign describing the geological history. It doesn't explain the name, and the geology can hardly be said to match the dramatic volcanic cliffs and columns that characterise the valley of the same name in South Africa. Maybe a Yorkshire explorer came back from Africa and coined the name for this more modest local valley.

At SE 0770 5632, 200m NNE on from the information board, take the grassy path to the east, by a line of saplings. It's a direct path to the North Nab pillar, not shown on the OS maps, but well walked. The route to the pillar is steep, going generally east alongside a young plantation. After 300m of climbing, the path comes to the SE corner of that plantation. Keep straight on up, turning NE after a further 100m and setting your sights on a rounded outcrop of rock (SE 0822 5640) alongside the fence that borders the open-access land.

From the rock, follow the fence north for only 20m to a stile that provides access to the open moor. The pillar is then 250m due east across the grass

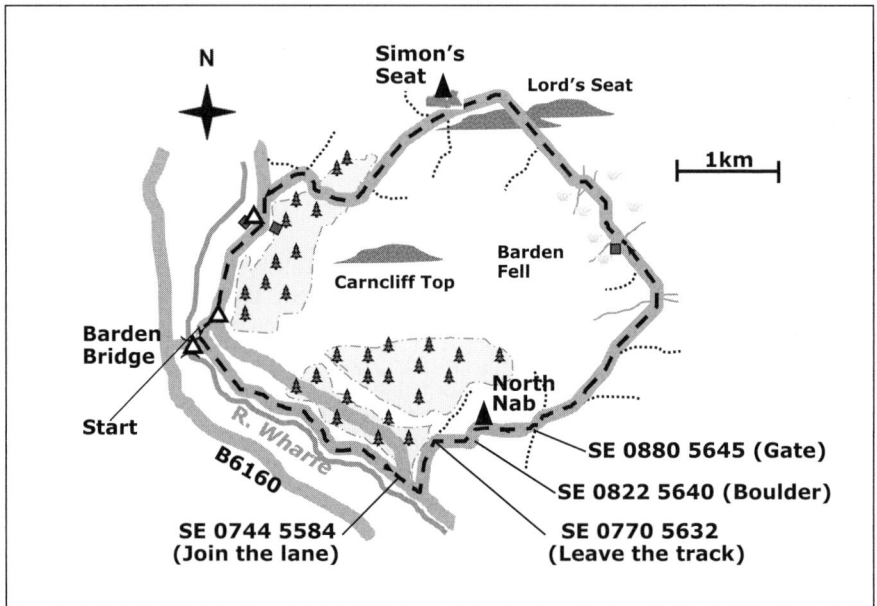

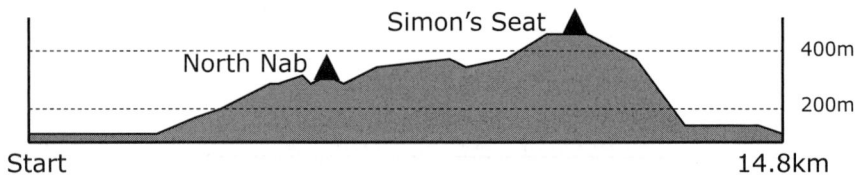

Route and height profile for North Nab and Simon's Seat

Pillar details for North Nab	
Name:	North Nab
Position:	SE 8471 56428
Flush-Bracket No:	S5296
Height:	319m (1047 ft)
Built:	May 1949
Historic use:	Secondary
Current use:	None
Condition:	Fair

North Nab pillar – Halton Height on the horizon

moor; it's not difficult. It's in fair condition, having been repaired around the top, and it's lost its OS plug. However, the flush-bracket and spider are intact and the main fabric of the base is sound.

To look for nearby pillars, start in the NW, the direction faced by the flush-bracket. The distant, gently rounded moorland hill is Thorpe Fell. Turning north, the Simon's Seat rock formations are visible on the horizon, with a track in the foreground. The pillar is on the right-hand rock outcrop, visible with binoculars. Round the east there is nothing to see except the distant Kex Gill Moor, where the pillar is missing.

Turning SSE, the low hill in the foreground is Brown Hill and the long hill behind it is Beamsley Beacon. The Beamsley pillar is on the high point at the western end, by a huge cairn. In the SE, the low Haw Pike summit is just about in line with the most westerly of the four wind turbines, and in front of it. The pillar is there, but not clear. Finally, to the WSW, there is the Halton Height peak, characterised by an escarpment on the south edge. When viewed from North Nab, the pillar is hidden behind a cairn. Also, on a clear day, the distant Pendle Hill is visible to the SW.

So what does 'Nab' mean? It's a common name for a hill, but I can find no reference to its literal meaning. All the 'Nabs' I know are rounded hills that overlook a valley.

From North Nab, walk due east, making for a track and a gate in a wall (SE 0880 5645). It's 350m across the grass moor, with a marshy area just before the track. Through the gate, follow the track that goes straight on (left is to Broadshaw House), going generally NE. It's then 2.3km of limestone track walking, with moorland as far as the eye can see, up to a wall with a gate where the route turns NW. On the way, two further tracks leave to the right; keep left both times.

As you continue to follow the wall the only point of interest comes after 650m – a shooter's hut with its characteristic heather camouflage. Does it fool the grouse? Or is it just a cheap thatch to hold down the tin roof? Whatever

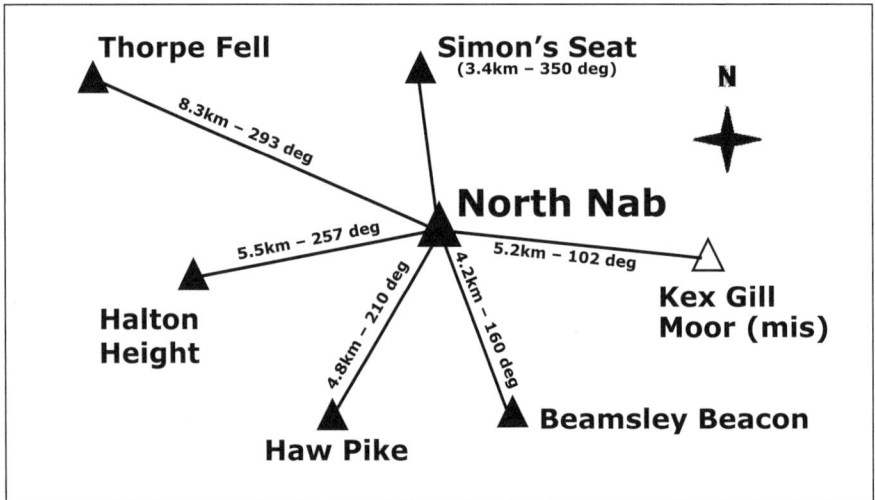

Nearby pillars in view from North Nab

the answer, the facilities dedicated to massacring the birds are evident all around, with numbered rocks and bunkers dotted amongst the heather.

300m on from the hut, the path goes to the NE of the wall, returning to the SW side again after 400m. It's then 1.2km of uphill walking, the final section increasingly boggy, to the distinctive 'Lord's Seat' rock outcrops. They are popular with the climbers, specifically for the sport of 'bouldering'. It's worth pausing to watch if there's any action when you arrive.

At Lord's Seat (SE 0846 5994), turn west and pick up the paved path that goes to the Simon's Seat gritstone outcrop, with the pillar perched dramatically on the top. Like many, those paving stones have been salvaged

Deluxe shooting hut

from old cotton mills – you can often see the machinery fixing points. They have been soaked in the sweat of a thousand mill girls, and I've heard it said that if you place your ear to the stone you can still hear the looms thrashing and the belts slapping! I don't believe it!

It's a scramble to reach the pillar, with a long drop on the north side to beckon the unwary. It's in fair condition, with some damage around the top and with the remains of a concrete plug. Both the flush-bracket and spider are intact.

Pillar details for Simon's Seat	
Name:	Simon's Seat
Position:	SE 07891 59808
Flush-Bracket No:	S5294
Height:	485m (1591 ft)
Built:	April 1949
Historic use:	Secondary
Current use:	None
Condition:	Good

Simon's Seat outcrop and pillar

The views to the north and NW are superb, stretching across the whole of the Yorkshire Dales. The 'Three Peaks' – Pen-y-ghent, Ingleborough and Whernside – are to the NW, about 30km distant, but generally obscured by closer peaks and moors. Looking back due east over Lord's Seat, 12km to the ESE are the distinctive white domes of the Menwith Hill Early Warning Centre. It's akin to the more well known Fylingdale, whose Motto is "Vigilamus", meaning, "We are watching". So let's hope they're all doing a good job.

Looking for surrounding pillars, there's again nothing to see in the east, but to the SSE North Nab is visible in the foreground, with Beamsley Beacon

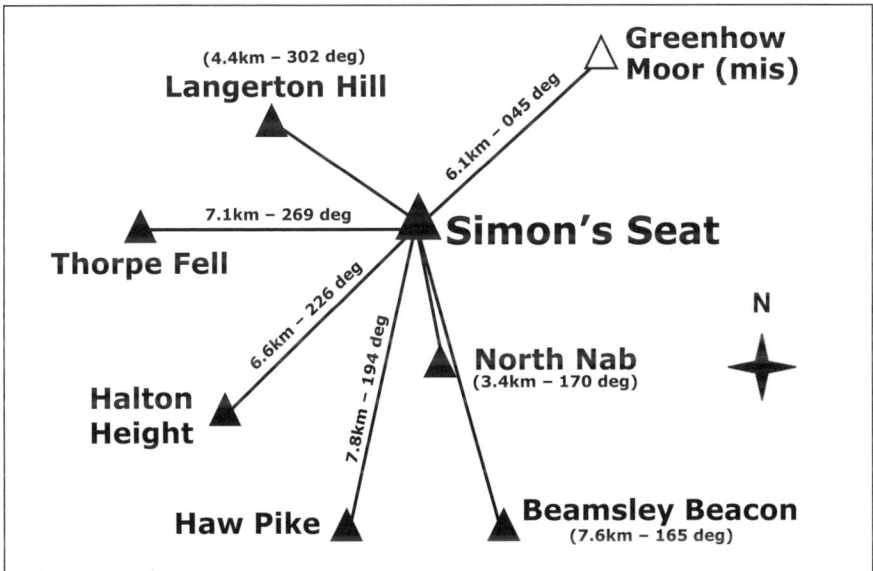

Nearby pillars in view from Simon's Seat

behind it. To the SW, Halton Height is just behind and to the left of the Lower Barden reservoir, with Haw Pike beyond it and to the left again (SSW). Thorpe Fell is due west, and just left of it and beyond it you should be able to make out the obelisk at Watt Crag. Finally, to the NW, Langerton Hill is the second low grassy hill in your line-of-sight, with a wall running across it. The pillar is hard to make out because it's near the wall and not on the skyline.

The meaning of 'Simon's Seat'? 'Simon' probably refers to the old English personal name 'Sigemond'. And most 'seats' I know are rocky outcrops looking out over a valley, presumably where the landowner might sit and survey his domain.

From Simon's Seat pick up the sandstone path that runs SW down to the plantation. (Avoid the path that leaves due south across Truckle Crags.) After 1.5km, at SE 0686 5883, the path turns through the plantation, becoming a track that zigzags down to Howgill Lane. Turn left there and walk SW to join Stangs Lane. 100m on from the junction see if you can find the cut-mark (BM No 2) on Wood View Farm; it's very faint.

From the farm it's another 1.5km of lane walking back to the car. There's one more cut-mark (BM No 3) to find on the way – somewhere near the sign for Barden, where a lane branches off left to Hazlewood.

Route summary for Walk 7

Your present location	Your next objective	Waypoint at next objective	Directions and distance
Car park, Barden Bridge SE 0527 5744	Footbridge over stream Then take the lane	SE 0744 5584	SE along the river – 3km. (Look for BM No 1 first.)
SE 0744 5584	Point to take rising path going east	SE 0770 5632	North along the Valley of Desolation – 800m
SE 0770 5632	Rounded rock outcrop	SE 0822 5640	Steeply uphill, east, then NE, by plantation – 400m
SE 0822 5640	North Nab pillar	SE 0847 5643	Along the fence to a stile (20m north), then east across the moor – 250m
SE 0847 5643	Gate	SE 0880 5645	East across moor – 350m
SE 0880 5645	Wall with gate, keep left of wall	SE 1009 5796	NE on track. Ignore two right forks – 2.3km
SE 1009 5796	Lord's Seat, turn west	SE 0846 5994	NW by a wall, past a shooter's hut – 2.5km
SE 0846 5994	Simon's Seat pillar	SE 0789 5981	West on paved path – 500m
SE 0789 5981	The path turns west through the wood	SE 0686 5883	SW, descending along a rough sandstone path – 1.5km
SE 0686 5883	Howgill Lane, then turn left	SE 0632 5915	West and NW, zigzagging through the wood – 1km
SE 0632 5915	Car park, Barden Bridge	SE 0527 5744	SW along Howgill Lane into Stangs Lane – 2km, with two BMs to find

Benchmark summary for Walk 7

BM No	Type of benchmark and location	Grid reference
Start 1	Cut-mark – Barden Bridge, south parapet, NW face	SE 0523 5739
Return 2	Cut-mark – Wood View Farm, NW side road, south angle, SE face (road-side, faint)	SE 0593 5876
3	Cut-mark – NW face of stone post, SE side of road, behind the 'Barden' sign	SE 0543 5765

Walk 8. New Pasture Edge

Start:	Car park, top of Main St., Grassington
Map reference:	SE 0034 6419
Distance:	6.8km (4.3 miles)
Total ascent:	190m (625 ft) – average climbing gradient 1 in 17
Estimated time:	2.5 hours
Walk grading:	Easy
OS map:	Landranger 98

Walk summary

The route uses a lane NE north out of Grassington, passing an old lead-mining area on the way to the pillar. Return is on grass pasture, with 'Bell-Pits' and ancient field enclosures as points of interest. It could be fitted either side of lunch with Walk 9.

The open-access land around the pillar might be subject to temporary closure, May and June being the most likely, as well as during the grouse-shooting season. Weather should not present any problems, and there are six benchmarks to look for.

Parking and access

From Skipton, take the A6265 north to Threshfield, via Cracoe. Then follow the B6265 into Grassington (16km, 10 miles from Skipton). Take the narrow 'Main Street' to the top, where there is parking under the trees.

The walk

The parking area might be called 'Chamber End Fold', because that's the name quoted for the position of the cut-mark (BM No 1) that's easy to spot on the house on the NW side. Having bagged that one, begin the walk by going NE up Moor Lane (signposted as a no through road, opposite Main Street). There's then 2.3km of quiet lane walking uphill to a track that goes left (SE 0155 6598) at Yarnbury.

On the way there are four more cut-marks to find, the first (BM No 2) being very faint, on a gatepost on the right after the lane has veered left and become steeper. I had to trace it with my fingers to find it. BM No 3 at Spring House is much easier; then there is a longer stretch before BM No 4, on a gatepost 40m on from a footpath sign to Hebden. It's from this point that you get your first view of the pillar, 1km away to the north. Finally, BM No 5 is 350m further on – another gatepost.

At Yarnbury, before you reach the track to go left, it's worth spending half an hour to look round the Grassington lead mining area. Study the display

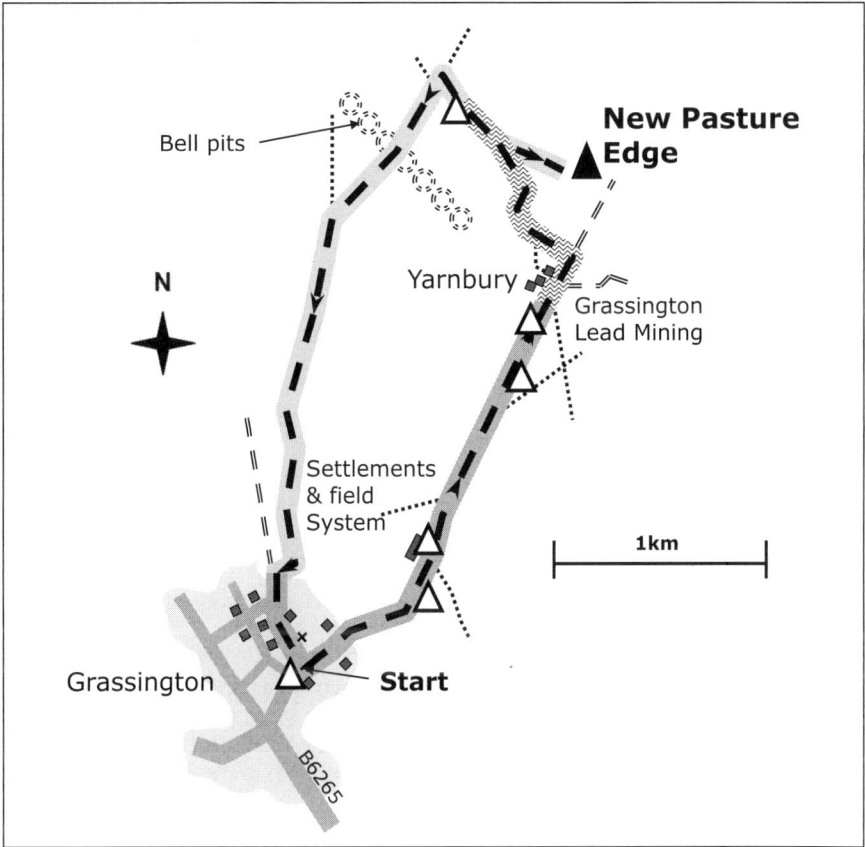

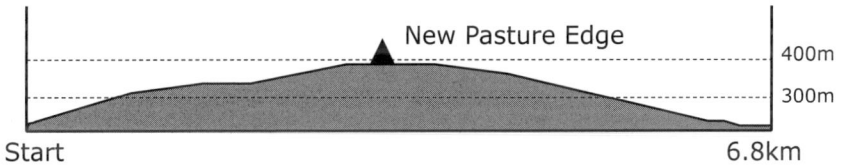

Route and height profile for New Pasture Edge

board and then follow the route, with more information panels to read on the way. I found it very interesting, but it said nothing about the life and death of the miners, or health and safety (or the lack of it). It was a very hard life, and goodness knows what long-term effects came from the heavy-metal exposure. (Note that, if there are any access restrictions to the moor, they will be posted by the display board.)

Pillar details for New Pasture Edge	
Name:	New Pasture Edge
Position:	SE 01383 66375
Flush-Bracket No:	S5193
Height:	396m (1299 ft)
Built:	August 1949
Historic use:	Secondary
Current use:	None
Condition:	Good

New Pasture Edge pillar – looking south to Thorpe Fell

100m on from the mining area take the track to the left signposted to Conistone and follow it NW. It veers right for a few metres, with the pillar then to the fore, but you have to walk on NW for a further 250m to find a gate (SE 0119 6654). Then walk back SE through the heather to reach the pillar.

When I arrived it was being used as a bird feeder, and at least 50 grouse got up as I approached, setting off in all directions. So where are the hawks and other birds of prey? With all that free bounty on offer? I live in Cheshire – nearly every day a Kestrel hovers over my back-garden looking for baby blackbirds, and when I walk the meadows, two buzzards circle overhead waiting for me to flush out a field-mouse or a young rabbit. However, I see no such opportunists on the Dales moors. I suspect that they've all learned a hard lesson at the hands of the gamekeepers.

Despite the wedge of turf holding the bird feed propped on top, the pillar was in excellent condition, with its original plug, and with the flush-bracket facing west. The area is pretty grim, with millstone grit under the heather, and moors as far as the eye can see to the east.

To the south, the long sweep of Thorpe Fell makes the horizon, with the pillar easy enough to find. (The Cracoe memorial is visible at the western end of the fell.) Turning SSW, and lower, the Swinden quarry is clear, where the pillar was dug up in 1985. WSW, The Weets is more difficult to find. It's the right-hand of the two modest hillocks on the horizon, the elusive pillar against the wall that goes over the top. Then due west, with the flush-bracket at your back, Kilnsey Moor is the long green hill that makes the horizon, it's pillar on the high point.

To the NW, the heather reaches of New Pasture Edge nearly cut off the longer view, but Middlesmoor Pasture is just showing, falling away on either side. It's 434m high, but as seen from New Pasture Edge, Firth Fell is directly behind it, 4km back and 607m high. Therefore, it's probably Firth Fell that

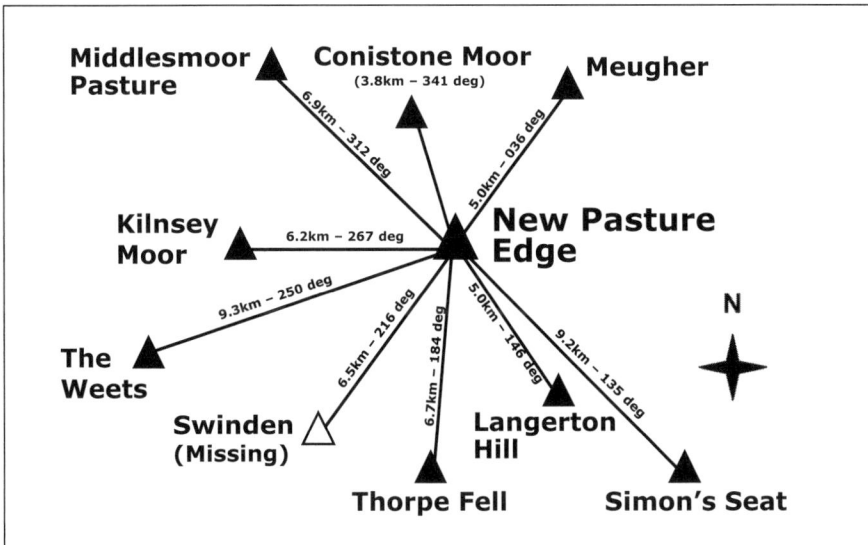

Nearby pillars in view from New Pasture Edge

makes the horizon, with the nearer pillar on Middlesmoor Pasture very difficult to resolve.

To the north, 8km away, Great Whernside is obvious, with the steep western side. The view is along the ridge, with Whernside Pasture (690m) to the fore hiding the pillar (further back, 704m). It makes the closer Conistone Moor easy to find – the green pasture hill forward and left (NNW) of Whernside. The pillar is in front of the wall that goes over the outcrop at the west side of the hill.

Scanning the NE horizon, I couldn't find Meugher. It is theoretically visible on a section of moor that just shows behind a closer line of moor top. It needs a very clear day to resolve it. In contrast, Simon's Seat on the SE horizon is easy – it's on the right-hand group of rocks, the left-hand one being Lord's Seat. Finally, the green Langerton Hill is closer and lower, on a line that is 'one reservoir width' right of the small Mossy Moor Reservoir visible in the foreground. The pillar is near a wall, so difficult to pick out.

Having completed the observations, retrace your steps NW to the gate and follow the track for 200m until it ends at another gate (SE 0106 6668). On the left there is then a wall stile, with a 'pivot' benchmark (BM No 6) on the bottom step. There's an engraved arrow, and on the top surface of the step there's a shallow depression (about 'thumb' size) where the surveyor would have stood his measuring staff. It's an alternative to a rivet benchmark, where the head stood proud and the staff was positioned on the top of that.

Take that stile, but don't cross the meadow. Go right and follow the left of the wall instead, walking 120m to where a wooden stile comes over the wall.

Now you can go left, with a very clear grass path to follow SW. After 180m you cross a line of what are called 'Bell Pits', shallow depressions in the ground about 6m apart. They are related to lead mining, but there are better examples during Walk 9 to Kilnsey Moor, so I'll save the details for that narrative.

After three wall-stiles the path joins one coming from the right, then crosses another wall stile and turns more south. 200m on, having gone through a gap in a wall, there is yet another wall stile, the path then leading to a junction of three walls, with a gap stile. The other side is a narrowing enclosure with two 'please keep close to the wall' signs. At the second of those (SE 0026 6489), look over the wall on the left to see a semi-circle line of old rocks (* on the field system map). The area is covered in a network of ancient enclosures, hardly recognisable as you walk, but very clear on Google Earth™ and nicely traced on the 25000:1 OS maps.

Their dating is very difficult to establish, but could be Roman or even older, when man first settled to farming and had a need to enclose his stock. Aerial views in oblique sun reveal the old boundaries as low mounds. As the odd solid remnants show, they were originally lines of rocks, probably topped off with a wooden palisade. (The existing stone wall you are looking over is likely to date from the 18th century.)

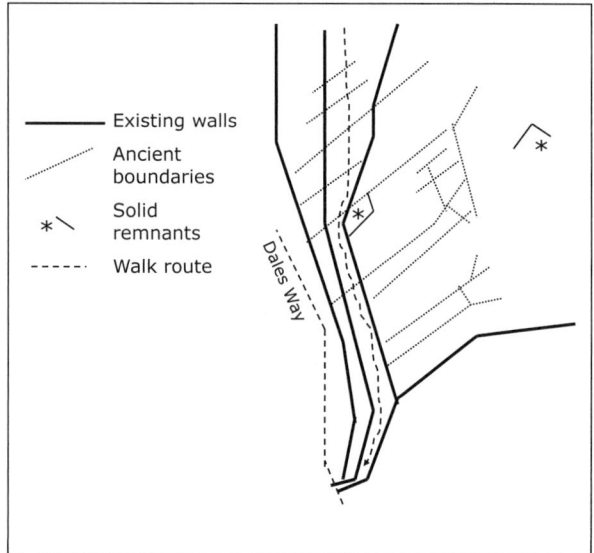

Ancient field system

From there, the path continues south through the narrowing enclosure, turns west over a stream and stile and joins The Dales Way. Go left there, south down to Chapel Street, and it's then 300m SE back to the car.

Route summary for Walk 8

Your present location	Your next objective	Waypoint at next objective	Directions and distance
Car park, Grassington SE 0034 6419	Track going left	SE 0155 6598	NNE on lane – 2.3km (Five BMs to find)
SE 0155 6598	Gate to right, beyond pillar	SE 0119 6654	NW on track – 800m
SE 0119 6654	New Pasture Edge pillar	SE 0138 6637	SE on moor – 280m
SE 0138 6637	Back to gate	SE 0119 6654	NW on moor – 280m
SE 0119 6654	Gate at end of track	SE 0106 6668	NW on track – 200m (BM near gate)
SE 0106 6668	Ancient enclosures, at second 'keep by the wall' sign	SE 0026 6489	Over stile by gate, 100m NW by a wall, then grass path SW and south, by Bell Pits and over seven stiles – 2km
SE 0026 6489	Dales Way, go left	SE 0024 6463	South, turning west over stream and stile – 300m
SE 0024 6463	Car park, Grassington	SE 0034 6419	South on Dales Way to join Chapel St, then SE – 500m

Benchmark summary for Walk 8

BM No	Type of benchmark and location	Grid reference
1	Cut-mark – No 2 Chamber End Fold, east face, SE angle	SE 0033 6420
2	Cut-mark – Gatepost, SE side of lane, NW face, 14m NE of wall angle	SE 0085 6455
3	Cut-mark – Gatepost, NW side of lane, NE face, SW side of entrance to Spring House	SE 0091 6467
4	Cut-mark – Gatepost, SE side of lane, NW face, 14m SW of wall angle	SE 0120 6534
5	Cut-mark – Gatepost, NW side of lane, SE face, 0.9m SW of a wall junction	SE 0137 6565
6	Pivot – Wall step, SW side of path, NE face 1.2m NW of wall junction	SE 0106 6667

Walk 9. Kilnsey Moor

Start:	'The Green', Kilnsey Village
Map reference:	SD 9741 6782
Distance:	7.9km (4.9 miles)
Total ascent:	350m (1150 ft) – average climbing gradient 1 in 13
Estimated time:	3 hours
Walk grading:	Easy to moderate
OS map:	Landranger 98

Walk summary

The route uses an old drover's track from Kilnsey village, crossing the Kilnsey Moor summit before returning to the track. There are 'Bell-Pits' and ancient field systems as points of interest. Weather will not be an issue, and there are 13 benchmarks to look for. It could be fitted either side of lunch with Walk 8.

Parking and access

From Skipton, follow the A6265 north to Threshfield, via Cracoe. Then take the B6160 to Kilnsey (19km, 12 miles from Skipton). Turn up the lane ('The Green') to the left, immediately after the trout farm, with roadside parking after 100m. From Grassington, if you've just completed Walk 8, it's only 4km (2.5 miles).

The walk

'The Green' is the start of Mastiles Lane ('The marshy track'), joining Kilnsey with Malham, with a history going back to Roman times. Soldiers marched it, medieval monks walked it, driving their sheep and transporting milk and cheese, 18th century drovers herded their stock along it, and finally, 21st century walkers use it. Its importance in the late 19th century is confirmed by the number of benchmarks recorded along it – 22 in the 3km stretch covered by this walk, most of which I couldn't find.

As you walk west from the car, BM No 1 is on a gatepost, before the lane turns left uphill and crosses a cattle-grid. (There's a useful information board just after the grid.) 120m on from that, look for BM No 2 on a wall base-stone, on the right. 250m further on, the track divides – go left down the limestone track, signposted to Malham. Kilnsey means 'The marsh by the kiln', and the 1852 OS map shows a limekiln on the left, near the area that is now the quarry – long gone now. (I talk more about limekilns in later walks.)

500m on (50m after a path leaves back left via a small walker's gate), you should be able to spot the rivet (BM No 3) on the large wall base-stone. Then BM No 4 (cut-mark) is somewhere near the entrance gate to Kilnsey Howgill

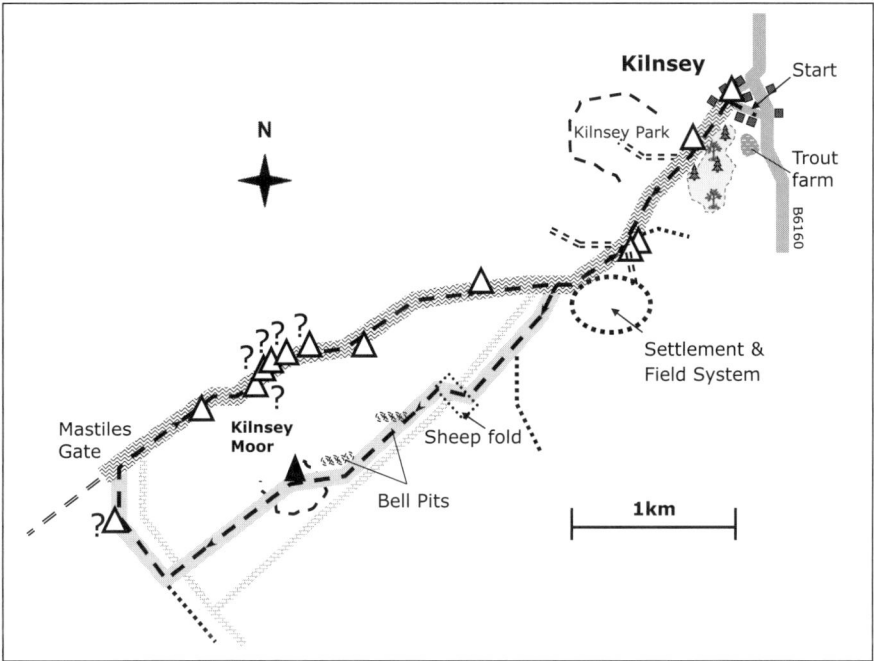

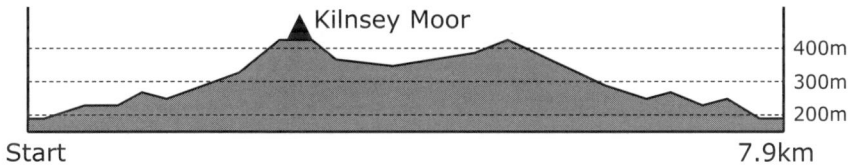

Route and height profile for Kilnsey Moor

Reservoir, and the point where the track divides again and you go left towards Malham Tarn.

250m on, with a view of the track dividing below you to the fore, pause to look around at the various walls. The half-fallen one to your right (northwest) is probably 17th century, whereas the intact walls to the west (your fore) are younger – 18th century or later. Looking to the southeast (left), there are the stony remains of much older walls (16th century or earlier) and the faint remnants of the raised boundaries of ancient enclosures, maybe Roman or earlier. There are more in the next small field to the SE – I've indicated them all with 'Here' on the picture. The ancient settlement is in the next (bigger) field SE, shown on the 25 000:1 OS map, and very clear on Google Earth™. On the 1852 map, that field is called 'Salisbury' – I wonder how far back that goes?

Ancient enclosure lines

Bell pits – with spoil

Continue into the dip (SD 9646 6701) and take the left track (public bridleway, going SW), leaving Mastiles Lane. After 150m continue along the left side of the fence and wall, keeping on that path as the main bridleway veers off to the south. After 400m you reach a sheepfold, where you cross to the right of the wall and continue SW along it. 200m on there are some Bell Pits, and then some better ones a further 500m on (SD 9543 6613), when you've completed the steepest part of the climb and the pillar has come into view.

The Bell Pits are relics of lead mining. The seams were usually vertical, and the miners dug a shaft downwards from the surface, opening it out below into a bell-shaped chamber, stopping only when there was danger of the top caving in. The lead ore was winched up through the shaft in buckets. Having exhausted one spot they moved a few metres along the seam and dug another one.

As you follow the line (near due west) towards the pillar you'll see that one pit is beginning to sink in. If you stood in the centre and stamped up and down, what would happen? I wasn't tempted! The shafts were capped with wood to stop sheep falling in. However, that rots, so the danger remains. And how many miners were buried, I wonder, when a roof did fall in?

The pillar is in excellent condition, with an original plug, and with the flush-bracket facing south. If it's a clear day the first direction to look is SSW to the distant Pendle Hill, then well forward and left of that (south), the small peak of Sharp Haw is right of the valley, with Rough Haw close by. The higher Crookrise is left of the valley, forming the wooded right-hand end of the long sweep of Cracoe Fell (with its obelisk) and Thorpe Fell (pillar easily visible). On the line to the obelisk, Swinden quarry is in the valley to the fore. If they hadn't taken the top off, with its pillar, it would just have been visible.

Turning SE, Simon's Seat is now 15km away, but the rocks are visible, with Lord's Seat to their left. The line across Langerton Hill (in the foreground) is then just left of Lord's Seat. It's a green hill with a wall, the pillar elusive.

Pillar details for Kilnsey Moor	
Name:	Kilnsey Moor
Position:	SE 95174 66060
Flush-Bracket No:	S5564
Height:	450m (1476 ft)
Built:	June 1949
Historic use:	Secondary
Current use:	None
Condition:	Good

Kilnsey Moor pillar – looking NNE to Great Whernside

Due East, New pasture Edge is close, with higher moors behind making it difficult to resolve. It's just left of the mast that's visible on the horizon. ENE, Coniston village is in the valley to the fore, with the 'Dib' gorge behind. Its line points directly at Meugher on the horizon. But I still couldn't find the pillar! NE, you'll see two small rectangular plantations – Coniston Moor pillar is just behind the left end of the left-hand plantation.

NNE, the long sweep of Great Whernside is obvious (as in the picture). The pillar is by a large cairn at the central high point. Left of Great Whernside, the next high point on the horizon is Buckden Pike, 13km away. Then Middlesmoor Pasture is on a line between Buckden and Whernside, close, the other side of the Littondale valley. I could see that pillar. To find Firth Fell,

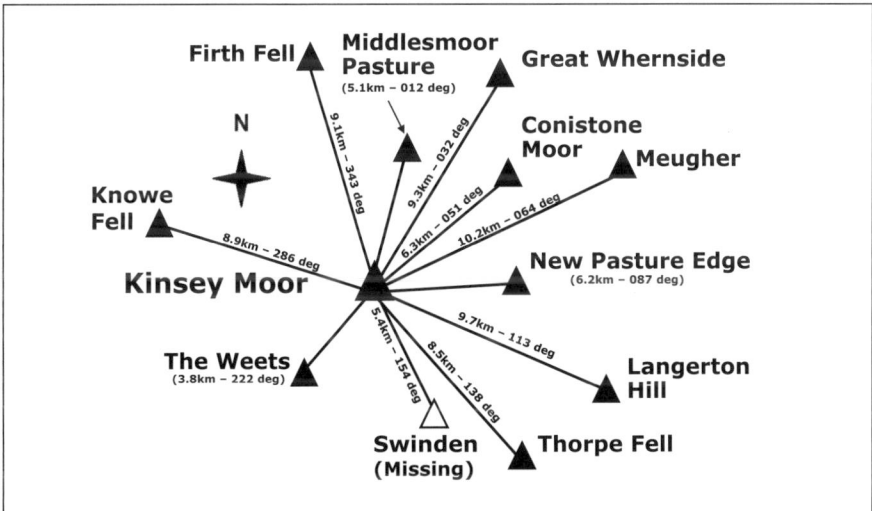

Nearby pillars in view from Kilnsey Moor

follow the rising hill left from Middlesmoor to the NNW, the top just visible behind the northern reaches of Kilnsey Moor. I couldn't find the Firth Fell pillar. (From New Pasture Edge, you were looking along the line from Middlesmoor to Firth, now you're looking across it.)

NW, there used to be pillar at Parsons Pulpit, only 4.3km away, but even if it was still there, the line is obscured by the nearby 'High Mark' peaks. WNW, Knowe Fell is just showing (I think I could see the pillar), whereas WSW, Rye Loaf is hidden by Kirkby Fell immediately in front of it. Finally, SW and very close, is The Weets, with a wall going across it. The pillar is by that wall.

To start for home, leave the summit to the SW (towards Pendle and Weets), dropping down the steep grass embankment to reach a gate (700m, at SD 9466 6563), with a bridleway on the other side. (The area is open-access, so there are no issues with climbing the gate.) Go right on the other side, following the bridleway along the wall. After 350m, the records showed a 'pivot' benchmark (BM No 5 – it should be a thumb-sized depression with an engraved arrow, dating to about 1860). It's on a stone, 20cm high and 6.1m west of the track centre. I found a likely stone, but not the mark. Will you have any better luck?

At Mastiles Gate, go right, and it's then 3.7km back to the car. Up to the point where you turned off during the outward leg, the records showed 11 rivets, of which I found only three. BM No 6 is easy to spot, 400m on from the Mastiles Gate, on the right. After the high point (422m spot-height on the OS map), there's a group of five BMs (Nos 7 to 11), all on boulders at the side of the track as you walk downhill, about every 100m. If you can find them, you're better than me! (There are plenty of candidate boulders to examine – look at the BM table for precise location details. Without a GPS, it's virtually impossible to find them.)

I did find BM No 12, on a rock on the right, as well as BM No 13 on the wall to the left, at an area where the track briefly widens. Between them were three more wall rivets that were far too difficult to locate.

Once back at the car, for one last treat, walk 300m north up the lane and have a look at Kilnsey Crag. It's an impressive overhang, and there may some climbers to watch.

Route summary for Walk 9

Your present location	Your next objective	Waypoint at next objective	Directions and distance
Kilnsey village SD 9741 6782	Track leaves left	SD 9646 6701	West and SW on Mastiles Lane – 1.4km (Four BMs)
SD 9646 6701	Bell Pits, veer right to pillar	SD 9543 6613	SW on track, then along wall via sheep fold – 1.4km
SD 9543 6613	Kilnsey Moor pillar	SD 9517 6606	WSW on grass moor, along Bell Pit line –280m
SD 9517 6606	Gate	SD 9466 6563	SW on limestone grass moor – 700m
SD 9466 6563	Mastiles Gate	SD 9441 6618	NNW on bridleway – 650m (One elusive BM)
SD 9441 6618	Kilnsey	SD 9741 6782	Generally ENE on Mastiles Lane track – 3.7km (Eight BMs to look for)

Benchmark summary for Walk 9

BM No	Type of benchmark and location	Grid reference
Start 1	Cut-mark – Gatepost to house 'Old Hall Farm', north side of road	SD 9736 6783
2	Cut-mark – Wall stone, 125m SW of building, NW side of track	SD 9720 6775
3	Rivet – Wall base-stone, 12.8m SW of wall junction, SE side of track	SD 9685 6725
4	Cut-mark – Gatepost, 0.9m SW wall junction, SE side of track (entrance to reservoir)	SD 9680 6717
Return 5	Pivot – Stone, 6.1m west of track centre (elusive)	SD 9446 6591
6	Rivet – Wall base-stone, SE side of track	SD 9472 6640
7	Rivet – Boulder, SE side of track, 0.9m out from the wall 20cm off the ground (elusive)	SD 9505 6657
8	Pivot – Boulder, NW side of track, 3.7m out from the wall, 40cm off the ground (elusive)	SD 9510 6661
9	Rivet – Boulder, NW side of track, 0.9m out from the wall, 20cm off the ground (elusive)	SD 9515 6663
10	Rivet – Boulder, NW side of track, 4.9m out from the wall, ground level (elusive)	SD 9519 6664
11	Rivet – Boulder, NW side of track, 0.9m out from the wall, 20cm off the ground (elusive)	SD 9528 6667
12	Rivet – Boulder, SE side of track, 0.9m out from the wall, 20cm off the ground	SD 9539 6669
13	Rivet – Wall base-stone, north side of track	SD 9606 6698

Part B. Walks based around Settle

Settle (meaning 'dwelling place') is a thriving market town dedicated to the tourist, granted its charter in 1249. It was market day when I visited, and the place was buzzing. The central feature is 'The Shambles', a Victorian two-storey building, now housing a predictable collection of fish and chip shops, pizza-houses and restaurants. In 1880 it would have been cobblers, tailors, drapers and fancy goods, and maybe even the local rat-catcher! Before that, back in the 17th century, it was a slaughterhouse, so it definitely has some history.

There's a theatre, the river to walk, some very old buildings to admire and it's one end of the famous Settle to Carlisle Railway. Take a ride – it's highly recommended, passing through parts of the Dales that are covered by these walks, including the Ribblehead Viaduct and the Blea Moor tunnel. Try www.settle-carlisle.co.uk for details of journey times and prices. And for an overview of Settle, with information on accommodation, try www.settle.co.uk.

The town is easily reached from the A65 via the B6480, with the B6479 providing good access to the SW Dales, as far as Horton and beyond. There are six walks centred on Settle, visiting 12 pillars:

10. Newton Moor and Hunter Bark
11. Langcliffe and Rye Loaf
12. Smearsett Scar and Moughton
13. Pen-y-gent
14. Sulber
15. Knowe Fell and Cow Close Fell
16. Cave Hill and Low Green Field Lings

There is also a missing pillar, 'Parson's Pulpit', at SD 91839 68748, 3km NE of Malham Tarn. It fell apart sometime between 1985 and 1987 and the spot is now marked with a concrete disc. For the keenest Trigpointer, the site can be visited during a circular walk from the Malham Tarn Field Centre (near the start of Walk 15). Take the path that leaves NE from the north of the tarn, climbing the escarpment to Parson's Pulpit through a gap at Dew Bottoms. Then you can carry on SSE to pick up the path that comes back to Malham Tarn via Gordale Beck.

For benchmarks, as you explore the town, there are a couple of flush-brackets that you might notice – on the SW battlement of Settle Bridge (No 1479, SD 8166 6408) and on House No 9, South Parade, Duke Street (No 1478, SD 8170 6316). They are part of the chain from Ribblehead to Skipton. There is also a cut-mark on the Town Hall (SE angle, SD 8199 6365) and a bolt on the tower of Holy Ascension church (SE angle, SD 8194 6389).

Walk 10. Newton Moor and Hunter Bark

Start:	Village square, Long Preston
Map reference:	SD 8341 5821
Distance:	14.5km (9.1 miles)
Total ascent:	330m (1080 ft) – average climbing gradient 1 in 18
Estimated time:	5.5 hours
Walk grading:	Easy to moderate
OS maps:	Landranger 98 and Landranger 103

Walk summary

The route leaves Long Preston eastwards, to reach Newton Moor via a complex route, needing a compass. The middle leg is NW along a track and lane, going by the Wild Share plantation. Return is south along the Pennine Bridleway and a lane, visiting Hunter Bark on the way. There are six benchmarks to look for, and the weather should not be an issue.

Parking and access

From Settle, take the B6480 and A65 SE for 8km (5 miles) to Long Preston ('The priest's farmstead'). Parking is around the village square.

The walk

Before you start, look at the ancient signpost near the phone box. How old? Probably about 150 years, and in excellent condition, declaring the distances to Settle and Skipton for the coachman. On the old maps the coach road followed the (now) A65, and the signpost is shown on the 1896 record. However, back in 1851, the position says 'pump', which will have been the village water supply.

Walk east from the square, up School Road and Back Lane, continuing along Scalehaw Lane, posted as 'Footpath only – No Through Road'. It becomes a track, and where it veers left over a cattle grid (SD 8404 5854) keep straight on along the walled track. It goes right, downhill, to a footbridge (SD 8419 5865) over Long Preston Beck. On the other side there is a round, walled

Ancient signpost

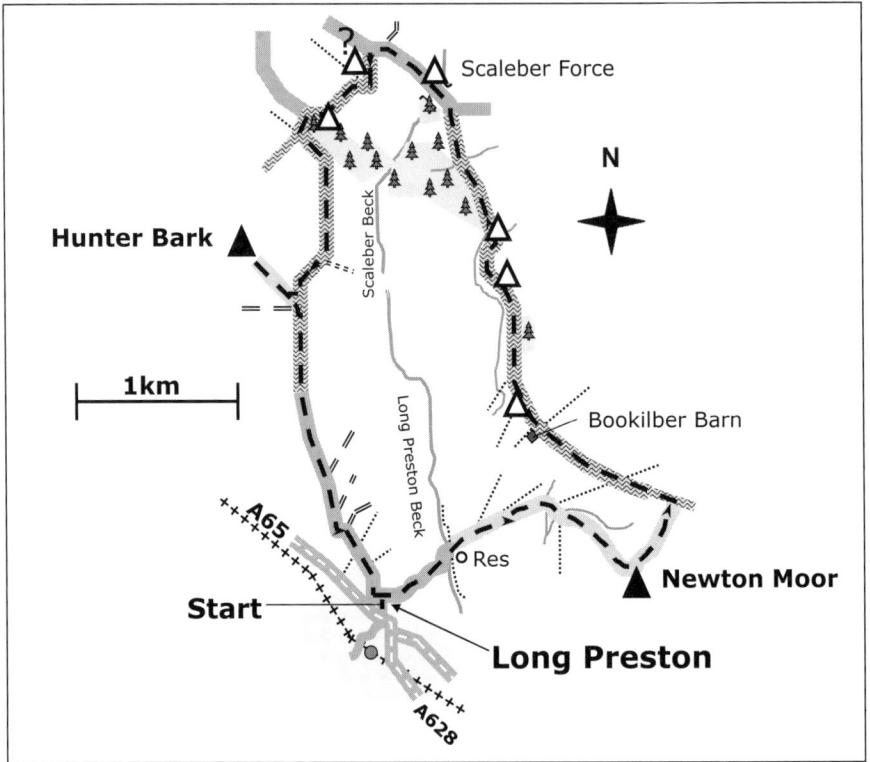

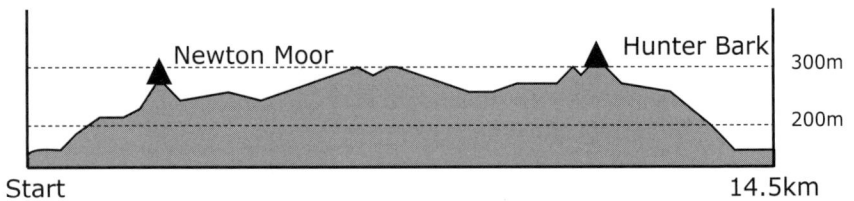

Route and height profile for Newton Moor and Hunter Bark

structure – a reservoir. Looking down with Google Earth™, it appeared to be empty, but that doesn't stop the Health and Safety people insisting on the 'Deep Water' signs.

Walk below the reservoir, then steeply NNE up the edge of the field, with the wall on your left, to a wall-stile (No 1 on the sketch) at SD 8433 5882. It's there that three paths divide (see your OS map), and the route follows the most southerly, going generally ENE and never clear on the ground. A compass helps.

On the other side of stile No 1 keep right (NE), cutting the corner of the rough field for 70m to a wall-stile (No 2) in the SW wall (SD 8437 5884). Over that one, turn more east, keeping a shallow gully to your right and crossing the field for 200m to the next wall and stile (No 3, SD 8458 5888). There is then another field to cross, again due east, 170m to wall-stile No 4 at SD 8472 5890.

In the next field, head NE to make a diagonal crossing, 350m up to a wall, with a small stream to cross near the end. Then you can follow the wall for 100m ESE to

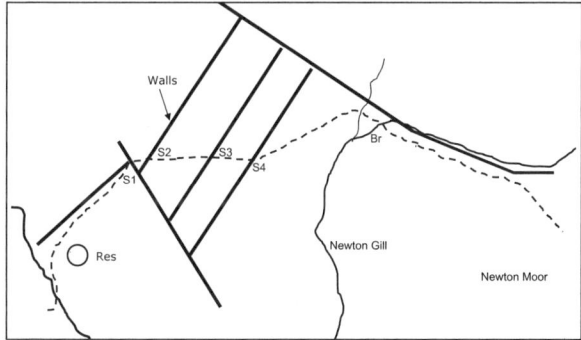

Walls and stiles to Newton Moor

cross the deeper Newton Gill on a bridge (SD 8513 5903), on to Newton Moor. 'Newton' means 'The new farm', probably referring to ancient properties east of Long Preston – 'New House' and 'Little Newton'.

To reach the pillar, first keep ESE along the wall, with Newton Gill on the other side. After 450m, where the wall turns away NE (SD 8548 5896), leave it and make for the pillar, 400m SE up the grass moorland hill. It's an undistinguished site, but the pillar is reasonably sound, with its spider, OS plug and flush-bracket (facing WSW) all intact. That WSW direction is towards Whelpstone Crag, across Ribblesdale, with Tosside to the SSW, both pillars on the ridge with Gisburn Forest behind. They are difficult to pick out. SSW, as always on a clear day, Pendle Hill is dominant, with a pillar on its east end. It's too far away (18km) to resolve.

Pillar details for Newton Moor	
Name:	Newton Moor
Position:	SE 85835 58744
Flush-Bracket No:	S5192
Height:	292m (958 ft)
Built:	June 1949
Historic use:	Secondary
Current use:	None
Condition:	Slightly damaged

Newton Moor pillar – on a bleak day

Turning NW, with Ingleborough making the horizon, Hunter Bark is the light-coloured hill in the immediate foreground. The pillar should be easily visible. NNW, Warrendale Knotts (its 'Langcliffe' pillar inside a cairn) with Sugar Loaf in front, is unmistakeable. NNE, Rye Loaf (its pillar behind a cairn) is the middle of the three high points (Kirkby Fell right, Scosthrop High Moor left, with an antenna).

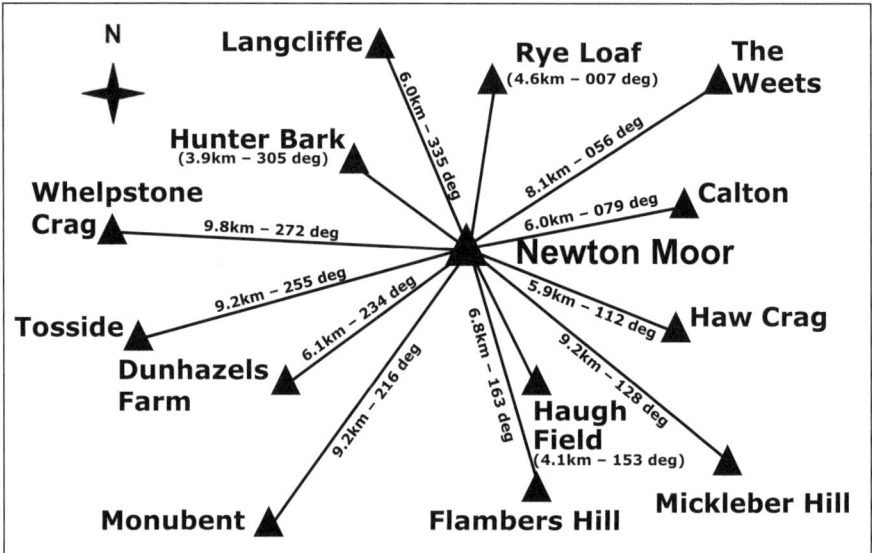

Nearby pillars in view from Newton Moor

NE, The Weets is the straw coloured peak across the valley, with Malham in the deep gorge to its left. The Weets hill then slopes southwards to Calton (ENE), which is too indistinct to find easily. Looking ESE, the horizon is Skipton Moor, with Sharp Haw and Crookrise in front and slightly left. Closer still, and low, Haw Crag is on the same bearing. You should be able to see that pillar.

In the SE, Haugh Field should be visible close by, just beyond the A65, but Mickleber and Flambers Hill, either side of it and further away, are indistinct. Likewise, to the SW, Monubent and Dunhazels Farm are low and difficult to spot.

From the pillar, walk 440m NNE (opposite the flush-bracket), down to a track (Langber Lane), with a loading platform at SD 8603 5911 giving access through the wall. There, go left (NW) and follow the track for 4km to the junction with Back Gill Lane at SD 8416 6245. It's plain walking, taking you alongside Bookgill Gill Beck, past a broadleaf woodland plantation ('The Hawes', opposite the small Langber Plantation on the right) and the Wild Share forestry plantation.

On the 1891 map this lane is a key route, which is clear from its width between the walls and the fact that it was surveyed with benchmarks. In medieval times it would have been a packhorse route. Up to Back Gill Lane I could find only three out of a dozen benchmark records, the first (BM No 1) coming on the west wall after 1.2km, about 20m beyond a path leaving west. The second (BM No 2) is on the right (NE) wall, 400m on from the end of the Langber Plantation, and the third (BM No 3) is on an emaciated gatepost, 200m further on, again on the right.

The lane continues past the Wild Share plantation, becoming 'High Hill Lane'. When it joins Back Gill Lane it keeps that 'High Hill' name and crosses the bridge over Scalaber Beck. Have a look for BM No 4, a rivet somewhere on the parapet. (You will also pass this one during Walk 11.)

Follow the lane 1km NW, then west as the Stockdale Lane track joins from the right. In the field to the north at that point, the old map says 'Roman camp', but there is nothing to distinguish the site now. At SD 8347 6302 go left (south) down the Pennine Bridleway (Lambert Lane, a walled track), following it 1.1km as it turns SW and west to become Mitchelle Lane. On the way there's a ruined barn on the right. There should be a cut-mark (BM No 5) on the NW angle (that's in the field), but I couldn't find it. Then the last one (BM No 6) is on a gatepost by the private track that goes back SE along Black's Plantation.

At SD 8284 6249 go left (south), following the signpost to Long Preston. As you reach the plantation on the left, where another path leaves to the right, keep left along the trees and follow the track SE and then south for 1.5km to arrive on the eastern side of Hunter Bark, with a fence barring your access. Carry on south to a gate and stile at SD 8283 6077 (footpath to Mearbeck), then return NW across the moor for 300m to reach the pillar.

The best I can come up with for 'Hunter Bark' is in relation to the covering of a (hunter's) hut with tree bark for weatherproofing. More common though, is the use of heather, as you saw during the moorland walks from Skipton.

Pillar details for Hunter Bark	
Name:	Hunter Bark
Position:	SD 82638 61045
Flush-Bracket No:	S5436
Height:	315m (1033 ft)
Built:	June 1949
Historic use:	Secondary
Current use:	None
Condition:	Good

Hunter Bark pillar – looking north to Langcliffe and Pen-y-ghent

The pillar is sound, with all its fittings intact, and the flush-bracket faces due west. That direction bisects Whelpstone Crag (WSW, which you looked at from Newton Moor) and New House Pasture (WNW). That's low and indistinct, left of the railway track. Looking north along the Ribblesdale valley is much more rewarding. (By now, the weather had cleared for me.) On the west side of the valley (looking NNW) Smearsett Scar and Moughton are on the same bearing, just right of Whernside on the horizon (Ingleborough and Park Fell are left of Whernside, and a bit closer). I could see the Moughton Pillar, but I couldn't find the closer Smearsett Scar. On the east side of the valley, sugarloaf is very close, with Warrendale Knotts (Langcliffe pillar) behind it, and the high peak just showing beyond its left flank is Pen-y-ghent.

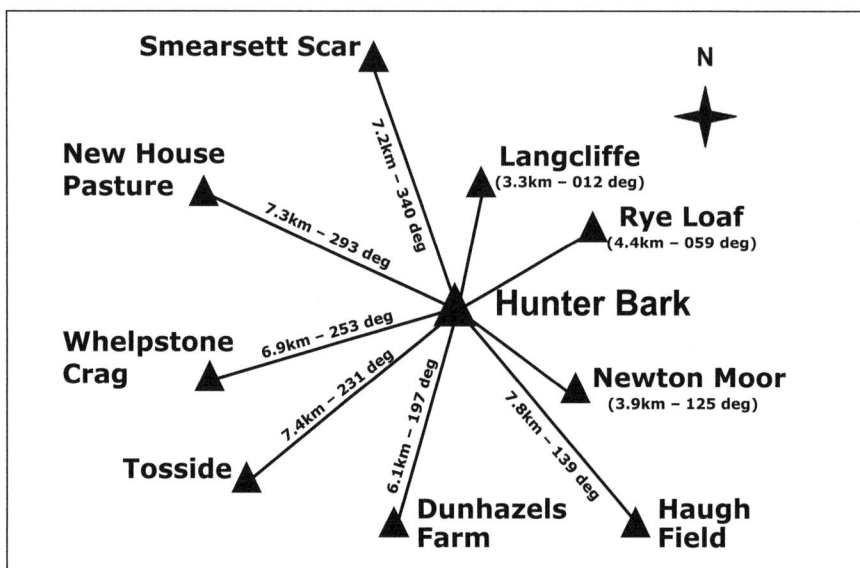

Nearby pillars in view from Hunter Bark

Looking NE, Rye Loaf is now behind Scosthrop High Moor and the peak is only just visible, left of the antenna. The views east are obscured by the nearby moorland, but SE, Newton Moor is easy to spot. Then further away and slightly right of the same line, Haugh Field is low and elusive. Finally, SSW, Dunhazels Farm is just right of the line to Pendle Hill, with an antenna nearby, and SW, Tosside is across Ribblesdale, at the southern end of the Gisburn Forest.

From the pillar, retrace your steps SE to the stile and follow the limestone track (Edge Lane) south. After passing an old way-marker for Long Preston and Settle, it becomes a tarmac lane (Green Gate Lane) and takes you back to the village and the car.

Route summary for Walk 10

Your present location	Your next objective	Waypoint at next bjective	Directions and distance
Village square, Long Preston SD 8341 5821	Track leaving Scalehaw Lane	SD 8404 5854	East along School Lane and Back Lane, then NE along Scalehaw Lane – 900m
SD 8404 5854	Footbridge	SD 8419 5865	NE on track – 200m
SD 8419 5865	Wall-stile No 1	SD 8433 5882	NNE, below the reservoir, then up along the wall – 200m
SD 8433 5882	Wall-stile No 2	SD 8437 5884	NE, across corner of rough field – 70m
SD 8437 5884	Wall-stile No 3	SD 8458 5888	East across field – 200m
SD 8458 5888	Wall-stile No 4	SD 8472 5890	East across field – 170m
SD 8472 5890	Bridge to Newton Moor	SD 8513 5903	NE across field and SSE along wall – 450m
SD 8513 5903	Point to leave wall	SD 8548 5896	ESE, along wall to last bushes – 450m
SD 8548 5896	Newton Moor pillar	SD 8584 5874	SE across grass moor – 650m
SD 8584 5874	Gate to track	SD 8603 5911	NNE across moor – 440m
SD 8603 5911	Back Gill Lane, go straight on	SD 8416 6245	Generally NW (Langber Lane and High Hill Lane) – 4km. Three BMs to find
SD 8416 6245	Pennine Bridleway – Lambert Lane	SD 8347 6302	NW and west on lane – 1km. One BM to find
SD 8347 6302	Lane to Long Preston	SD 8284 6249	South, SW and west on walled track – 1.1km. Two BMs to look for
SD 8284 6249	Stile and gate to Hunter Bark	SD 8283 6077	Generally south on track – 1.8km
SD 8283 6077	Hunter Bark pillar	SD 8264 6105	NW across grass moor – 300m
SD 8264 6105	Return to stile and gate	SD 8283 6077	SE across grass moor – 300m
SD 8283 6077	Town Head	SD 8315 5889	Generally south on track and then Edge Lane – 2km
SD 8315 5889	Village square Long Preston	SD 8341 5821	SSE along Green Gate Lane – 700m

Benchmark summary for Walk 10

BM No	Type of benchmark and location	Grid reference
1	Cut-mark – Wall, 18.9m NW of path leaving SW, SW side of Langber Lane	SD 8491 5976
2	Cut-mark – Wall, 10.4m SE of a wall angle, NE side of lane	SD 8460 6098
3	Cut-mark – Gatepost, 30m south of wall junction, east side of High Hill Lane	SD 8447 6116
4	Rivet – Top of parapet, Scalaber Bridge, NE side of lane, centre (common to Walk 11)	SD 8411 6256
5	Cut-mark – NW angle of Preston's Barn, west side of Lambert Lane (elusive)	SD 8344 6287
6	Cut-mark – Gatepost, angle of wall, south side of Lambert Lane	SD 8301 6246

Walk 11. Langcliffe and Rye Loaf

Start:	Chapel Square, Settle
Map reference:	SD 8204 6350
Distance:	13.0km (8.1 miles)
Total ascent:	560m (1840 ft) – average climbing gradient 1 in 10
Estimated time:	5 hours
Walk grading:	Moderate to strenuous
OS map:	Landranger 98

Walk summary

The route leaves Settle to the NE, crossing the Langcliffe pillar summit and following a path eastward, below a series of escarpments, and then south to Rye Loaf. Return is across open-access land (no grouse restrictions, often wet) to Black Gill Lane. There are nine benchmarks to find.

Parking and access

In Settle, locate Duke Street (B6480) through the town centre. Just north of Station Road (going west) take Chapel Street going east and then go right into Chapel Square. The pay-and-display car park ('Greenfoot') is at the end of that road.

The walk

From the car park, walk north to Chapel Street and then along Main Street, before turning right up Castle Hill and right again to join the lane called 'Highway'. After 150m, at SD 8212 6375, beyond a pair of gates, go right up the walled limestone drive. It rises steeply, with the view of Settle expanding below, eventually ending at a gate.

Walk start in Settle

On the other side take the grassy path that goes right (NE). It crosses a low wall and cuts the corner to the main path that runs eastwards. Follow that, again rising steeply, with the Blua Crag escarpment coming into view to the fore, the route eventually following a wall. At SD 8294 6407 there is a gate, with the path beyond dividing. Keep left along the wall until you reach a ladder stile at SD 8319 6408, which leads to a steep, narrow path up to the Warrendale Knotts escarpment and the Langcliffe pillar. Langcliffe means 'long cliff', and the name is very apt.

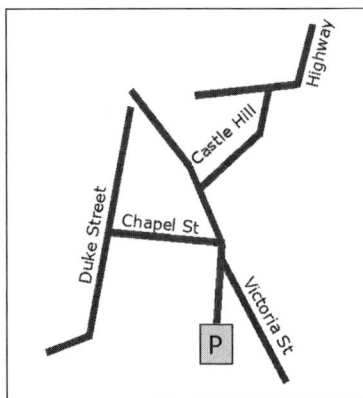

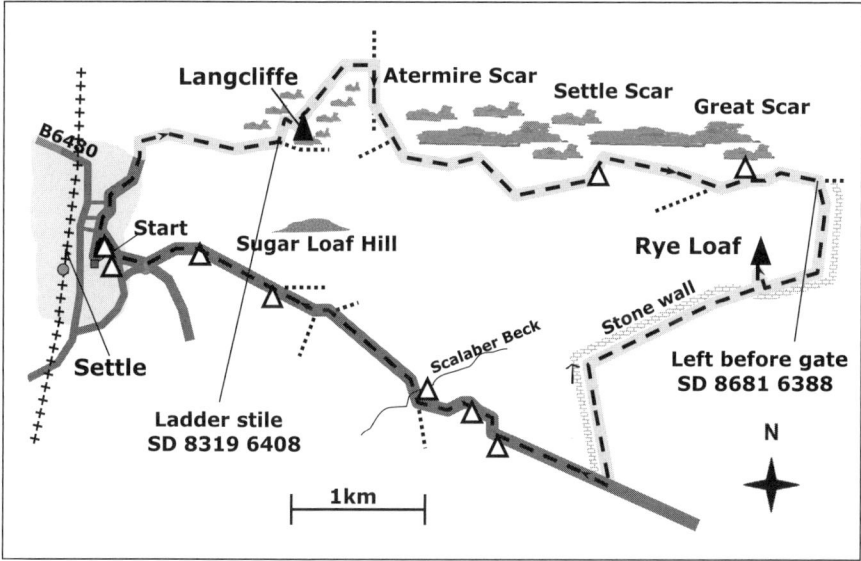

B6480

Langcliffe Atermire Scar Settle Scar Great Scar

Start Sugar Loaf Hill Rye Loaf

Scalaber Beck Stone wall

Settle

Left before gate
SD 8681 6388

Ladder stile
SD 8319 6408

N

1km

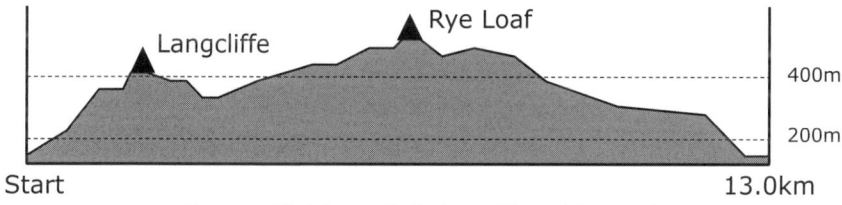

Rye Loaf

Langcliffe

400m

200m

Start 13.0km

Route and height profile for Langcliffe and Rye Loaf

It's a stiff climb, with the path zigzagging through a gap in the escarpment. Near the top there is a low, crumbling wall; go right after that, and the pillar will soon come into view.

It's still sound, with its spider and flush-bracket, but half buried in the rubble from what used to be a shelter. Its plug is missing. Establishing your bearings is best done via the small cairn about 50m away – it's NNE from the pillar, with Pen-y-ghent just to its left, due north. Knowe Fell is 5km away to the NE, but is just obscured by Brent Scar in the foreground. The higher, more distant hill, right of Pen-y-ghent, is Fountains Fell.

Turning ESE, Rye Loaf is the rounded hill, with the pillar and cairn easily visible. The hill to the right of Rye Loaf (SE) is High Greet, with an antenna, visited later in the walk. Looking SSE, the distinctive Sugar Loaf Hill is below in the foreground. You'll pass by the other side of it later in the walk, its name deriving, like hundreds of other cone-shaped hills, from its resemblance to a 'conical pile of refined sugar'.

Pillar details for Langcliffe	
Name:	Langcliffe
Position:	SD 83372 64226
Flush-Bracket No:	S5521
Height:	440m (1444 ft)
Built:	July 1949
Historic use:	Secondary
Current use:	None
Condition:	Good, but buried

Langcliffe pillar – Cairn to NNE

Over the eastern side of Sugar Loaf, Newton Moor is the low hill on the horizon. Near due south, over the tip of Sugar Loaf, Hunter Bark is just behind it. Looking down, and maybe into the sun, spotting the pillar will be very difficult. But if it's a clear day, the best view on this bearing is again to the distinctive Pendle Hill, 23km away on the horizon.

The two pillars in the SW and west are more distant and not against the horizon, so are difficult to spot. But to the NW (Ribblesdale valley to the right), on a nice day the profile of Ingleborough is unmistakable, with its flat top

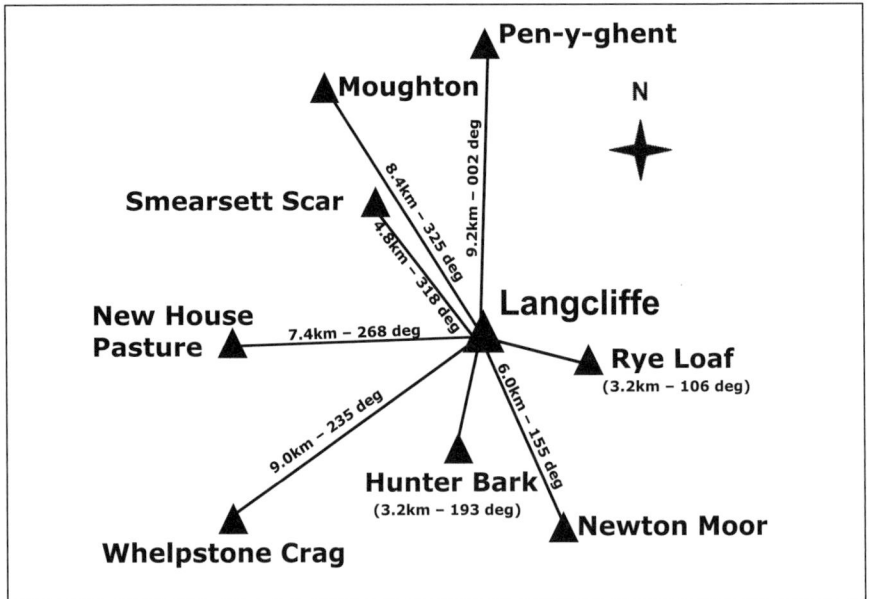

▲**Pen-y-ghent**

▲**Moughton**   **N**

Smearsett Scar ▲   8.4km – 325 deg
                        4.8km – 318 deg
                        9.2km – 002 deg

New House   **Langcliffe**
Pasture ▲   7.4km – 268 deg ▲
                                 ▲ **Rye Loaf**
                                 (3.2km – 106 deg)

         9.0km – 235 deg
                                 6.0km – 155 deg
              ▲ **Hunter Bark**
              (3.2km – 193 deg)
▲   ▲**Newton Moor**
Whelpstone Crag

Nearby pillars in view from Langcliffe

Warrendale Knotts and Attermire Scar from the SE

and ledges. On the same line, in the foreground, look for Smearsett Scar and Moughton. Smearsett is a low, rounded peak, whereas Moughton (behind it) is a high, flat limestone plateau. (I talk about 'Limestone Pavements' in later walks.)

From the pillar, walk NNE past the cairn. There is a clear, meandering path, your first target being SD 8366 6461, a high point with a splendid view of Bent Scar (left) and Attermire Scar (right) to the fore. The large 'Victoria Cave' is clear to the NE. It boasts some fascinating archaeology, suggesting the first humans habited the Dales around 11,000 years ago, leaving behind relics of their primitive weapons.

From the vantage point you'll see below the path that runs under Attermire Scar. Drop down and turn right along that path, following it south and then SE below the scar for 1.8km. There are three gates, a nature reserve, some wet areas, some friendly highland cattle, and the path eventually reaches Stockdale Lane at SD 8474 6382. Before you get there, take time to look back – it's often the case that

Can you spot this boulder with its cut-mark?

the best views are behind. Certainly, the pillar summit and the various scars look impressive from this angle.

Follow Stockdale Lane eastwards. At the gate to Stockdale Farm keep left on the path by the wall, following it into open country, with the Rye Loaf summit always on your right. On this stretch of the walk there are two cut-marks to search for; one on a gatepost (BM No 1) on the lane, the other (BM No 2) on a large rock to the side of the track, more or less when you are due north of the Rye Loaf peak.

At SD 8681 6388 you reach a gate. Don't go through it; turn right instead, through another gate (or over it – this is all open-access land) to pick up a little used path on the other side. Keep close to the right of the wall, with some boggy areas to negotiate, following it SW and then west round to the south of the summit. Then it's a short climb back northwards to reach the pillar and cairn shelter on top.

Pillar details for Rye Loaf	
Name:	Rye Loaf
Position:	SD 86421 63313
Flush-Bracket No:	S5231
Height:	547m (1795 ft)
Built:	August 1949
Historic use:	Secondary
Current use:	None
Condition:	Good

Rye Loaf pillar – Langcliffe behind to the WNW

Having named Sugar Loaf nearby, it's understandable that a rounded, vaguely loaf-like hill nearby might be called Rye Loaf, but I can't say why a rye loaf might be shaped any different from an ordinary loaf. Anyway, the pillar is in excellent condition, with all its original fittings, and the cairn and small shelter are due south, so direction finding is easy. Look first to the WNW, back to the Langcliffe pillar. It's easy to spot, sticking up out of the rubble. In the NW, Ingleborough is on the horizon, but the two closer pillars at Moughton and Smearsett Scar are now obscured by Attermire Scar. Pen-y-ghent is just west of north and again on the horizon, Cow Close Fell is just east of north. Between them is Fountains Fell, with the Knowe Fell pillar summit in front of it and lower.

To the NE, the nearby Kirby Fell gets in the way, but The Weets is just about visible due east. Its pillar is by a wall, so you won't see it. In the SE and south, the four pillars at Calton, Haw Crag, Haugh Field and Newton Moor are each theoretically visible, but are all on low, indistinct summits. The same applies

Knowe Fell
(5.2km - 001 deg)

N

Langcliffe
(3.2km - 286 deg)

Rye Loaf

The Weets
(6.1km - 090 deg)

Hunter Bark
(4.4km - 239 deg)

6.3km - 123 deg

8.4km - 144 deg

Calton

Newton Moor
(4.6km - 187 deg)

8.3km - 171 deg

Haw Crag

Haugh Field

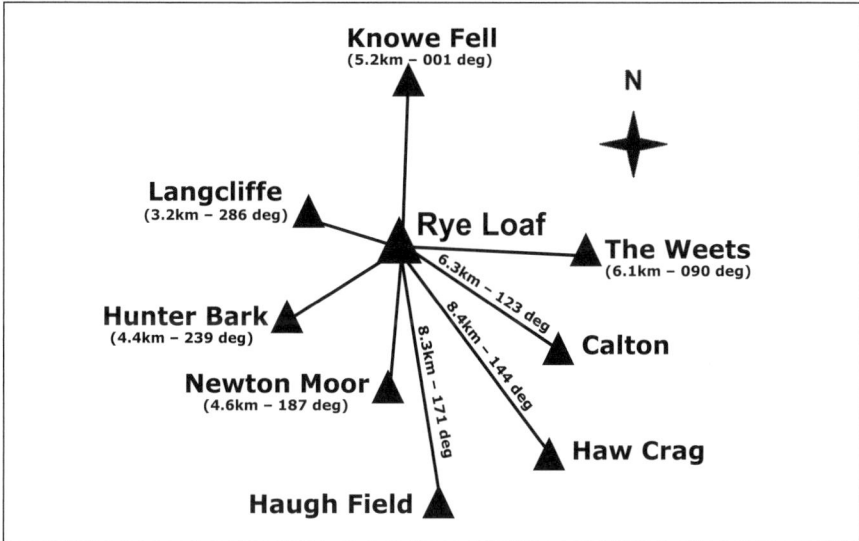

Nearby pillars in view from Rye Loaf

to Hunter Bark in the SW, right behind and in line with the antenna. So it's only Pendle Hill, 22km to the SSW, which again catches the eye if the day is clear.

From the summit, retrace your steps south, down to the wall and stone stile giving access to the other side. From there your objective is the antenna (SD 8525 6261), 1.5km to the SW. You can follow the wall, but boggy areas may force you into several detours. The area is open-access, and there is just one wall to cross, with at least three spots where you can step over it. Just before the antenna there is one very boggy stream – that's best crossed close by the wall, with a fence to hold on to.

The antenna is rusty and neglected, with no obvious function, but there is a vehicle track from it that you can follow SSE to the lane (at SD 8544 6194, 800m). There you turn right, with 4km of pleasant lane walking back to Settle, and with seven benchmarks to look for.

BM No 3 (a cut-mark) is easy – somewhere on the drystone wall on the SW side of the lane, 100m on from the 'bends for half mile' sign. No 4 is also on a wall, 30m on from a 'passing place' sign just after turning first sharp right, then sharp left. Walking on from there for about 600m, joining High Hill Lane, see if you can find BM No 5, a rivet, on one of the bridge parapets over Scalaber Beck. If you're doing the walks in order, you'll have passed here on the Newton Moor/Hunter Bark route, so you will already have found it.

It's 1km to the next cut-mark (BM No 6), under the lee of Sugar Loaf Hill, having passed the bottom end of Stockdale Lane. It's on a gatepost, not far on from a lone bush/tree on the left. Whilst you're searching, you might be

lucky enough to witness some paragliding from the Sugar Loaf summit. BM
No 7 is also on a gatepost, with a cracked top, about 700m further on, as you
go down hill and approach a left-hand bend.

Finally, as you bear right going into Settle, walk down Albert Hill and into
Victoria Street. BM No 7 is near a playground sign at the bottom of Albert Hill,
and BM No 8 is the easiest of them all, on house No 7, Victoria Street.

Route summary for Walk 11

Your present location	Your next objective	Waypoint at next objective	Directions and distance
Car park, Chapel Square SD 8204 6350	Right turn up limestone drive after big gates	SD 8212 6375	NE via Main St, Castle Hill and the lane called Highway – 400m
SD 8212 6375	Ladder stile to path for pillar	SD 8319 6408	NE on track to gate, then east on grass path – 1.5km
SD 8319 6408	Langcliffe pillar	SD 8337 6423	NE, zigzagging through the escarpment – 200m
SD 8337 6423	High point on Warrendale Knotts	SD 8366 6461	NNE from pillar on meandering grass path – 400m
SD 8366 6461	Join Stockdale Lane	SD 8474 6382	South and SE on grass and lime- stone path below the scar – 1.8km
SD 8474 6382	Gate (Go right, not through it)	SD 8681 6388	East on Stockdale Lane, then path, with two BMs to find – 2.2km
SD 8681 6388	Rye Loaf pillar	SD 8642 6331	South over gate, follow wall round SW, to pillar from south – 600m
SD 8642 6331	Antenna	SD 8525 6261	South, over wall stile, SW along the wall – 1.5km
SD 8525 6261	Black Gill Lane	SD 8544 6194	SSE along track – 800m
SD 8544 6194	Car park, Chapel Square	SD 8204 6350	WNW on lane and streets – 4.3km, seven BMs to find

Benchmark summary for Walk 11

BM No	Type of benchmark and location	Grid reference
After Langcliffe 1	Cut-mark – Gatepost, south side Stockdale Lane, entrance to farm drive	SD 8529 6389
2	Cut-mark – Boulder, north side of track, 7.3m north of wall	SD 8628 6386
Black Gill 3 Lane	Cut-mark – Wall stone 54.3m SE of a wall junction, SW side of road	SD 8470 6224
4	Cut-mark – Wall, 69.0m west of a culvert, SW side of lane	SD 8458 6239
5	Rivet – Top of parapet, Scalaber Bridge, NE side of lane, centre (common to Walk 10)	SD 8411 6256
6	Cut-mark – Gatepost, 13.4m SE of a wall junction, SW side of lane	SD 8324 6312
7	Cut-mark – Gatepost by wall junction, south side of lane	SD 8261 6340
8	Cut-mark – NW angle of house, corner of Commercial Street and Albert Hill	SD 8215 6338
9	Cut-mark – NE angle No 7, Victoria Street	SD 8208 6349

Walk 12. Smearsett Scar and Moughton

Start:	Car park by camp site, Little Stainforth
Map reference:	SD 8153 6716
Distance:	13.7km (8.6 miles)
Total ascent:	500m (1640 ft) – average climbing gradient 1 in 10
Estimated time:	5.5 hours
Walk grading:	Moderate, but with difficult areas
OS map:	Landranger 98

Walk summary

The route starts NW to Smearsett Scar, before reaching Wharfe via field paths and a lane. The Moughton pillar is accessed via a track and a scramble up Studrigg Scar; then the return is over the limestone pavements to the Dry Rigg Quarry and a lane across Swarth Moor. There is one benchmark to spot, and weather should not be an issue.

Parking and access

From Settle, take the B6479 north to Stainforth (2km, 1.5 miles). Two lanes lead into the village, going right off the B6479 – note the second of them; there's a car park by the main road (SD 8206 6726). You might need to use it.

I chose to drive on a further 150m to the lane on the left into Little Stainforth (signposted 'no caravans'). It was very narrow, with a 2m (6 ft) packhorse bridge to negotiate. My VW Golf only just squeezed through. Also, the 'hump' would threaten the underside of a long wheelbase vehicle. If in doubt (there's no turning back), park at Stainforth and walk to Little Stainforth. It adds 1.8km to the route.

The walk

Go north along the lane out of Little Stainforth, with Pen-y-ghent impressive to the NE, and walk 550m to a walled grassy track that leaves from the left (SD 8117 6770), signposted to Fiezor Nick. It ends with a gate, with two more gates then side-by-side to the fore. Ignore those and go left around the wall, keeping to its left side and crossing two stiles. A third stile takes you over the wall and across open pasture to a fourth stile (SD 8046 6803), the boundary to open-access land.

From the other side, leave the grassy path to ascend the hill SW to the rocky Smearsett Scar summit. The pillar is sound, but with no plug, and the flush-bracket faces SW, that's opposite to Pen-y-ghent. So NE is the best direction to begin your observations, as shown in the picture.

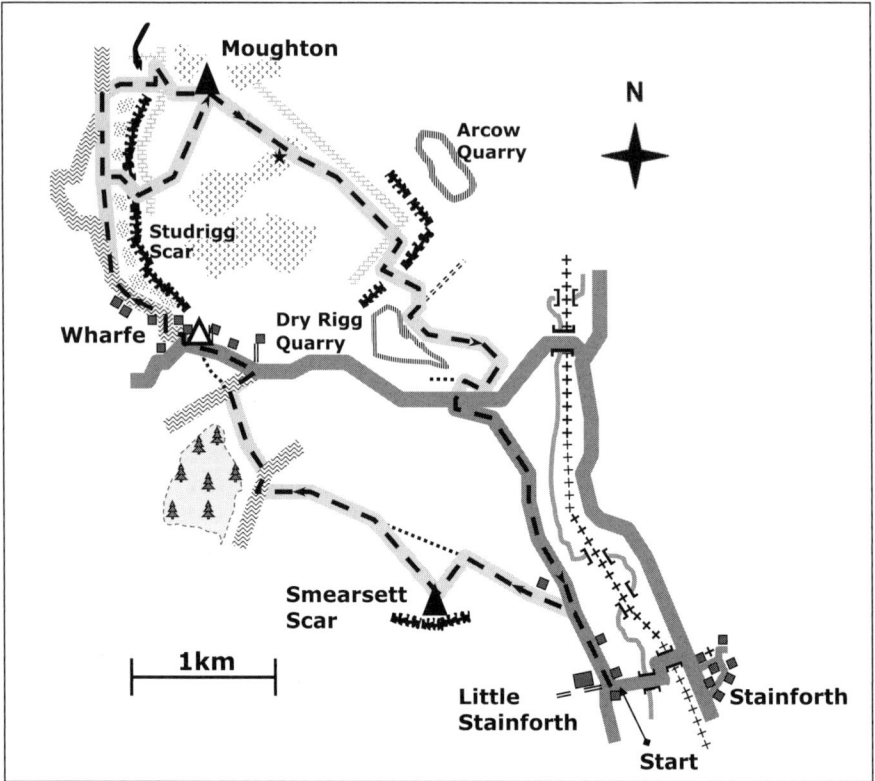

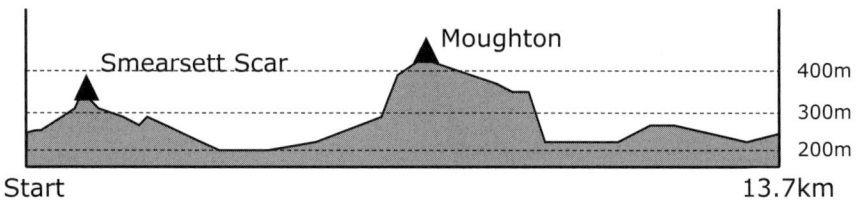

Route and height profile for Smearsett Scar and Moughton

To find the pillar on Pen-y-ghent look for the path to the summit – the pillar's at the top, right of the wall. To the ENE, the steep-sided hill is Fountains Fell, and the Knowe Fell pillar is on the other end of that long moorland top, near due east. It was very clear. Looking SE, the Langcliffe pillar is on Warrendale Knotts, which is the broad rocky hill with the steep right-hand side. The cairn, with the pillar inside it, is just discernable. SSE, slightly further away, behind Settle, Hunter Bark is the low, rounded hill with a wall crossing it, the pillar clear on the summit.

Pillar details for Smearsett Scar	
Name:	Smearsett Scar
Position:	SD 80248 67805
Flush-Bracket No:	S5449
Height:	363m (1191 ft)
Built:	July 1949
Historic use:	Secondary
Current use:	None
Condition:	Good

Smearsett Scar pillar – Pen-y-ghent behind, to the NE

Due south, the unmistakeable Pendle Hill is 26km distant, then SW, New House Pasture is too low and nondescript to find, even though it's quite close. To the NW, the distinctive profile of Ingleborough is obvious. Its pillar is left of centre on the plateau, and I think I could see it. (But, during Walk 17, looking back from Ingleborough to Smearsett Scar, I was not so sure there was line-of-sight.)

NNW, following the line of the hill down from Ingleborough, Park Fell is at the eastern end, with the long sweep of Whernside behind and slightly left. To find Moughton, the other pillar on this walk, look along the bearing to the

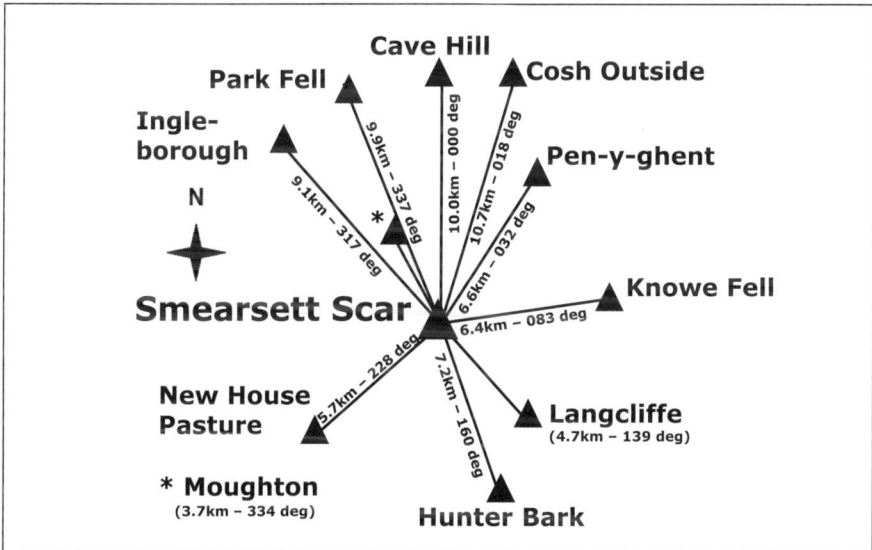

Nearby pillars in view from Smearsett Scar

Whernside summit – the white pillar is easy to spot, close by on the other side of the valley. Due north, Cave Hill is low, at the western end of the Langstrothdale plantation. I couldn't find the hill, let alone the pillar. Finally, ENE, there's a finger of trees pointing at the end of the Cosh Outside hill that forms the horizon. There's a cairn on that end, but the pillar is right, on the next high point. I found it on my photograph, but not with my binoculars.

'Smearsett' means 'The butter pasture', and it's across those pastures (now supporting sheep, not cows) that you leave the pillar, walking 600m NW to regain the main field path at a gate (SD 7981 6829). As you descend, there is a good view of the Moughton escarpment, with the two quarries at the eastern end. The way off later in the walk is down the steep grassy slope between them.

From the gate, the path crosses pasture to another gate, then follows a wall and emerges on to a track (SD 7899 6847). Go right there and follow it 150m to a right-hand bend and take the field path over the wall on the left, finger-posted to Wharfe. It goes NNW by Wharfe Wood, downhill, through two gates and over three stiles, to a ford and a track. Go right there, to the lane (at SD 7904 6932), and then turn left towards Wharfe. (The onward field path from the ford will also take you to Wharfe, but it looked vague and messy.)

It's 600m to the track into Wharfe (SD 7846 6949), leaving off a bend in the lane, finger-posted to Crummock. About 30m before that turning look for a wall junction on the right, with a rivet at ground level. It's the clearest wall rivet I've seen. The route through Wharfe goes left, then right, following the bridleway signs around the north of the hamlet. It becomes a pleasant walled track, rising steadily for 350m to a highpoint (SD 7800 6995). There, take the wall-stile on the right and follow the field path, generally running parallel to the track.

It's good walking, with the cliffs and screes of Studrigg Scar on the right, and you'll not be surprised to learn that reaching the top of Moughton is difficult. The first opportunity comes after 700m (SD 7790 7060), when the path has climbed over a 'nick' between two escarpments, marked by an old tree stump. On the other side, my preferred route continues down to the stream and stile by the gate, but you could go right, along the stream, up to the Studrigg escarpment, and clamber up on the left side of the cascade. There's a faint path, but the ascent is not easy, and best avoided during icy conditions. It's open-access and clearly a popular way up, because there's a stile over the wall at the top (SD 7820 7055, the only one I could find in that continuous wall). On the other side, it's 800m to the pillar, first NE, then NNE, for the best route amongst the limestone outcrops.

Having reconnoitred that route, I tried the better alternative, that is to continue on the field path below the escarpment, walking 600m to a low, bent gate (SD 7792 7118) that is easy to step over. The path actually rejoins the track on the left, but the bent gate takes you into open-access land, with a grassy vehicle track to the fore, winding up the slope. Follow it NE and east for 400m – it takes you up to the wall at the top without the need to clamber up streams.

To get over the wall, go north (left) along it for 100m to a corner, where it's fallen and has been protected by a fence (SD 7828 7134). It was in two halves, top and bottom, and I was able to undo the string ties and squeeze through over the bottom half, making good the ties afterwards. That was fine, but if the wall were ever rebuilt you'd be faced with climbing over it, obeying the rules by causing no damage.

On the other side, go back SE to make a diagonal ascent up the rocky slope, before the final approach east to the Moughton summit. The name means 'The hill with the pile of rocks,' and you'll see later that it lives up to its description.

The pillar is sound, with no plug, and with a cairn close by. The flush-bracket faces NE, but it's NW where you start your observations, to Ingleborough. The pillar was just visible, along with about 50 people! The good weather really brought them out.

Pillar details for Moughton	
Name:	Moughton
Position:	SD 78683 71185
Flush-Bracket No:	S5230
Height:	428m (14043 ft)
Built:	September 1949
Historic use:	Secondary
Current use:	None
Condition:	Good

Moughton pillar – Ingleborough behind, to the NW

NNW, at the end of the ridge from Ingleborough, Park Fell is easy to see (with Whernside left a bit and behind), but due north, low and closer, Sulber is more difficult. It's right of the wall that runs north-south near the eastern end of the escarpment, just poking up. (It was easier to see Moughton from Sulber, see Walk 14.)

Right of the bearing to Sulber, Cave Hill is in line with the NW tip of the plantation reaching up the side of the fell, and just beyond a line of trees and a farmstead in the foreground. Despite that confidence, I still couldn't find the pillar! NNE, Cosh Outside is easier. There's a finger of trees pointing at the end of the hill, (where there's a big cairn), and the pillar is on the slightly higher point above the top of the 'finger'.

ENE, Pen-y-ghent stands out, but its pillar is obscured by the wall across the summit. Right of that is Fountains Fell, so that you should again be able to find Knowe Fell right of that. The perspective is similar to that from Smearsett

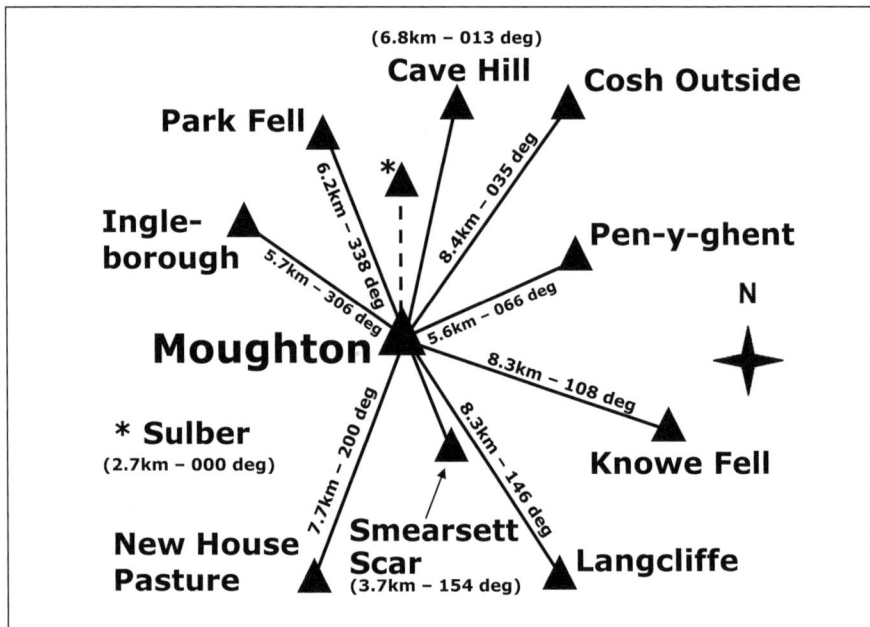

(6.8km – 013 deg)

Cave Hill   **Cosh Outside**

Park Fell

Ingle-borough   **Pen-y-ghent**

                                                    N

Moughton

***** **Sulber**
(2.7km – 000 deg)

                                             Knowe Fell

New House Pasture   **Smearsett Scar**
                         (3.7km – 154 deg)   **Langcliffe**

6.2km – 338 deg
5.7km – 306 deg
8.4km – 035 deg
5.6km – 066 deg
8.3km – 108 deg
8.3km – 146 deg
7.7km – 200 deg

Nearby pillars in view from Moughton

Scar. SSE, Warrendale Knotts (Langcliffe pillar) looks much the same, but is now further away, with Smearsett Scar much closer, just right of that bearing. The green pasture hill with a rocky top is easy to spot. Finally, due south, Pendle Hill is now 30km away, and SSW I soon gave up trying to find New House Pasture.

Leave the pillar to the SE, in the direction of the adjacent cairn. Your first objective is to pass about 100m to the left of a large, well-made cairn that is about 300m away, before keeping on a SE course until you eventually reach a wall, about 1km from the pillar. On the way you must cross some classic limestone pavement, long stretches of narrow outcropping rock formations interwoven with crevices ('grikes') and holes, with the odd wobbly bit thrown in to increase the walking hazards. Such pavements are formed in the harder type of limestone, after the rock has been exposed and scoured by retreating glaciers. Then 10,000 years of acid rain dissolve and expand the natural joints and plains in the bedrock, as well as leaching out any softer bits as holes. It all adds up to a fascinating geological feature, one well worth the photograph.

Once at the wall (around SD 7956 7063), follow it 600m SSE to a corner (SD 7998 7017), then SSW. On the way, you'll pass a fenced gap that allows you a glance down the huge drop into Arco Quarry. 220m on from the corner, at SD 7992 6998, there's a brand new stile over the wall, with a steep grassy slope to negotiate on the other side. At the bottom, take the path going right along the fence, to the edge of the Dry Rigg Quarry. The path then follows the edge of the quarry, emerging alongside the access road and on to the lane crossroads (SD 8038 6912). Go straight on there and it's 2.4km back to the car.

Limestone pavement – ankle breaking ground!

Route summary for Walk 12

Your present location	Your next objective	Waypoint at next objective	Directions and distance
Little Stainforth SD 8153 6716	Track leaving WNW	SD 8117 6770	NNW on lane – 550m
SD 8117 6770	Wall stile, leave path	SD 8046 6803	WNW on track to gate, then left of wall, three stiles, across pasture to fourth stile – 800m
SD 8046 6803	Smearsett Scar pillar	SD 8025 6780	SW across grass pasture – 300m
SD 8025 6780	Regain path at gate	SD 7981 6829	NW across pasture – 600m
SD 7981 6829	Track, go right	SD 7899 6847	NW, then west on path by wall – 1.1km
SD 7899 6847	Stile to field path on left	SD 7906 6860	NNE on track – 150m
SD 7906 6860	Track at ford	SD 7880 6913	NNW on field path – 600m
SD 7880 6913	Lane	SD 7904 6932	NE on track – 200m
SD 7904 6932	Track from right of bend	SD 7846 6949	WNW on lane – 600m, one BM to spot
SD 7846 6949	Wall stile on right	SD 7800 6995	NWN and finally NW through Wharfe on to walled track – 700m
SD 7800 6995	Stream and stile	SD 7790 7060	North on grassy path, over 'nick' – 700m
At SD 7790 7060, after the 'nick' you could go right, along the stream to the escarpment, and clamber up on the left side of the cascade (not easy). There is a stile over the wall at the top (SD 7820 7055). Then it's 800m to the pillar, first NE, then NNE for the best route amongst the limestone outcrops.			
SD 7790 7060	Low gate	SD 7792 7118	North on field path – 600m
SD 7792 7118	Wall breach	SD 7828 7134	NE and east on grass track, then north along wall – 500m
SD 7828 7134	Moughton pillar	SD 7868 7118	SE, then east across grass moor and outcrops – 450m
SD 7868 7118	Wall	SD 7956 7063	SE across limestone pavement – 1km
SD 7956 7063	Wall corner	SD 7998 7017	SSE along wall – 600m
SD 7998 7017	Wall-stile	SD 7992 6998	SSW along wall – 220m
SD 7992 6998	Path, go right	SD 8018 6979	SE down grassy slope – 350m
SD 8018 6979	Lane junction, go straight on	SD 8038 6912	SW, then south, SE and SW around the quarry on path – 1.5km
SD 8038 6912	Little Stainforth	SD 8153 6716	SSE on lane – 2.4km

Benchmark summary for Walk 12

BM No	Type of benchmark and location	Grid reference
1	Rivet – Wall junction, north side of road	SD 7850 6948

Walk 13. Pen-y-ghent

Start:	Car park, Horton
Map reference:	SD 8077 7265
Distance:	9.6.km (5.9 miles)
Total ascent:	490m (1610 ft) – average climbing gradient 1 in 11
Estimated time:	4 hours
Walk grading:	Moderate
OS map:	Landranger 98

Walk summary

A straightforward loop over one of the most famous Yorkshire Dales peaks, starting in Horton, using the Pennine Way by Horton Scar and returning via Brackenbottom. There are two benchmarks, and icy conditions would make the descent hazardous. The walk could be paired either side of lunch with Walk 14 to Sulber, which starts further north and is very easy.

Parking and access

From Settle, take the B6480 and B6479 10km (6 miles) north to Horton in Ribblesdale. There's a pay-and-display car park 100m south of the river bridge. In mid-week I escaped payment by parking on the road south of the car park, but weekends might be different.

The walk

Go south on the B6479 for 250m and take the Pennine Way track leaving to the east (SD 8089 7241). After 200m, go left at the sign for 'Pen-y-ghent via Horton Scar' and follow the walled track NNE for 2.6km until it runs out at SD 8229 7428. There, go right (east), following the Pennine Way path for 2.6km up to the summit of Pen-y-ghent, passing the entrance to Hunt Pot on the way. Near the top, the path veers south, diagonally up the slope, before turning SE for the final stretch up to the wall and the pillar.

'Pen-y-ghent' might mean 'Hill of the border country', with a mixture of Welsh and old French. There is a parallel with mountains like Pen-y-fan and Pen-y-parc in Wales, so one theory is that this Yorkshire peak marks a longer surviving Welsh kingdom. But no one is sure.

The pillar is not very special – a rather crooked stone construction close to the wall. But it's sound enough, with a stone plug, and the flush-bracket faces SSE, which is towards Knowe Fell. The easiest pillar to find first is near due east, Cow Close Fell, which is the rounded hill to the left of the long sweep of Fountains Fell, and to the right of Littondale. Near the eastern end of

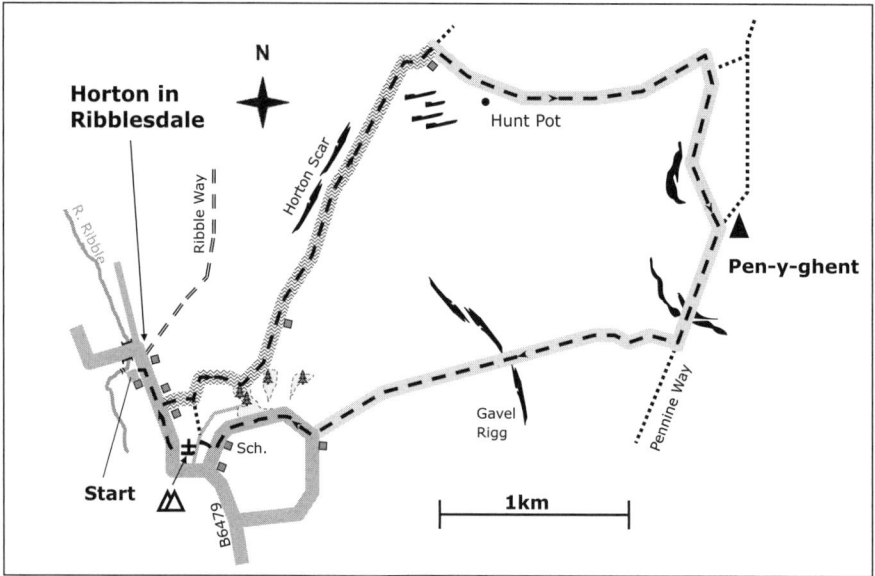

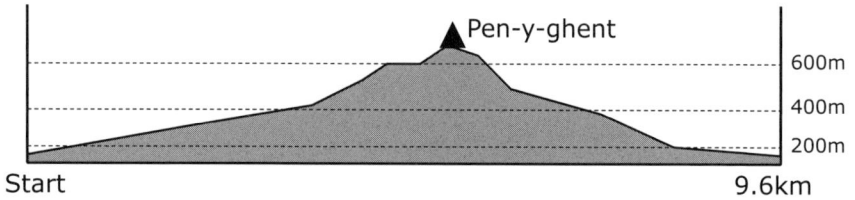

Route and height profile for Pen-y-ghent

Fountains Fell you should be able to spot the two cairns that are on the Pennine Way path at that point. (You pass them during Walk 15.)

To find Knowe Fell, put your back to the flush-bracket and scan the far south of the Fountains Fell ridge. It was too misty for me to see the pillar, but you should be able to spot it. Due south, Warrendale Knotts, with the 'Langcliffe' pillar on top inside a cairn, is the individual 'knotty' hill dropping away steeply into the Langcliffe valley. The higher ground to its left is Attermire Scar.

SSW, Smearsett Scar is low, on the line of the path that leaves from your feet. Then WSW, the flat-topped Moughton is in line with the wall. On a clearer day, both pillars should be visible. Looking over the wall, just north of west, Ingleborough is unmistakeable, and your height on Pen-y-ghent means that you should be able to see the pillar. (Often, it's too far back on the flat top to be seen from lower vantage points.) On the same line, Sulber is close and low, but the wall on Pen-y-ghent gets in the way.

Pillar details for Pen-y-ghent	
Name:	Pen-y-ghent
Position:	SD 83853 73383
Flush-Bracket No:	S5776
Height:	695m (2280 ft)
Built:	November 1949
Historic use:	Secondary
Current use:	None
Condition:	Good

Pen-y-ghent pillar – looking NE

Immediately right of Ingleborough is Simon Fell. Then right of that (WNW) is Park Fell. Again, the pillar should be easy to find. In contrast, NNW, the low-lying Cave Hill is near impossible to find, let alone look for its pillar. You might have more luck than me on a better day. (You have to look over the wall.) Between the bearings for Park Fell and Cave Hill, Whernside should be easily visible, 13km distant.

Due North, again over the wall, Cosh Outside was visible, even in the mist. There is a finger of trees pointing up the slope of the western end of that hill – the pillar is right of that line. Looking NE along the wall, Horse Head is only just visible over the NE ridge of Pen-y-ghent itself. Finally, ENE, Firth Fell is on the horizon, looking along the valley containing Pen-y-ghent Gill.

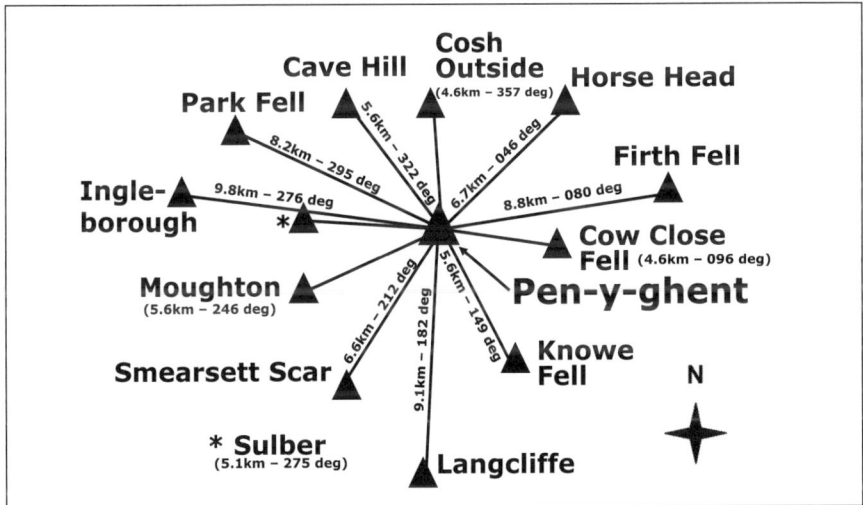

Nearby pillars in view from Pen-y-ghent

Looking back at Pen-y-ghent

From the pillar, continue SSW on the Pennine Way, picking your way carefully down the steep, rocky staircase. After 700m, at SD 8362 7276, take the path right, through the gate signposted to Brackenbottom. It's then 2.1km of easy walking on a limestone path, with Horton Quarry dominant to the fore on the east side of Moughton. As you walk, take the occasional look back for the best appreciation of the Pen-y-ghent summit.

The path meets a lane by a farm at SD 8169 7226. Go right there and follow the road as it loops round NW to SW, through a pleasant woodland glade. There's a school, with a footbridge soon after across the stream on the right. Take that and go left on the other side, walking 150m to find the east entrance to St Oswalds Church (SD 8099 7211).

There are two benchmarks on the church tower, one a cut-mark dating to about 1850, and the second a rare

Protruding bracket benchmark

projecting bracket. That one was part of the 1920 Ribblesdale to Skipton survey line (Second Geodetic Survey) and you can see the rounded head where the surveyor will have stood his measuring staff.

Finally, exit from the west of the church and go right, with the pub to the fore a serious temptation, and then 350m along the B6479 to complete the walk.

Route summary for Walk 13

Your present location	Your next objective	Waypoint at next objective	Directions and distance
Horton car park SD 8077 7265	Track left	SD 8089 7241	South on road – 250m
SD 8089 7241	Path, go right	SD 8229 7428	NNE on track – 2.6km
SD 8229 7428	Pen-y-ghent pillar	SD 8385 7338	East, south and SE on path – 2.6km
SD 8385 7338	Path, go right	SD 8362 7276	SSW on steep path down – 700m
SD 8362 7276	Lane, go right	SD 8169 7226	WSW on path – 2.1km
SD 8169 7226	Church	SD 8099 7211	NW, west and SW on lane, crossing bridge after school – 800m. (Two BMs on the church)
SD 8099 7211	Horton car park	SD 8077 7265	North on B6749 – 340m

Benchmark summary for Walk 13

BM No	Type of benchmark and location	Grid reference
1	Cut-mark – West face of St Oswalds Church tower	SD 8099 7211
2	Protruding bracket – South face of St Oswalds Church tower	SD 8099 7211

Walk 14. Sulber

Start:	Off-road parking, B6479 near Selside
Map reference:	SD 7879 7464
Distance:	3km (1.9 miles)
Total ascent:	80m (260 ft) – average climbing gradient 1 in 20
Estimated time:	1.2 hours
Walk grading:	Easy
OS map:	Landranger 98

Walk summary
A short, easy walk on paths and across open-access land. It includes a visit to the Ribblesdale Fundamental Benchmark, and I've added more detailed discussion of how the levelling system worked, to complement that provided in the main introduction.

Parking and access
From Settle, take the B6480 and B6479 for 13km (8 miles) north to the track access to South House (1km south of Selside). Off-road parking is on the east side of the lane.

The walk
Take the track west from the road, going left where it divides, following the South House B&B sign. Having passed by the house and farm buildings, keep left through the field gate when you are faced with a 'keep-out' sign on the continuation of the track. Cross the small pasture, take the wall-stile at the

Pillar details for Sulber	
Name:	Sulber
Position:	SD 78749 73879
Flush-Bracket No:	S5623
Height:	349m (1145 ft)
Built:	July 1949
Historic use:	Secondary
Current use:	None
Condition:	Good

Sulber pillar – looking NE to Cosh Outside

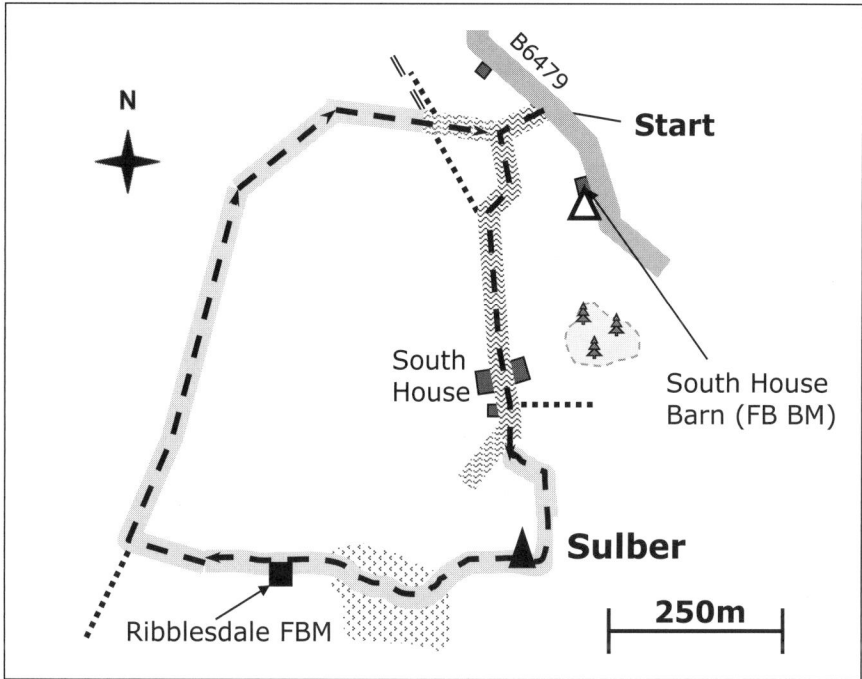

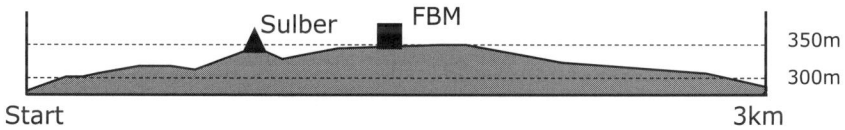

Route and height profile for Sulber

bottom (into open-access land) and follow the left side of the wall on the right, going south and west to the pillar.

The Sulber pillar looks well, with its original plug intact, and with the flush-bracket facing NNW towards Blea Moor. Sulber means 'The sunny hill', and it lived up to its name for my visit, with a blue sky and cotton-bud clouds.

Start your observations due east, to Pen-y-ghent, which is easy to spot. Its pillar is hidden, though, behind the wall on the summit. To the SE the perspective on Fountains Fell and Knowe Fell is similar to that from Pen-y-ghent, but further away. I couldn't find the Knowe Fell pillar. Due south, looking over the southern stretch of the Sulber hill, Moughton is just showing. You can see the pillar and the cairn side-by-side.

Turning west, Ingleborough is poking out from behind Simon Fell, but the pillar is definitely too far back to see. In contrast, Park Fell, right of Simon

N

Blea Moor

Low Green Field Lings

Cave Hill
(4.3km – 022 deg)

8.8km – 350 deg

035 deg

Cosh Outside

Park Fell
(3.9km – 322 deg)

8.6km – 049 deg

Ingle- borough
(4.7km – 278 deg)

6.4km – 123 deg

Sulber

Pen-y-ghent
(5.1km – 095 deg)

9.5km – 123 deg

Moughton
(2.7km – 181 deg)

Knowe Fell

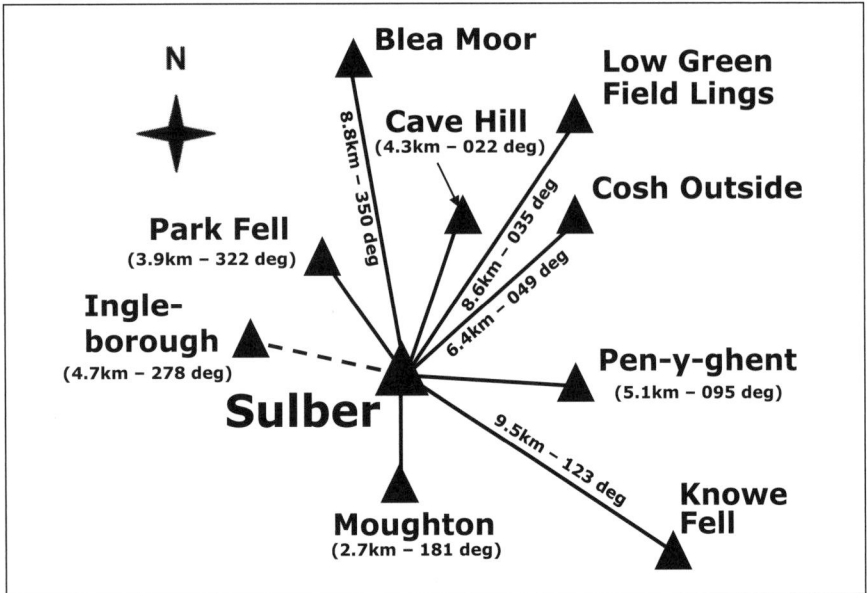

Nearby pillars in view from Sulber

Fell, is easy to spot. NNW, with the flush-bracket at your back, Blea Moor is the gently rounded straw-coloured hill. It was too misty for me find the pillar. As usual, Cave Hill to the NNE was elusive, let alone its pillar. (It's definitely there, and in line-of-sight, see Walk 16 later). Slightly east of that bearing, Low Green Field Lings is just to the north of the Langstroth plantation, on a line with the corner of the wall that you followed on the way up. Finally, on the south side of the plantation, Cosh Outside is much easier to locate, even if the pillar is elusive on the right (back) of the two humps. (The feature on the forward hump is a cairn.)

To reach the Ribblesdale Fundamental Benchmark from Sulber is a little awkward, so there's a wall map to help. It's 450m west of the pillar, against the north side of a wall. The area around Sulber and the FBM is all open-access, and I easily crept through the 'sheep-creep' in the wall west of the pillar, pushing my rucksack through first to lift up the gate (secured again afterwards, obviously).

On the other side skirt round the left side of the rocky depression (going SSW) and cross the limestone outcrops (west) to a gate at SD 7835 7384, with the FBM then about 50m west along the wall. It's a granite pillar, set securely on solid bedrock that is never likely to be disturbed. The tip of the rounded cap on the top is a height reference point, levelled as 356.052m above the Newlyn datum in 1921. That's to within 1mm. But that's only half of it. In a chamber below the pillar there is the absolute, official datum point, seen only by the OS, one that cannot be chipped, bent, corroded or stolen. The one on the pillar top is for everyday easy access.

As declared on the pillar, it is an OS Passive Station, regularly levelled, nowadays by GPS. In October 1999 it was measured as 356.033m, which is 18mm lower. Apparently, that is less than the expected statistical error, so that no conclusion about land movement can be reliable made – a pity.

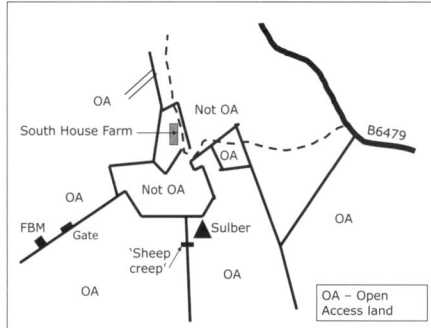

Wall map to find the Fundamental Benchmark

The height quoted is called 'orthometric', which is an 'on the ground' measurement relative to Newlyn. In 1921 it was measured by painstaking steps along the chains of flush-brackets, the closest one (No G2085) being on South House Barn. It's 200m south of the starting point of this walk, on the west side of the road (SD 7885 7446, SE face of building, 2.5m from the east angle, height 289.966m). Then there are more flush-brackets going south and north, linking with the FBMs at Kirby Stephen and Skipton, the latter line including the projecting bracket you saw on the church during Walk 13. So the first steps the surveyor would have taken would probably have been a series of precise theodolite measurements from the FBM, across the fields to the farm, along the drive to the lane, then south to the flush-bracket on the barn.

In 1999 the height was more likely measured by GPS – an important difference. It's purely mathematical, where there is an imaginary ellipsoid that best fits the shape of the earth. It is the height to that ellipsoid (at the specific longitude/latitude co-ordinates of the BM) that is measured, before a complex computer programme does its best to convert it back to the orthometric height, the 'real' ground under your feet. Before that conversion, the height from the ellipsoid at the FBM location was 407.894m – hugely different.

Ribblesdale Fundamental Benchmark

The ellipsoid fits better to some parts of the earth than others, so individual countries adopted their own local ellipsoids (including the UK), ones that fitted best to them – forget the rest of the world! So you can see how complicated it gets. As another point of interest, between 1921 (when the Newlyn datum was established) and 1999, global warming has elevated the sea level. By how much I don't know, but possibly a few mm. But that doesn't matter, since the datum at the Newlyn Tidal Observatory is a bolt in the floor, not the actual sea. Then the 4.751m is added to allow for the height of that bolt above the water.

That 'mean sea level' was determined as the average of thousands of measurements with floating gauges rising and falling with the tide under the observatory, taken every 15 minutes for six years up to 1921. That period allowed for most of the tidal extremes, as the weather, moon and sun conspired to produce them, to be included in the average. So what is that gap now? If they repeated the experiment? Surely, the 4.751m will have shrunk? One day, if the pessimists are correct, the sea could overwhelm the bolt, then what would the measurements mean?

From the FBM, continue west along the grass track, about 30m from the wall. After 300m (at SD 7804 7383), go right (north), following the right-of-way grass path that comes through a gate from the left. 200m on, the path divides – keep left, following it for another 600m. At SD 7827 7461 take the gate and veer right, through another gate – then it's east for 600m on a path and track back to the lane.

Route summary for Walk 14

Your present location	Your next objective	Waypoint at next objective	Directions and distance
Off-road, B6479 SD 7879 7464	Sulber pillar	SD 7875 7388	West and south on track though farm, then pasture and stile, then south along wall – 900m
SD 7875 7388	Gate	SD 7835 7384	Through the sheep-creep, then SSW and WNW around rocky depression – 550km
SD 7835 7384	FBM	SD 7829 7382	West along wall – 60m
SD 7829 7382	Go right on field path	SD 7804 7383	West along wall – 300m
SD 7804 7383	Gate, go right	SD 7827 7461	North on field path – 800m
SD 7827 7461	Car, B6479	SD 7879 7464	East on path and track – 600m

Benchmark summary for Walk 14

BM No	Type of benchmark and location	Grid reference
1	Ribblesdale FBM – North side of wall, 60m west of gate	SD 7829 7382

Walk 15. Knowe Fell and Cow Close Fell

Start:	Verge, Brootes Lane, NW of Malham Tarn
Map reference:	SD 8832 6846
Distance:	15.7km (9.8 miles)
Total ascent:	460m (1500 ft) – average climbing gradient 1 in 13
Estimated time:	6 hours
Walk grading:	Difficult
OS map:	Landranger 98

Walk summary

This is a difficult walk, and will not be to everyone's taste. But it's the only way to visit these two isolated pillars in one walk. The route follows walls that define the National Trust boundary line (purple) shown on OS maps, from Knowe Fell, across Fountains Fell and Barbrook Fell, and on to Cow Close Fell. I did the walk in the July 2009 Monsoon season, and the inward leg back to Brootes Lane was very wet. I stepped in two thigh-deep bog holes. So choose a dry spell, and certainly not when there is lying snow. There are three benchmarks to look for on Brootes Lane.

Parking and access

From Settle, take the B6479 to Langcliffe and turn right up the lane indicated to Malham. It's single track, steep and winding, but with numerous passing places. After 7km (4 miles) keep left at the fork (right is to Malham) and follow the lane NE, with Malham Tarn then to the right. The lane turns north, uphill, and crosses a cattle grid. Parking is 600m on from there, on the grass verge by the wall leaving westward.

The walk

Go WNW along the wall, following the path marker sign. After 350m a path joins from the right – follow that left (SW) along a wall and then across open moor to a gate (SD 8772 6828). Go right after that, WNW. (The bearing is 281 deg – the short section of wall to the right there bears 290 deg.) It's then 1.1km uphill across grass moor, with bogs and 'Shake Holes' to negotiate, the target being SD 8665 6851. (They are also called 'Sink Holes'; areas of ground that collapse when the underlying limestone is dissolved and washed away by underground water.) SD 8665 6851 is where you cross a fallen wall and an insulated section of an electric fence to reach the pillar (then only 50m away to the NW). The fence will be live, so be careful. (To test it, pick a length of reed and lay it on the wire. Depending on how wet it is, you'll feel the faint pulses increasing as you push your hand closer to the wire.)

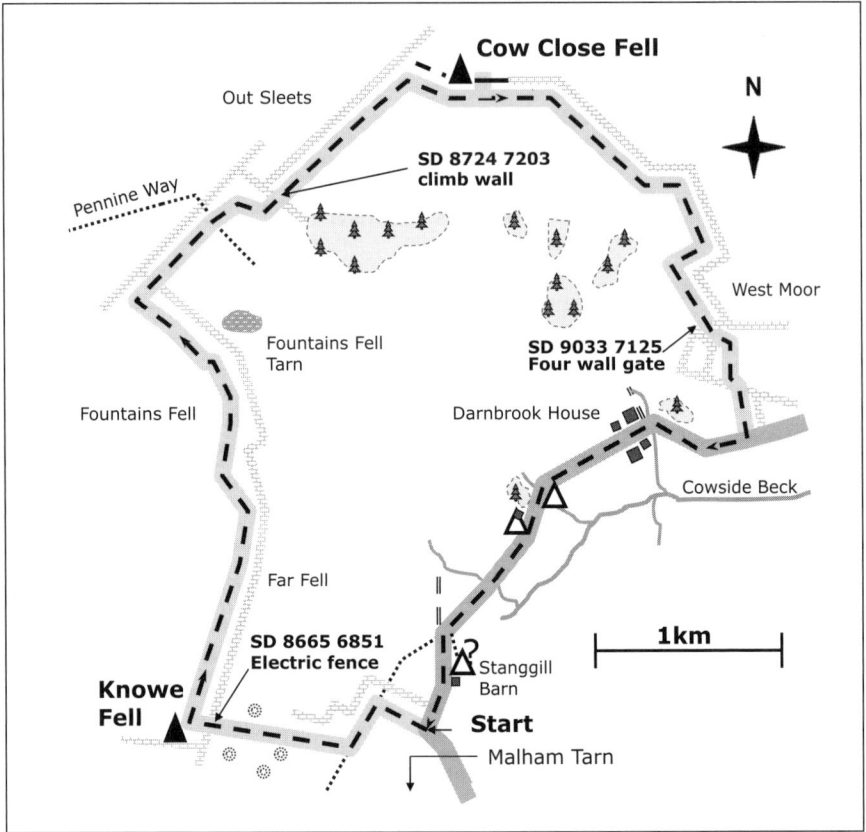

Cow Close Fell

N

Out Sleets

SD 8724 7203
climb wall

Pennine Way

West Moor

Fountains Fell
Tarn

SD 9033 7125
Four wall gate

Fountains Fell

Darnbrook House

Cowside Beck

Far Fell

SD 8665 6851
Electric fence

1km

Stanggill
Barn

Knowe
Fell

Start

Malham Tarn

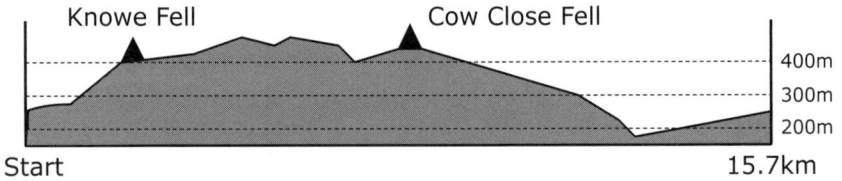

Knowe Fell   Cow Close Fell

400m
300m
200m

Start   15.7km

Route and height profile for Knowe Fell and Cow Close Fell

Knowe Fell pillar is in good condition, with no plug, and its flush-bracket faces south. Knowe means 'Knoll' (Nordic) – a small, rounded hill, which is fair enough, the fell being the southern end of long hill that stretches north to Fountains Fell.

NNW is the best direction to look first, with Pen-y-ghent dramatic in the foreground (its pillar by the wall across the top – difficult to see). Further back, and left, are Ingleborough (flat top) and Whernside ('Whaleback' shape). Due north is Fountains Fell, the next stage of the walk. It means 'The hill belonging to Fountains Abbey' – of French origins, related to the monks who used the abbey. Then right of that (NNE), Cow Close Fell is the rounded, heather-clad hill. The pillar is clear, and looks very tall – for a reason you'll see later.

Pillar details for Knowe Fell	
Name:	Knowe Fell
Position:	SD 86629 68551
Flush-Bracket No:	S5526
Height:	593m (1946 ft)
Built:	August 1949
Historic use:	Secondary
Current use:	None
Condition:	Good

Knowe Fell pillar – looking NW to Pen-y-ghent

NE, Buckden Pike, 15km away, makes the horizon, with Firth Fell on the same line just showing. Its pillar is hidden behind a wall. Turning ENE, Great Whernside is visible, but the closer Middlesmoor Pasture is obscured by the wall you crossed coming up. East, the broad expanse of Parson's Pulpit is close, but now with no pillar to see, and ESE Kilnsey Moor is the hill just left of a small clump of trees in the middle ground. I found the pillar on my photograph.

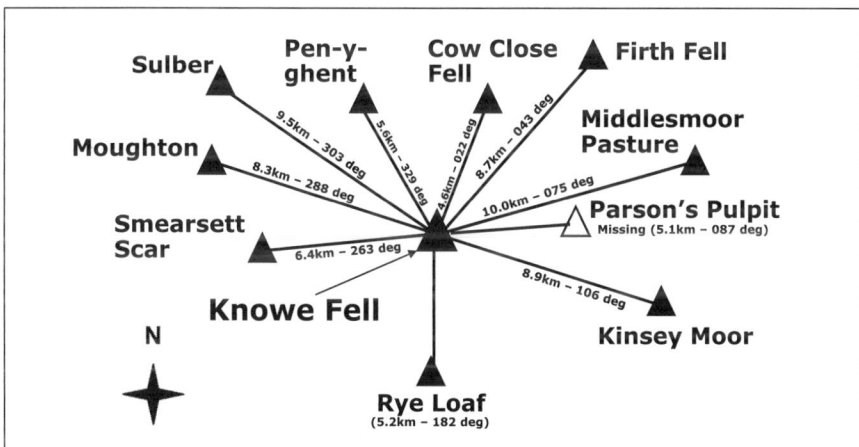

Nearby pillars in view from Knowe Fell

SE, the nearby ground cuts off the view to The Weets and Calton, but south, Rye Loaf is easy to spot, with its cairn and pillar. SW, Warrendale Knotts (with the Langcliffe pillar) is just hidden by Langcliffe Scar in front.

West, Smearsett Scar is the left one of the two green hillocks in the foreground, dropping away steeply on the south edge. The pillar is clear. WNW, the wide expanse of Moughton is backed by the southern slopes of Ingleborough, the Moughton pillar on the high point just left of the line to the Ingleborough summit. Finally, Sulber is low and indistinct to the NW, somewhere right of the large Horton Quarry. I couldn't find it.

From the pillar, walk north, following the left (west) side of the electric fence and wall, with a view down to Malham Tarn. It's 3.2km across Fountains Fell to another wall crossing your path (at SD 8619 7140), where you go right, through a solid gate. During that 3.2km, the maxim is 'keep close to the wall'. There're several bogs to negotiate, and where the wall turns east for 100m, before turning back north, don't cut the corner.

From the solid gate, keep close to the right side of the new wall, eventually crossing the Pennine Way (SD 8679 7201), marked by two cairns, as it comes up from the direction of Pen-y-ghent. (From this area, the views NW should be superb, but I was enveloped in rain clouds so I can't comment.) 270m further on, the wall turns SE. Follow that for 330m to a wall junction (SD 8724 7203), a wall branching from the other side, going NE. Climb your wall at the junction, with two robust posts to help (causing no damage – this is all open-access land, so you can do this) and follow the right-hand side of the wall going NE.

As you walk NE, on difficult ground (even by the wall), Cow Close Fell is to the fore. After 350m there is a stream to cross, and it was from there that I decided to head direct for the pillar. Big mistake! Don't even think about it. It's much more difficult than the stretch of heather moor from Crookrise in Walk 3. Keep to the wall instead, following it a further 1km to the boundary fence at SD 8815 7294. Go right there, along the fence (more difficult ground to negotiate), with the pillar on the other side (north) after 330m. Then walk on a further 70m to the fence corner, where you can climb it easily to visit the pillar close up, again without causing damage.

The area is millstone grit, topped by metres of peat – unlike Knowe Fell, which is limestone. Cow Close Fell reminds me of the most inhospitable parts of the Derbyshire Peaks – Kinder and Bleaklow – where the ground changes on a yearly basis. When they erected Cow Close Pillar 60 years ago it would have been level with the peat. Now it's three feet higher, the surrounding peat having been washed away at the rate of half an inch per year. That's not a general level of erosion – I think the act of erecting the pillar, digging a four foot hole and filling it with concrete, and then encouraging thousands of walkers to visit the site, causes the localised loss of the peat. Eventually, it will fall over, like several in the Peak District. For now, it's intact, with an original plug (too difficult for people to climb up and steal it!) and the flush-bracket faces east.

Pillar details for Cow Close Fell	
Name:	Cow Close Fell
Position:	SD 88453 72795
Flush-Bracket No:	S5618
Height:	624m (2047 ft)
Built:	September 1949
Historic use:	Secondary
Current use:	None
Condition:	Good

Cow Close Fell pillar – looking east towards Great Whernside

As the cloud rolled in, I got a fleeting glimpse of Pen-y-ghent to the west, and I managed the photograph to Great Whernside in the east. Then I was engulfed. To the NW, Cosh Outside should be visible over the right of Plover Hill, and Horse Head should be clear to the north, the other side of the Littondale valley. Beyond that (NNE), across the next valley (Langstrothdale), the bleak Yockenthwaite Moor will form the horizon, then with Buckden Pike to the NE and Great Whernside to the east. The line to Great Whernside

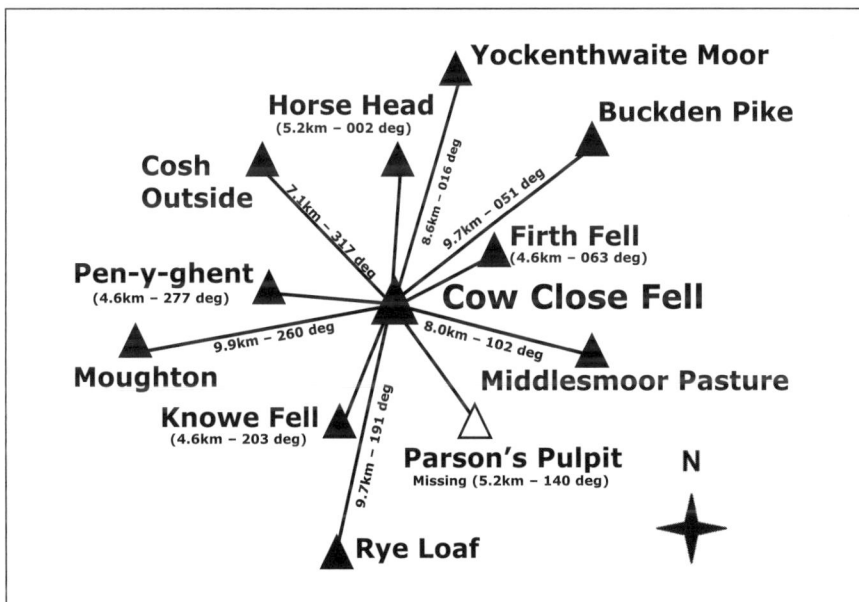

Yockenthwaite Moor

Horse Head
(5.2km – 002 deg)

Buckden Pike

Cosh Outside

7.1km – 317 deg

8.6km – 016 deg

9.7km – 051 deg

Firth Fell
(4.6km – 063 deg)

Pen-y-ghent
(4.6km – 277 deg)

Cow Close Fell

9.9km – 260 deg

8.0km – 102 deg

Moughton

Middlesmoor Pasture

Knowe Fell
(4.6km – 203 deg)

9.7km – 191 deg

Parson's Pulpit
Missing (5.2km – 140 deg)

N

Rye Loaf

Nearby pillars in view from Cow Close Fell

crosses the middle of the closer 'Old Cote Moor Top' ridge, sloping down to the SE. Firth Fell (left) and Middlesmoor Pasture (right) are both on that ridge.

SE, the horizon will be Thorpe Fell, with the Parson's Pulpit site to the fore. South, you will be looking down the valley, the way back, with Knowe Fell left and Rye Loaf on the horizon. Finally, WSW, Moughton might just be visible left of Pen-y-ghent.

From the pillar, regain the south side of the fence and follow it east. After 300m it reaches a wall, where you continue east. 600m further on (on West Moor), the wall turns SSE, then makes an east-south-west excursion, before going SSE again and eventually reaching a makeshift gate (SD 9033 7125) at a junction of four walls. From the pillar to that gate is 3.2km, and the maxim is 'don't take any shortcuts – keep to the wall'. It's difficult walking, and when I tried to cut across the 'excursion', it got even harder.

Go though the gate and follow the left of the wall that continues SE, turning the corner after 200m and going SW. 100m down the hill, the rough pasture becomes more grassy – turn SSE there and pass under the pylons, heading 250m to a gate in the wall that crosses NW-SE at the bottom. Then you can follow the right side of yet another wall for 350m down to the lane. Strictly, at that point I think the limit of open-access is the left of that wall, but by then you won't care!

From there to the car is 3.5km, on a very quiet lane, with pleasant limestone scenery to the left – Cowside and Cowside Beck. On balance, I think 'Cow' refers to a 'Dam' (to create a weir in a stream), rather than the bovine meaning – there are quite a few 'Cowsides' in the Dales. As you consider that, look for two cut-marks, close together, one on the bridge parapet over Thoragill Beck (after 1.6km – for once, not on the road side of the wall) and one soon after on a barn on the right. There were numerous rivets I couldn't find, and there should be a cut-mark on the Stanggill Barn just after the cattle-grid 300m short of the car. I searched in vain.

Route summary for Walk 15

Your present location	Your next objective	Waypoint at next objective	Directions and distance
Lane side, SD 8832 6846	Gate, go right	SD 8772 6828	WNW and SW on grass path – 750m
SD 8772 6828	Wall and electric fence	SD 8665 6851	WNW (bearing 281 deg) across rising moor – 1.1km
SD 8665 6851	Knowe Fell pillar	SD 8663 6855	NW on moor – 50m
SD 8663 6855	Wall junction and gate – go right	SD 8619 7140	NNE, north and NW along fence and wall – 3.2km
SD 8619 7140	Cross Pennine Way	SD 8679 7201	NE along wall – 850m
SD 8679 7201	Climb wall and go left, right of new wall	SD 8724 7203	NE along wall, then SE along next wall to wall junction – 500m
SD 8724 7203	Boundary fence	SD 8815 7294	NE along wall – 1.3km
SD 8815 7294	Cow Close Fell pillar	SD 8845 7279	ESE along fence – 320m
SD 8845 7279	Gate at four walls junction	SD 9033 7125	East along fence and wall, SSE, east, south, west, SSE along wall – 3.2km
SD 9007 7165	Lane	SD 9060 7044	SE, then south by wall, SSE across meadow to gate, south by wall to lane – 900m
SD 9060 7044	Car, lane side	SD 8832 6846	West round to south – 3.5km (Three BMs to look for)

Benchmark summary for Walk 15

BM No	Type of benchmark and location	Grid reference
1	Cut-mark – SE face of SE parapet of bridge, 3.7m NE of stream centre	SD 8915 7008
2	Cut-mark – East face, 3.7m north of SE angle, building, west side of lane	SD 8905 6995
3	Cut-mark – NW angle of Stanggill Barn, east side of lane (elusive)	SD 8842 6874

Walk 16. Cave Hill and Low Green Field Lings

Start:	Old Ing, north of Horton in Ribblesdale
Map reference:	SD 8028 7715
Distance:	13.5km (8.4 miles)
Total ascent:	300m (980 ft) – average climbing gradient 1 in 19
Estimated time:	5 hours
Walk grading:	Difficult
OS map:	Landranger 98

Walk summary

This is a pure trigpointing walk, typical of the fanatical, even masochistic, pursuit of pillars by the enthusiasts. It's one you might leave to the end if you don't relish ploughing across rough grass moor and through dense forests. The walk takes in a section of the Pennine Way for the first pillar (with a couple of benchmarks), but the second can only be reached via the Langstrothdale plantation, and what you see on Google Earth™ and the OS maps is probably not what you'll find when you get there. So don't try it in winter, or when it's wet.

Parking and access

From Settle, take the B6480 and B6479 10km (6 miles) north to Horton in Ribblesdale. After the humped bridge, go left and then immediately right on the lane marked as a no-though road. It's single track with passing places, but on on a fine August day I met no traffic either way. Follow it for 5km (3 miles) through the gate at High Birkwith, where the tarmac gives way to limestone, so go carefully. Parking is on the grass verge 400m up the hill, as a track leads off right.

The walk

Walk 250m NE to the gate and then go left (north), joining the Pennine Way. The whole route is surveyed with old benchmarks, but you'll have to look very hard to spot the one on the gatepost - it's badly eroded.

200m along the Pennine Way you come to a gate (SD 8038 7756), with Cave Hill to the fore and, over the wall to the right, a stream that pours into the Calf Holes cave. There was no one caving whilst I was there, but it's a popular challenge for the pothole enthusiasts. On the old maps (1896 and 1910), it's called Dry Lathe Cave, the area itself being called Dry Lathe (a 'Lathe' being an Anglo Saxon land division, or a granary).

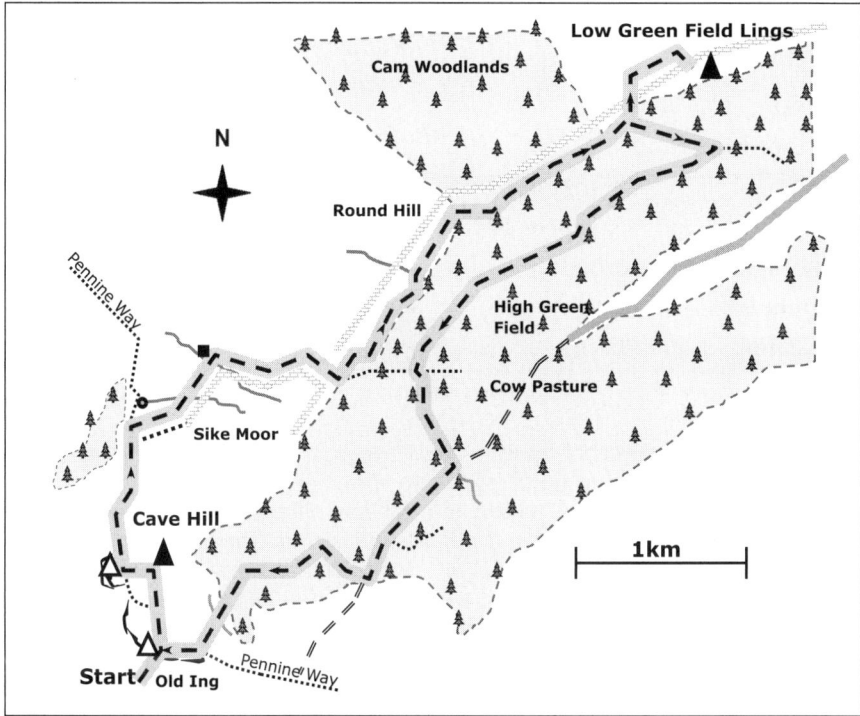

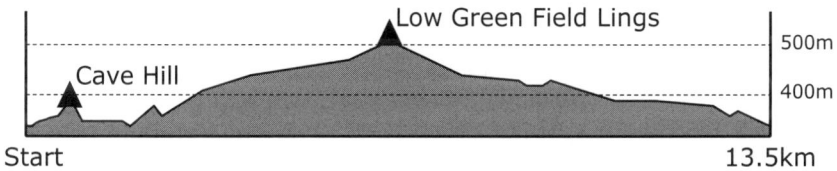

Route and height profile for Cave Hill and Low Green Field Lings

There are numerous caves in the area, so that name for Cave Hill is not surprising. It's easy to reach the pillar; just walk north up the grassy slope – it's open-access.

It's an undistinguished hill, and it's not surprising that it's hard to locate when looking down from nearby higher peaks. However, it's probably the most central location within the circle of the 'Three Peaks', so the views are not bad. The pillar is sound, with its original plug, and the flush-bracket faces just west of due south.

Start by looking WSW towards Ingleborough, as in the picture. You can just see the right-hand end, above Simon Fell, with a stone shelter (it's actually cruciform shaped). The pillar is left of that shelter, but I think it's too far back

Pillar details for Cave Hill	
Name:	Cave Hill
Position:	SD 80378 77850
Flush-Bracket No:	S5227
Height:	385m (1263 ft)
Built:	September 1949
Historic use:	Secondary
Current use:	None
Condition:	Good

Cave Hill pillar – looking WSW to Ingleborough and Park Fell

on the flat top to be visible. Right and forward (right of the pillar in the picture), is Park Fell. That pillar is easy to spot.

WNW is the long sweep of Whernside, with its pillar hidden behind the wall along the top. Likewise, Blea Moor pillar is not visible (the low, fawn-coloured hill to the NW, right of Whernside); it's again too far back. Then NNW, Great Knoutberry Hill is on the horizon, with its squat stone pillar theoretically in

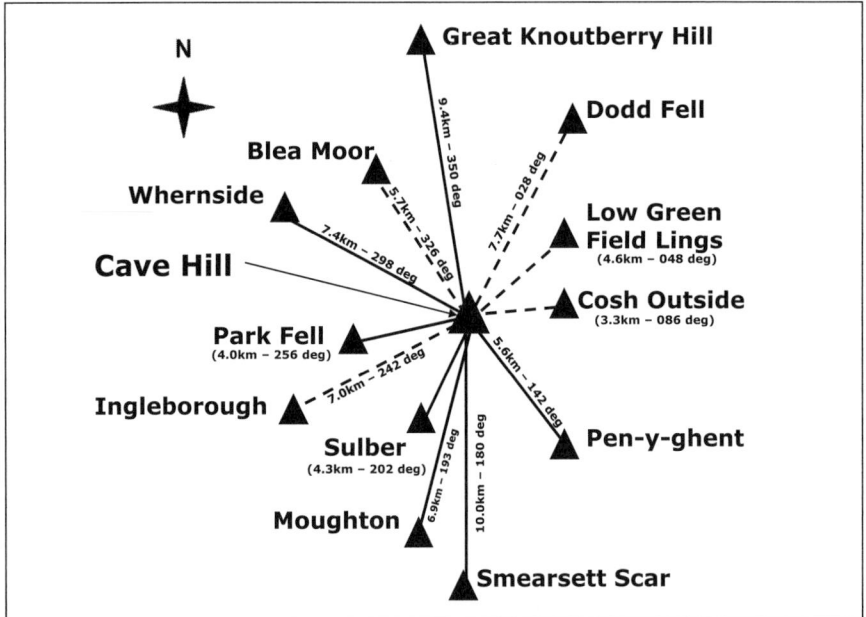

Nearby pillars in view from Cave Hill

view. It blends in with the end of the wall that snakes up to the summit. NNE, Dodd Fell is another pillar that's too far back to see. It's a rounded peat moor top, and the ground 500m in front of the pillar site (from this line-of-sight) is only 10m lower.

The second pillar on this walk, Low Green Field Lings to the NE, would have been in view if the forest weren't there. The trees just obscure it. Looking due east, over the plantation, Cosh Outside has a large cairn on the end prominence. Then the pillar is 300m behind that, and obscured. So why not put the pillar on the end by the cairn, where you could see it? I can't imagine.

SE, Pen-y-ghent is showing clear enough, but that's another pillar well hidden by a wall. SSW (with your back to the flush-bracket), the long flat top of Moughton has its cairn and white pillar on the right-hand side. Left of Moughton, due south, the small prominence is Smearsett Scar (with, on a clear day, Pendle Hill behind it). I found that pillar on my zoomed photographs. Finally, right of Moughton, near SW, Sulber is low and close, left of the farm with the long line of trees below it. On my photographs, I could even make out the sheep-creep in the wall behind it! Overall, though, Cave Hill has poor line-of-sight to its surrounding pillars.

Leave the summit due west, 270m across the rough grass back to the track. The target is SD 8020 7784, which is BM No 2, a pivot. See if you can find it on the wall under the tree. Then go right (north), following the Pennine Way for 900m to the Ling Gill Nature Reserve.

There's a fence gate on the right (SD 8026 7869), and an information board on the left, describing the merits of the Reserve. It has a map (indicating a benchmark which is now missing), on which it shows the footpath to the moor leaving alongside the fence going east. In contrast, the OS maps show it leaving further north, on the other side of the steam that ends in a pothole (see the sketch).

I went east along the fence, where there was evidence it was walked. It was tough going, the fence and wall veering NNE after 250m and crossing the stream (which was awkward). Then it's 400m (left of the fence) to a building and wall junction alongside another stream. There, take the gate on the right, cross the

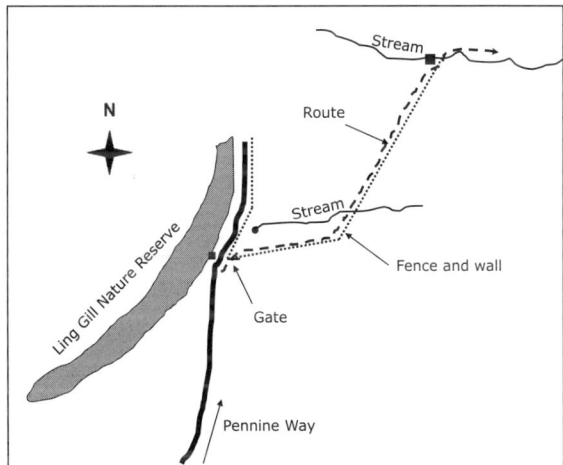

Route off the Pennine Way

stream and follow its north side (going ESE). After 150m, the wall crosses the stream and you then follow that for another 900m up to the plantation (SD 8158 7896). I found it hard work, after some very wet weather.

Turn left at the tree-line, walking between the wall and the plantation. You can then follow that wall all the way to the next pillar (2km), generally on its right (SE) at first, but changing to the left (north) on the NE side of the northern 'arm' of the forest. It's more hard walking, with boggy bits, deep heather and grass, a difficult stream to cross and with the trees sometimes overhanging. As you enter the plantation at Round Hill, the wall turns east across a clearing for 300m, before going NE again along an 'avenue'.

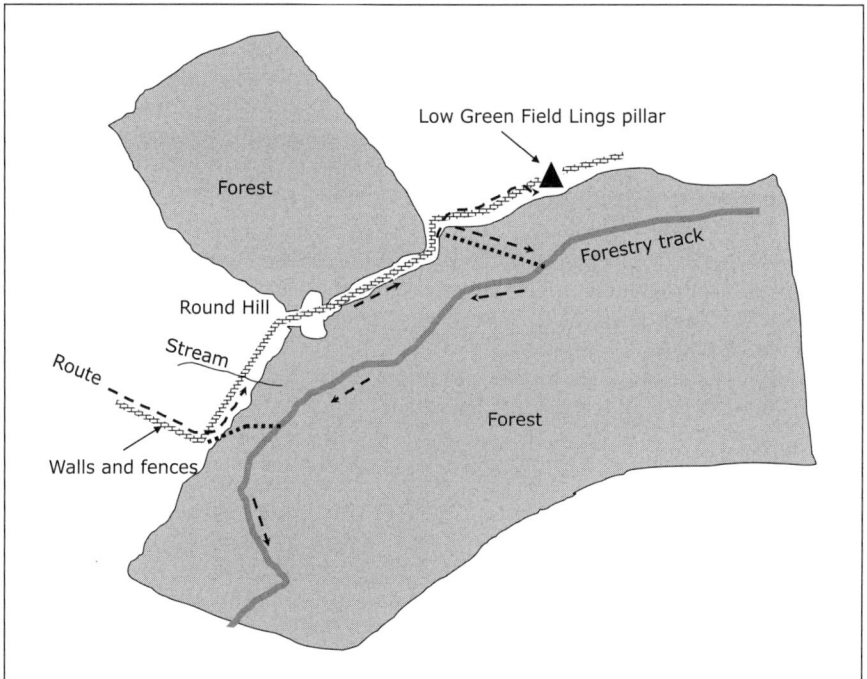

The route through the forest

200m after you emerge on the NE side, you'll pass a stile (SD 8337 8054) into the trees. It's the point you'll return to after visiting the pillar. From there to the pillar, now using the north side of the wall, is better walking, with quad-bike tracks to follow. (Cross back 100m before the pillar.)

There's another map to help, which you should look at alongside your OS map. Note that the alternative of using the forestry track, first fighting your way to it along the marked right-of-way through the trees, and then fighting your way back again later on nearer the pillar, is even more difficult.

Pillar details for Low Green Field Lings	
Name:	Low Green Field Lings
Position:	SD 83834 80881
Flush-Bracket No:	S5744
Height:	501m (1644 ft)
Built:	September 1949
Historic use:	Secondary
Current use:	None
Condition:	Good

Low Green Field Lings pillar – looking SW to Ingleborough

The 'lings' in Low Green Field Lings means, I think, some sort of heather. And I assume that the valley was originally described as having two green field areas, one high and one low (see your OS map). Whatever the origin, the pillar is in good shape, with a stone plug and with a flush-bracket that faces SE.

SW, Ingleborough is now 12km away, but more visible over Simon Fell. This time you can see the pillar, just left of the shelter. In contrast, Park Fell pillar is now more difficult to spot, because you're looking from a higher vantage point. It's not quite against the horizon, left of the wall on the top. West, Whernside looks much the same, and NW, Great Knoutberry Hill is now obscured by Oughtershaw Side. But north, I think that the Dodd Fell pillar is just visible – there is a candidate feature right on the top, beyond a wall in the foreground.

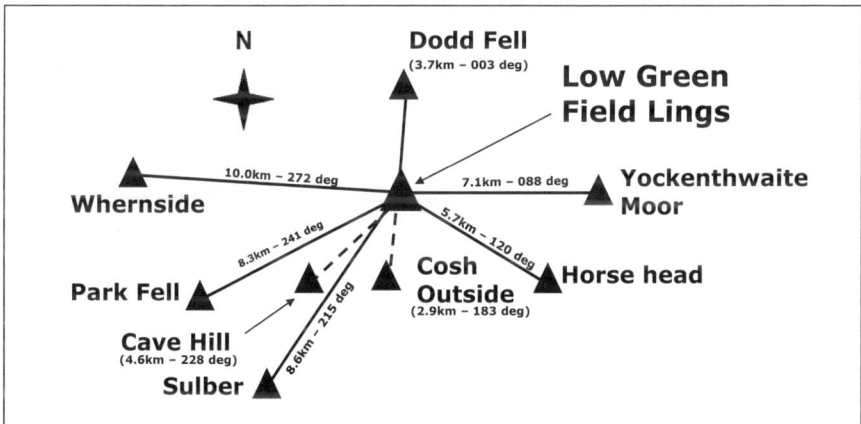

N

Dodd Fell
(3.7km – 003 deg)

Low Green Field Lings

10.0km – 272 deg

Whernside

7.1km – 088 deg

Yockenthwaite Moor

8.3km – 241 deg

5.7km – 120 deg

Park Fell

Cosh Outside
(2.9km – 183 deg)

Horse head

2.5km – 215 deg

Cave Hill
(4.6km – 228 deg)

8.6km – 221 deg

Sulber

Nearby pillars in view from Low Green Field Lings

Due east, diagonally across the fence, Yockenthwaite Moor is the long sweep of moor sloping down to the right. The pillar should be visible, but I couldn't find it. Back and right of that, on the horizon, is Buckden Pike, then right again, SE, Horse Head is across the forest. The pillar is just visible in front of a wall.

South, the cairn on the end of Cosh Outside is clear, but the pillar is well left of that, behind the wall that runs along the top. I don't think it's visible. Finally, the Cosh ridge now obscures Pen-y-ghent, but SSW, diagonally across the fence, you can still see the farm by Sulber. And, nearer SW, Cave Hill is definitely obscured by the trees.

From the pillar, retrace your steps to the stile (SD 8337 8054) that enters the forest. (There's a fence in your way by that stile – if you climbed it on the way out like I did, you won't have noticed that it's only 40m long, and you can walk round it!) The path through the forest is clear enough, but it's more hard walking I'm afraid. After 170m there's a huge Shake Hole in the way, surrounded by dense trees. I edged around it very gingerly – it's a significant hazard, so be careful. From there it's another 400m until you emerge on to the forestry track (SD 8391 8041); a hard limestone surface that comes as a great relief.

That track takes you back to the Old Ing gate and the car, snaking its way generally SW through the plantation for 6km. One thing that struck me was the absolute silence, except for the odd Magpie chattering in the distance – no bird song, no walkers, no rustling creatures. But I did pass a logger, piling up the timber, the driver coaxing and nudging the logs into position as if the massive steel grab was a delicate extension of his own hands – it was fascinating.

Looking at the piles, and the notices warning you not to climb on them, I visualised the effect of removing a key log, like a river log jam, and watching the whole lot cascade down the slope, back to where the logger had just brought them from. I moved on hurriedly, lest the temptation grow.

Logger at work

Route summary for Walk 16

Your present location	Your next objective	Waypoint at next objective	Directions and distance
Verge, Old Ing SD 8028 7715	Gate (with BM)	SD 8042 7735	NE on track – 250m (One BM)
SD 8042 7735	Calf Holes	SD 8038 7756	North on track – 200m
SD 8038 7756	Cave Hill pillar	SD 8038 7785	North on grass hill – 300m
SD 8038 7785	Rejoin track	SD 8020 7784	West on grass hill – 270m (One BM)
SD 8020 7784	Fence gate, go right	SD 8026 7869	Generally north on Pennine Way track – 900m
SD 8026 7869	Reach plantation	SD 8158 7896	East and NE by fence to building, cross stream and follow it ESE, then follow wall east and SE to plantation – 1.7km
SD 8158 7896	Low Green Field Lings pillar	SD 8383 8088	NNE, then ENE, following wall by trees, through the forest, and by trees again – 2km
SD 8301 8030	Back to path into trees	SD 8337 8054	Retrace the route WSW to stile into forest – 600m
SD 8337 8054	Forestry Track	SD 8391 8041	ESE through trees, past a deep Shake Hole – 600m
SD 8391 8041	Car, Old Ing	SD 8028 7715	Generally SW on track – 6km

Benchmark summary for Walk 16

BM No	Type of benchmark and location	Grid reference
1	Cut-mark – Gatepost, north side of track, NE face	SD 8042 7735
2	Pivot – Wall, west side of track, 116.0m north of wall junction	SD 8020 7784

Part C. Walks based around Ingleton

Ingleton is easily accessible from the A65 trunk road, and the small town provides an ideal gateway to two of the most striking of the Dales' fells, Ingleborough and Whernside. Driving NE, Kingsdale and Chapel-le-Dale exhibit the classic Dales scenery; limestone scars, caves and potholes, and provide onward access to Deepdale and Widdale.

There is an excellent website at www.ingleton.co.uk, including information on accommodation and camping. There is also a webcam at www.ingleboroughwebcam.co.uk, trained on the Ingleborough mountain. It's a useful way of assessing the weather before you make a journey.

The town is built on two levels, with the valley crossed by the disused railway viaduct. You can't walk it, which is a great pity – an opportunity missed by the tourist board, I'd say. Parking is at the SW end of that viaduct, with access from both Bank Top and the B6255. All the shops, with the usual tourist emphasis, are up top, and the lower level gives access to the eye-catching 'waterfall walks' along the Twiss and Doe rivers. They are splendid walks, but they'll cost you money I'm afraid – £4.50 when I was there in April 2009.

I've designed four walks from the town, visiting seven pillars:

Walk No 17	Park Fell and Ingleborough
Walk No 18	Gragareth Fell and Tow Scar
Walk No 19	Blea Moor and Whernside
Walk No 20	Great Knoutberry Hill

On the way to three of the walks, along the B6255, you'll pass by the entrance to White Scar Cave. That too is worth a visit; it's the longest show cave in Britain. If you follow the links on the Ingleton website you can go on a virtual tour of the cave – it's quite entertaining.

Ingleton has only one remaining benchmark, a cut-mark on St Mary's Church (SD 6949 7325) – see if you can find it.

Walk 17. Park Fell and Ingleborough

Start:	Lay-by, B6255, Chapel-le-Dale
Map reference:	SD 7454 7780
Distance:	12.2km (7.6 miles)
Total ascent:	510m (1670 ft) – average climbing gradient 1 in 6
Estimated time:	5 hours
Walk grading:	Moderate to strenuous
OS map:	Landranger 98

Walk summary

The route begins across Scar Close and up to Park Fell via Colt Park. After traversing the ridge along Souther Scales Fell, up to Ingleborough, the return is via Black Shiver Moss and Souther Scales. The climbs are short and steep, and the ground underfoot will never be too wet. There are no benchmarks to find, unless you have a pint in 'The Old Hill' and look for the cut-mark around the back of the building opposite.

Parking and access

From Ingleton, take the B6255 NE to Chapel-le-Dale (5.5km, 3.5 miles). Parking is in the lay-by, 300m past 'The Old Hill' public house.

The walk

Follow the lane NE for 850m to a track leaving from the right (SD 7526 7820). It goes SE for 600m, following a wall, then alongside the Scar Close outcrops towards a gate (SD 7571 7777). Go left before the gate (there's a short-cut), following the wall NE for 500m to a walker's gate at SD 7609 7807. You pass through one field gate on the way.

On the other side of the walker's gate the path goes east for 1.1km across the Gauber High Pasture scar (picking your way carefully) and then grass moor, rising gently up to Colt Park (SD 7715 7791). There's a second walker's gate and a wall stile on the way. At Colt Park, turn right and begin the steep ascent (gradient 1 in 3.5) SW up Park Fell. It's 1km of hard slog, following the wall until you reach another wall branching right (SD 7651 7714). There, use the stile and walker's gate to access the other side, with the pillar in view 170m further on.

It's in reasonable condition, with a bit of cracking, and a make-do asphalt plug. The flush-bracket faces just east of south, and the best direction to start your observation is near opposite to that, NW towards the distinctive whaleback of Whernside, with Crag Hill/Great Coum behind its left flank.

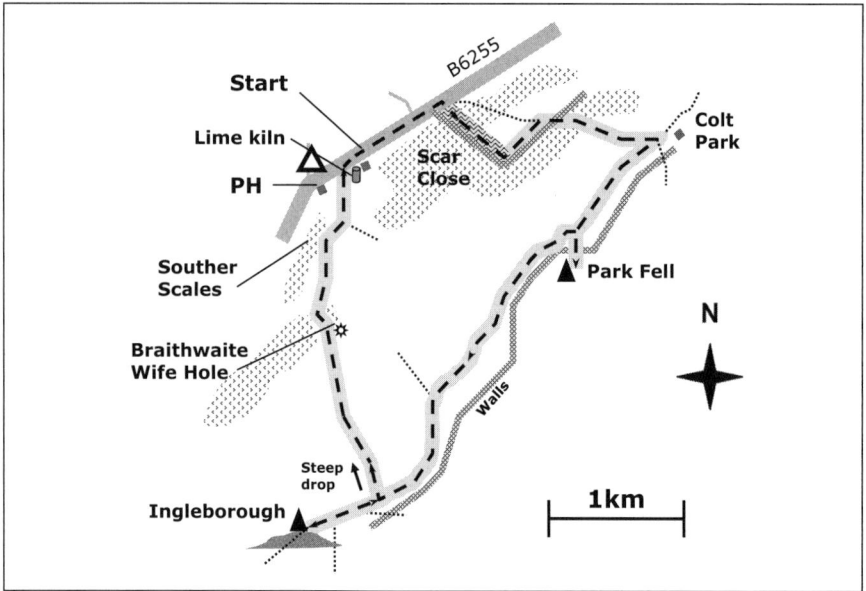

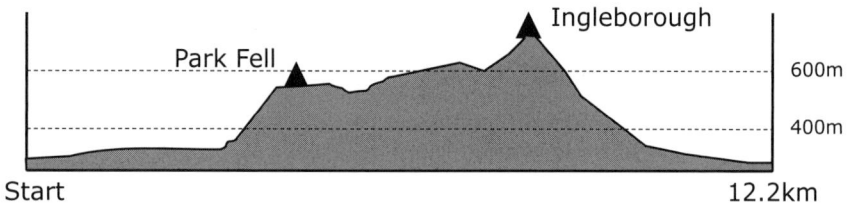

Route and height profile for Ingleborough and Park Fell

Right of Whernside is Little Dale, with the railway, and Blea Moor is right of that, with Widdale around its SE side. Then Great Knoutberry Hill is directly behind it, and higher.

NE, Low Green Field Lings is beyond the tree-line on the left-hand hill of the large plantation. Then east, Cosh Outside is the other side of the plantation valley, again above the tree-line. On the same bearing, Cave Hill is lower, in the foreground by the westerly tip of the forest. Although I located all those peaks with my monocular, on a misty day I couldn't resolve the pillars.

ESE, the double-humped profile of Pen-y-ghent is unmistakeable (pillar on the right, higher end, behind a wall), and SSE, Moughton is the long, flat hill (limestone pavement) with, I think, Langcliffe peeping up behind it (on Warrendale Knotts). In front, and left (SE) Sulber is closer, but lower, on indistinct terrain. Looking the other way was much easier.

Pillar details for Park Fell	
Name:	Park Fell
Position:	SD 76447 76965
Flush-Bracket No:	S5534
Height:	564m (1850 ft)
Built:	August 1949
Historic use:	Secondary
Current use:	None
Condition:	Good

Park Fell pillar – looking NNE to Blea Moor

SW, Ingleborough is sticking out above the nearby Simon Fell. I could see the walker's shelter, but not the pillar. To the WSW, the direction to Tow Scar, the higher ground and the wall are in the way, but WNW, the long ridge of Gragareth Fell is in view. That way, you're looking across Scales Moor, the SW end of the ridge that slopes down from Whernside. The valley below you is Chapel-le-Dale and the one on the other side of Scales Moor is Kingsdale. They meet at Ingleton, and if you look from that town up the valleys, you can imagine the glaciers of 10,000 years ago ploughing their way towards you, fed from the snows on the surrounding fells. And to the NW again is yet another glacial valley – Barbondale, under the shadow of Calf Top.

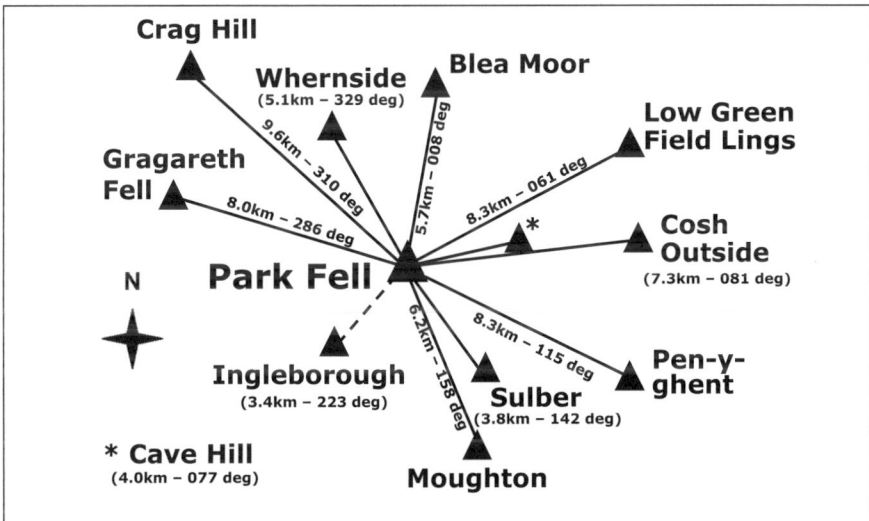

Crag Hill

Whernside (5.1km – 329 deg) **Blea Moor**

Low Green Field Lings

Gragareth Fell

9.6km – 310 deg
8.0km – 286 deg
5.7km – 008 deg
8.3km – 061 deg

N

Park Fell

Cosh Outside (7.3km – 081 deg)

8.3km – 115 deg
6.2km – 158 deg

Ingleborough (3.4km – 223 deg)

Sulber (3.8km – 142 deg)

Pen-y-ghent

* Cave Hill (4.0km – 077 deg)

Moughton

Nearby pillars in view from Park Fell

Looking from Ingleton, it is clear that the lower scars (White Scar, Twistleton Scar and Tow Scar) are all the same height, each part of one strata of limestone. Sat on top of that, preserved as Ingleborough, Whernside and Gragareth, is the harder sandstone and gritstone, and it is that geological sequence that defines much of the Dales, producing the distinctive flat-topped peaks.

From Park Fell, retrace your steps to the stile in the corner and get back over the wall. (This is preferable to carrying on SW from the pillar through an area of bog, and where you would be on the wrong side of the wall for the best views.) The route then follows the north and then NW side of the wall, tracing the edge of the hill for 3.2km, with a splendid outlook into Chapel-le-Dale and back to the Ribblehead Viaduct.

At first, the path keeps by the wall, but as you climb up South House Moor it keeps more NW before passing through a rock field and over a wall stile. On the other side you get a fine perspective on Ingleborough, including the harder seams of rock that characterise its flanks. The most obvious one is about 10m thick. So how long under the ocean to lay that seam down? I'd say 100,000 years, the rivers washing in the hard silt, layering it on the sea-bed, compressing it into rock, and then some major upheaval lifting the whole lot into the light of day, only for the elements to begin their relentless erosion all over again.

At SD 7473 7480 you reach a stream and walker's gate. It's the point you will return to after visiting Ingleborough. From there it's 660m of steep ascent to the summit, an old hill fort dating back to the Iron Age. 'Ingleborough' comes from the Old English 'burh' – 'fort on the hill', and I assume that 'Ingle' is the 'hill' part, since 'Ingleton' means 'farmstead by the hill'. Equally, 'Ingle' could have been someone's name.

Remains of Iron Age huts have been found, with later contributions from the Romans, with a walled camp, the Celts, with some vague stone circles, and in 1830, a hospice, would you believe? That didn't last long – it was meant as a tower, but all that remains is the pile of rocks, with traces of a wall, 100m WNW of the pillar.

The pillar is built in stone, with the flush-bracket facing east, and it remains in sound condition. The plug went years ago. The views are good (once the cloud had cleared!), but from the edges of the plateau rather than from the pillar itself. You can see to the Lakes (NW), to the Howgills (north, between Whernside and Crag Hill), over the north end of Pen-y-ghent to Great Whernside (east) and to Pendle Hill (south, with its steep left-hand edge).

Approaching Ingleborough

Pillar details for Ingleborough	
Name:	Ingleborough
Position:	SD 74119 74559
Flush-Bracket No:	S5619
Height:	724m (2375 ft)
Built:	August 1949
Historic use:	Secondary
Current use:	None
Condition:	Good

Ingleborough pillar – looking NNE to the shelter

In theory, there are 12 pillars in view within 10km, most of them ones you could see from Park Fell, so you should be able to work out what's what. But the flat top, and the various shelters, cairns and rock piles get in the way. I could not see Park Fell, but it might be in sight from a theodolite placed on top of the pillar. (I'm only 5ft 3in!) Likewise, I couldn't see any of the three low pillars round south to west, and I proved one by looking back to Ingleborough from Linghaw (a very undistinguished spot). I could see the Ingleborough shelter, but not the pillar.

Around east, Cave Hill and Sulber (same bearing as Pen-y-ghent) are too low to be seen from the pillar. SE, I could see the Moughton escarpment, but the

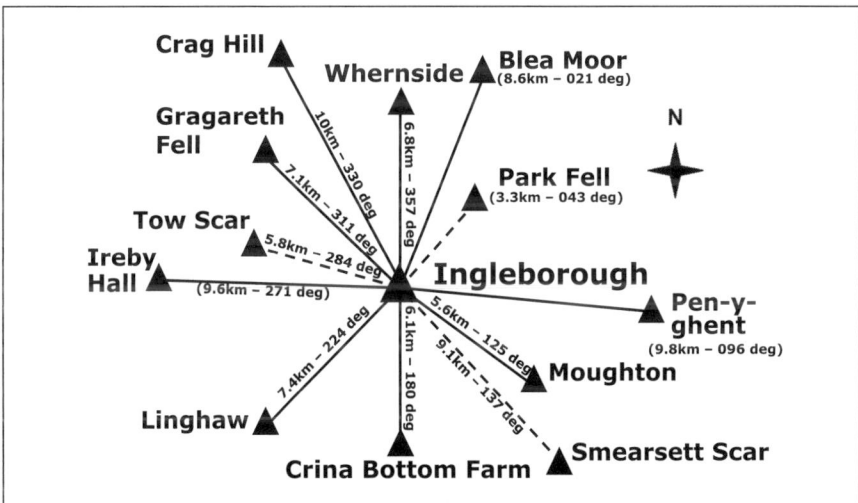

Nearby pillars theoretically in view from Ingleborough

lower Smearsett Scar was doubtful. Finally, WNW, the remains of the hospice definitely block the line to Tow Scar.

From the pillar, retrace your steps ENE to the walker's gate, ready for the very steep descent off the edge. It's a formidable stone staircase that drops 100m with a 1 in 2 gradient, so it's hard on the knees. I did it in snow – it was very tricky. Then the route is clear, flagstones at first, and some boarded stretches, crossing the moor

Looking back to Ingleborough from Linghaw

to reach a 'his and hers' pair of wall stiles – most unusual – on to the Souther Scales nature reserve. You pass by the 'Braithwaite Wife Hole', a huge 'Sink Hole' created when the underlying limestone was dissolved and washed away. Who was Braithwaite? And why did his wife deserve a mention? I couldn't find out.

After the scar, i.e., a limestone pavement eroded by eons of rain and frost, the path becomes grassy and passes through a couple of walker's gates. There's an information board about the area that is most helpful, then there's a nice limekiln set in the embankment just before the lane. (More on limekilns in later walks.)

Route summary for Walk 17

Your present location	Your next objective	Waypoint at next objective	Directions and distance
Roadside lay-by, B6255 SD 7454 7780	Track leaving lane to SE	SD 7526 7820	NE along the lane – 850m
SD 7526 7820	Gate, go left before it	SD 7571 7777	SE along track – 610m
SD 7571 7777	Walker's gate	SD 7609 7807	NE on grass moor path along wall – 500m
SD 7609 7807	Colt park	SD 7715 7791	East through scar and then moor path – 1.1km
SD 7715 7791	Stile, corner of walls	SD 7651 7714	SW and SSW on path by wall, steeply uphill – 1km
SD 7651 7714	Park Fell pillar	SD 7645 7697	SSW on path – 170m
SD 7645 7697	Stile, corner of walls	SD 7651 7714	Retrace your steps NNE, back over the wall – 170m
SD 7651 7714	Walker's gate after stream and path	SD 7473 7480	Generally SW along edge of Souther Scales Fell – 3.2km
SD 7473 7480	Ingleborough pillar	SD 7412 7456	WSW up to summit – 660m
SD 7412 7456	Path for descent	SD 7473 7480	Retrace your steps, ENE – 660m
SD 7473 7480	Car, lay-by	SD 7454 7780	NNW down steep descent, across moor, then NNE on grass path – 3.3km

Walk 18. Gragareth Fell and Tow Scar

Start:	Roadside parking, Ireby
Map reference:	SD 6538 7542
Distance:	14.7km (9.2 miles)
Total ascent:	580m (1900 ft) – average climbing gradient 1 in 11
Estimated time:	5.5 hours
Walk grading:	Moderate
OS map:	Landranger 98

Walk summary
The route begins in Ireby, following a track and lane NNE to Gragareth Fell.
Return is SW along the ridge, and via Masongill, with an excursion to Tow Scar.
There are six benchmarks to find, and the route should be possible in all
weathers.

Parking and access
From Ingleton, take the A65 NW for 5km (3 miles) and turn right down the
lane (Todgill Road) indicated to Ireby. Parking is by the telephone box.

The walk
From the car, take the lane that is signposted 'Leck 1' and follow it 500m NW
to a sharp left turn, looking for BM No 1 on the way – a cut-mark on a house
after about 100m from the start. As the lane turns left, go straight on (north)
up the track, with Brownthwaite eventually coming into view to the fore. It's
quiet, pleasant walking – a nice gentle start to the route.

Along the track, there's a rivet to find (BM No 2, after about 800m) in the
first wooded area, near a field gate that gives access west towards Overleck
Hall. Then look for two cut-marks, one on the right (BM No 3) only 170m
further on, and then one on the left (BM No 4) after the track has crossed a
stream and turned NE. The records show that one as a 'ruined house', but the
remains have now been converted into a well-made walled recess. It looks like
the stone with the cut-mark was repositioned, since the mark is now higher
up than was originally recorded.

Just after that, when I was walking alongside the plantation on the right, a
Brown Owl appeared from the trees and flew down the track straight towards
me. A round head and two large penetrating eyes – such an unpromising
aerodynamic shape. But when it peeled away, only yards in front of me, there
was not a breath of sound. No rush of ruffled air. No beat from the wings. A
truly memorable moment.

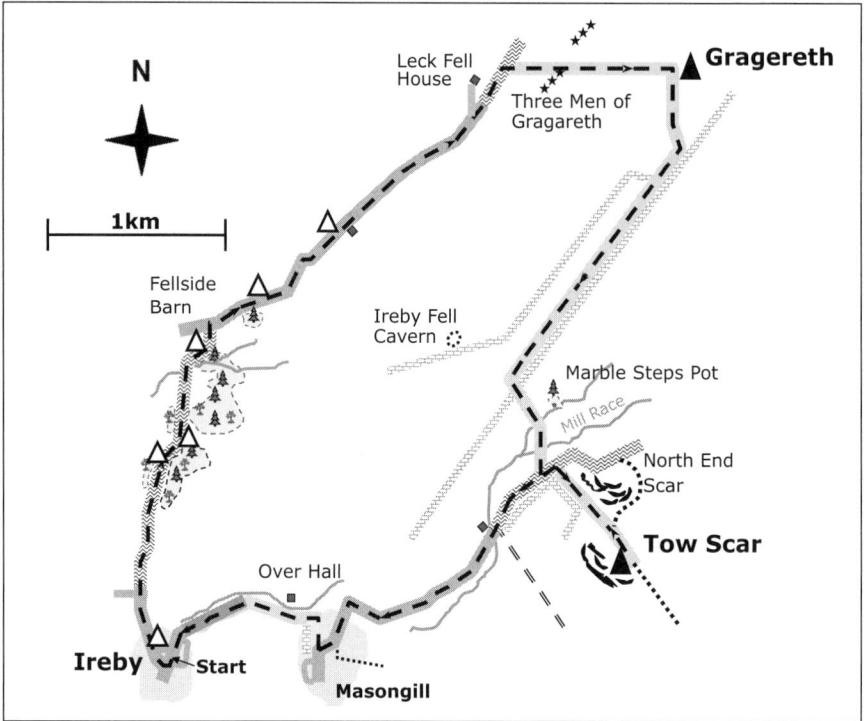

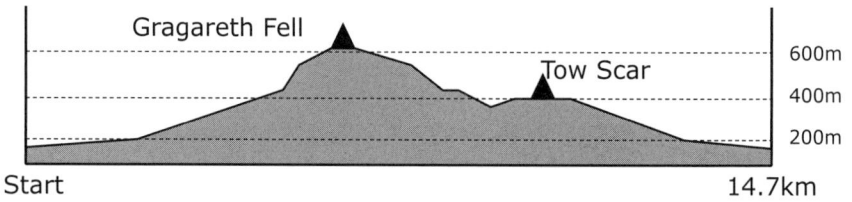

Route and height profile for Gragareth Fell and Tow Scar

After the plantation, not long before you reach a lane (2km from the start of the track, at SD 6570 7764), there is an old marker stone engraved with two place-names, something like K???leworth and Gawthorpe. It's a mystery, since Gawthorpe is near Wakefield, 60 miles away, and I couldn't match up the first word using any letter combinations.

At the lane, go right, walking NE, and with your first sight of Gragareth and its many cairns coming into view. It's then 2.5km of more quiet walking, rising steadily, with two more cut-marks (BMs No 5 and No 6) to look for, both on gateposts on the left. Neither was shown on the old records; I just happened to notice them. Maybe I missed some others.

Three Men of Gragareth – Brownthwaite behind

My 'Three Ladies' – looking west

At SD 6756 7914, as the lane turns left down to the Leck Fell property, take the gate to the moor on the right and follow the grassy track below the rocky hillside. After 250m, opposite the NE end of the Leck Fell farm, you can strike eastwards up the hill, with a grass avenue through the rock fields to ease the ascent. It's a steep 1 in 3 climb for 250m to the three cairns, called 'The Three Men of Gragareth'.

In fact, they look more like three women to me, dragging their skirts. Just to the NE there are three more cairns in a row, but they are not afforded any masculine status. So, in the interests of equality, I hereby name them 'The Three Ladies of Gragareth'. But, to be honest, the word 'men' might come from the Welsh 'mein', meaning 'rocks'. So that the three cairns are 'The three rocks at the limit of the city wall', 'Gragareth' being corrupted from the Welsh 'gor' (limit) and 'gaered' (city wall). Well, that's one theory anyway.

From the cairns to the pillar is 850m across the grass moor, with a clear path to help. It was mercifully dry when I was there. The pillar is sound, without its plug, and the flush-bracket faces ENE. The views are not special, but WNW, Brownthwaite is clear (pillar on the central 'hump') and the Calf Top ridge stretches away to the NNW, with a wall over the summit (pillar next to it). Then NNE, the Crag Hill pillar is at the left end of the hill, behind the section of wall that dips down.

ENE, the long sweep of Whernside forms the skyline. You can see the wall along the top, but its pillar is hard up against it. Then ESE and SE, the line of Park Fell along to Ingleborough is obvious, with the shelter on top of the plateau clear as usual. But I couldn't make out either pillar. Low in the SW, Ireby Hall is theoretically visible, but it might depend how tall you are. (You can see that pillar when you drive back, turning out on to the main road.) Finally, WSW, Sellet Hall should be in view, but it was too misty for me to locate.

Pillar details for Gragareth	
Name:	Gragareth
Position:	SD 68791 79306
Flush-Bracket No:	S5404
Height:	627m (2057 ft)
Built:	May 1949
Historic use:	Secondary
Current use:	None
Condition:	Good

Gragareth pillar – looking NNE to Crag Hill

From the pillar, walk due south for 350m to pick up the county boundary wall, then follow it south for 270m to a makeshift wall stile where the wall divides into two (SD 6882 7873). Negotiate that very carefully and then follow the left-hand of the two walls that form the long, narrow enclosure. Again, this was easy, dry walking – not what I'd expected. As you walk SW the view to the SE expands, so that Twisleton Scar and Tow Scar come into sight, and after 1.9km, at SD 6768 7722, you reach a new wall stile taking you left on a path across to the track near Tow Scar.

There's a path that joins from the right just there, coming from Ireby Fell Cavern. And when you go left over the wall and cross the grass moor to the track near Tow Scar, Marble Steps Pot is below the square of trees on the left. What are these 'pots'? Holes in the ground, to put it simply, carved out by

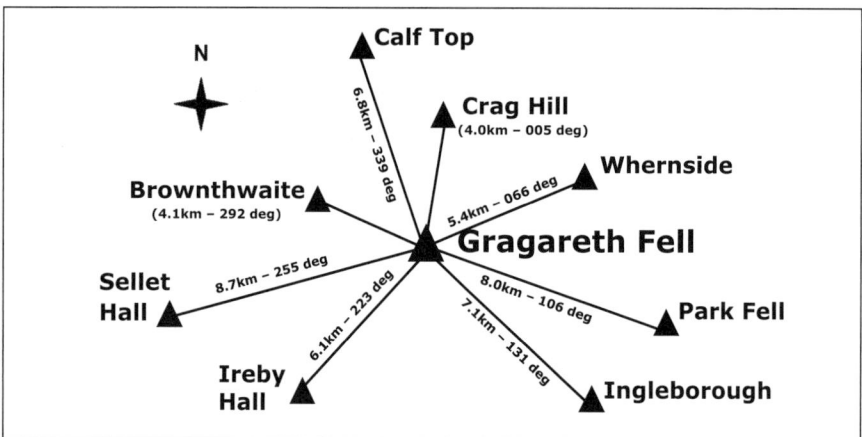

Nearby pillars in view from Gragareth Fell

Pillar details for Tow Scar	
Name:	Tow Scar
Position:	SD 68469 76003
Flush-Bracket No:	S5397
Height:	383m (1257 ft)
Built:	May 1949
Historic use:	Secondary
Current use:	None
Condition:	Good

Tow Scar pillar – looking NE – Whernside just showing

eons of rushing water, dissolving and sculpturing the limestone rock. The word comes from the way pebbles and rocks are spun in whirlpools, scouring out a circular depression, or 'pot'. Given enough pebbles and rocks, and enough time, you end up with a hole that some people can't resist going down. They talk of pitches and pipes, caverns and caves – it all sounds very claustrophobic to me; give me the outdoors anytime.

Having resisted the temptation to walk over to the trees and peer into the pot, when you reach the track (wall stile at SD 6792 7667), go left to the gate

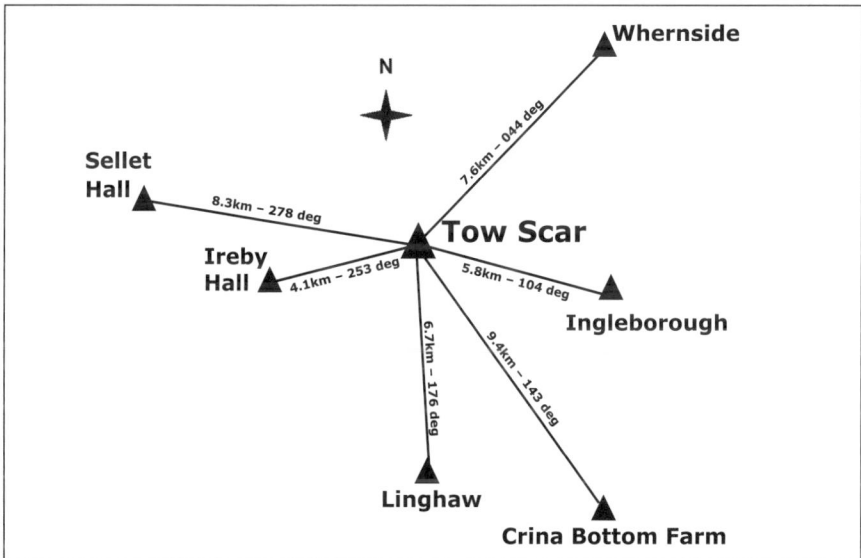

Nearby pillars in view from Tow Scar

(only 50m). Then you can walk along the wall, keeping SW of North End Scar, and pick up the path that skirts Tow Scar. It's open-access land, and you can easily walk up to the pillar (800m from the gate – watch out for Sink Holes). It's another sound pillar, without a plug, and this time the flush-bracket faces NE, looking over the nearby Low Plain outcrop to Whernside. Looking east and SSE, the Park Fell ridge along to Ingleborough is clear, but I know from looking the other way that the Park Fell pillar is too far back to see and the Ingleborough pillar has some rocky remains in its line-of-sight.

SE, Crina Bottom Farm is low and indistinct, but you should be able to spot the mast that is next to the Linghaw pillar, due south. I could see the pillar at Ireby Hall (WSW), but not the one near Sellet Hall (WNW), even though I could make out Kirkby Longsdale nearby. Finally, looking north along the Gragareth ridge, we already know that the pillar is too far back to see. So, Tow Scar is not a very exciting viewpoint.

And 'Tow'? Other than the obvious meaning, it is the fibre of flax or hemp, before spinning. It's ragged and coarse – perhaps that was how some long past inhabitant saw the appearance of the area. It's a guess – 'Tow' could equally be a corruption of another word.

From the pillar, retrace your steps back to the track and then follow it SW for 2.2km, past the closed reservoir (where the track becomes a lane), to the point where it goes left into Masongill (SD 6641 7553). There, go right through the gate (it's a right of way, but the fingerpost is missing) and walk along the wall. Go left at the end, through the pasture, with the stream to your right, and go between the two stone walls that form a short grass track. After two gates, the path follows the south side of the stream on the meadow embankment (SD 6583 7575), having been rerouted from its original course through the Over Hall property. There're a couple of path markers and a new kissing gate taking you on to the farm drive. From there it's 600m to the village, crossing the stream by either of the two bridges, and back to the car.

Route summary for Walk 18

Your present location	Your next objective	Waypoint at next objective	Directions and distance
Ireby SD 6538 7542	Lane goes left, go straight on	SD 6519 7587	NNW on Leck Lane – 500m
SD 6519 7587	Lane, go right	SD 6570 7764	NNE on track – 2km
SD 6570 7764	Gate	SD 6756 7914	NE on lane – 2.5km
SD 6756 7914	Three Men of Gragareth	SD 6795 7930	NE on track (250m), then east up steep rocky moor – 300m
SD 6795 7930	Gragareth Fell pillar	SD 6879 7931	East on moor path – 850m
SD 6879 7931	Join county boundary wall	SD 6881 7896	South across moor – 350m
SD 6881 7896	Wall divides, take east one	SD 6882 7873	South along wall – 270m
SD 6882 7873	Wall stile	SD 6768 7722	SW along straight wall – 1.9km
SD 6768 7722	Wall stile to track	SD 6792 7667	SW and south past pots – 700m
SD 6792 7667	Tow Scar pillar	SD 6847 7600	Left to gate, then SE along the wall – 800m
SD 6847 7600	Back to track	SD 6798 7670	Retrace your steps NW – 800m
SD 6798 7670	Gate near Masongill, go right	SD 6641 7553	Generally SW on track and lane – 2.2km
SD 6641 7553	Past Over Hall	SD 6583 7575	North, then west on path by stream – 700m
SD 6583 7575	Parking point at Ireby	SD 6538 7542	SW on farm drive and lane – 600m

Benchmark summary for Walk 18

BM No	Type of benchmark and location	Grid reference
1	Cut-mark – West angle of building, north side of road	SD 6536 7548
2	Rivet – Top of gatepost, junction of fence and wall, NW side of track	SD 6537 7672
3	Cut-mark – Gatepost, 0.4m north of wall junction, east side of track	SD 6547 7684
4	Cut-mark – NE angle of building ruin, west side of track, SE face	SD 6552 7737
5	Cut-mark – Gatepost, north side of track, east face	SD 6599 7780
6	Cut-mark – Gatepost, NE side of track, SW face	SD 6643 7816

Walk 19. Blea Moor and Whernside

Start:	Lay-by, B6255, Ribblehead
Map reference:	SD 7662 7932
Distance:	14.6km (9.1 miles)
Total ascent:	610m (2000 ft) – average climbing gradient 1 in 9
Estimated time:	5.5 hours
Walk grading:	Moderate to strenuous
OS map:	Landranger 98

Walk summary

The route begins by the Ribblehead Viaduct, reaching Blea Moor via Little Dale and then following the county boundary fence in a loop to Whernside. Return is steeply down from the ridge and back to the viaduct. There are three benchmarks. Lying snow would make the route dangerous, and it's best undertaken in dry weather.

Parking and access

From Ingleton, take the B6255 NE, via Chapel-le-Dale, for 10km (6 miles) to Ribblehead. Parking is on the lay-by after the junction with the B6479.

The walk

Before you start, look at the information sign near the stream. They used navvies to build the viaduct and Blea Moor tunnel, and when they died on the job they were buried in unmarked graves at Chapel-le-Dale. Now there's employee recognition for you! Then see if you can find the bolt (BM No 1) on the stream culvert, SE side of the road – that's easy. It's one of the BMs from the Third Geodetic Line between Kirkby Stephen and Ribblesdale (1952). Curiously, the location is referred to as 'Batty Wife Hole' on the OS records.

To begin, use the grass path opposite Gauber Road (B6479) to cut the corner to the limestone track that takes you alongside the viaduct. Near the start of that grass path, BM No 2, a rivet, is on a small boulder a few metres SW along the road from the footpath sign to Blea Sidings, and a few metres off the verge to the NE – not so easy as the bolt.

The viaduct dates to 1875 and, worryingly, the information cairn under the centre arch declares that the crumbling limestone may fall on your head. Indeed, you can see the large number of tension bars and plates that keep it all together. Don't go under the viaduct; take the path that leaves the track from the bend (SD 7607 7951) and follow it up Little Dale. There's another small information board that's worth reading, about the locomotive depot and brickworks.

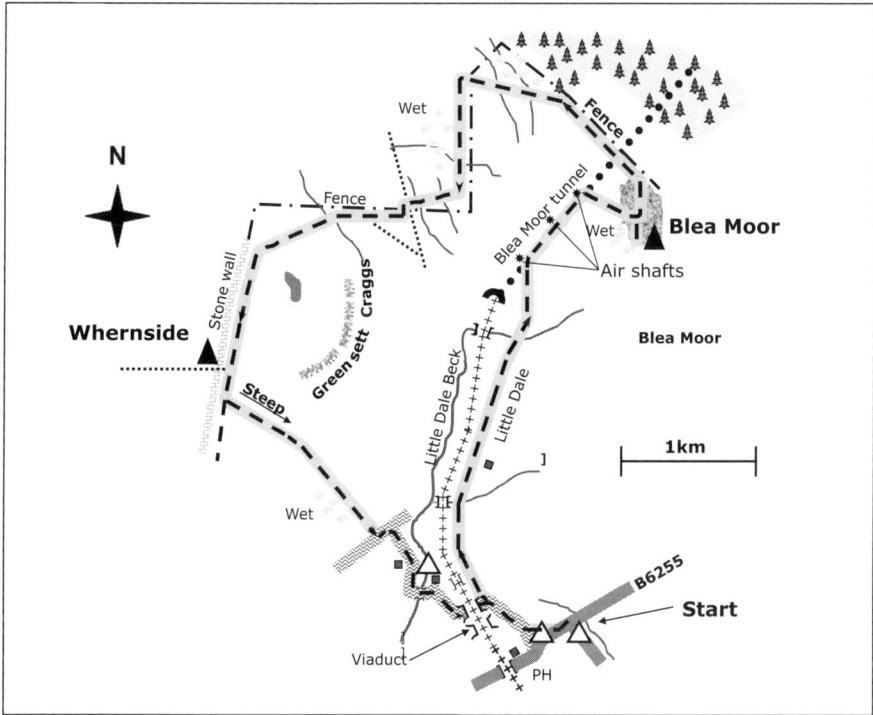

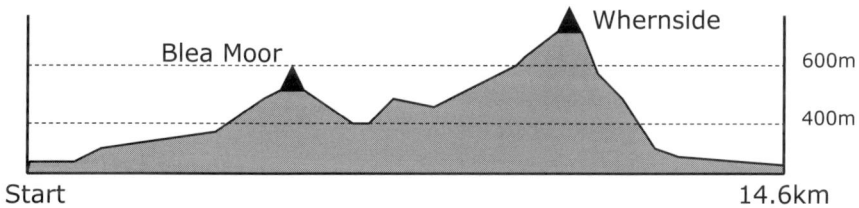

Route and height profile for Blea Moor and Whernside

The well-made path follows the railway line, with an old-fashioned signal box and signal, as well as a dilapidated station, one that now seems to be a smallholding. An irritable bird of prey screamed at me from its cage – probably the only way of brightening its day.

At SD 7609 8137, just before the main track turns NW over the railway, take the path that keeps straight on (NNE), with the three spoil heaps to the fore. They represent just a fraction of the material hued out of the hill by the navvies, hauled up the shafts (now used for tunnel ventilation) by steam engines. How many men died? Too many. In those days they had proper winters, with blizzards and floods that could catch anyone out.

Pillar details for Blea Moor	
Name:	Blea Moor
Position:	SD 77264 82584
Flush-Bracket No:	S5228
Height:	536m (1759 ft)
Built:	September 1949
Historic use:	Secondary
Current use:	None
Condition:	Good

Blea Moor pillar – looking WSE to Whernside

50m on from the third spoil heap, at the top of a rise (SD 7678 8283), strike off ESE across the grass moor to find the Blea Moor pillar (600m distant). It's not difficult at first, but 100m before the last ridge there's a wide marshy area. Go round it on the left (north), keeping to the peaty outcrops, so you'll eventually approach the pillar from the NW.

It's another sound pillar, with a stone plug, and the flush-bracket faces NW. So WSW, Whernside is obvious, but its pillar is behind the wall. NW, the white Ayr Gill Pike pillar is at the left end of the hill, with the Howgills behind. (You'll visit those in a later walk.) East Baugh Fell is behind the right end of Aye Gill Pike (looking NNW) and then Swarth Fell and Wild Boar Fell are even further back, due north.

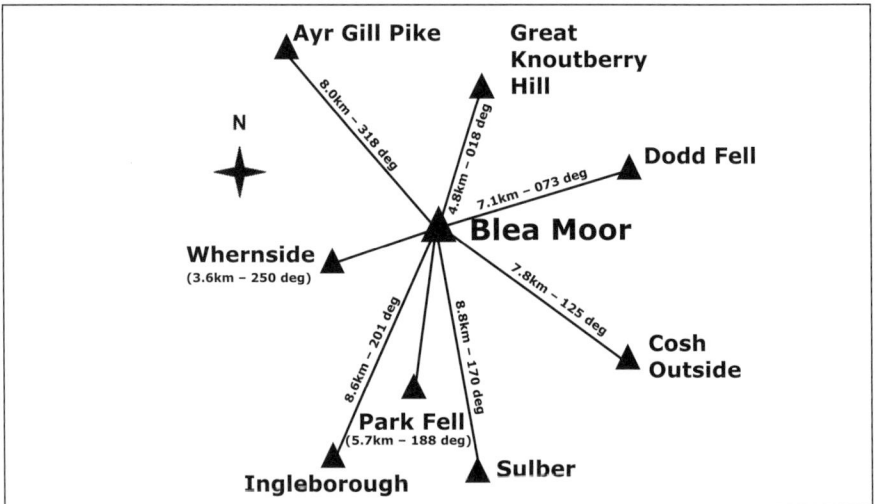

Nearby pillars in view from Blea Moor

On Great Knoutberry Hill (NNE), the squat pillar is easy to see at the end of the wall, and I could also see the pillar on Dodd Fell, which forms the horizon to the ENE. SE, the plantation in front of Cosh Outside is clear, but the pillar is elusive. And more SSE, I think that Cave Hill, which is on the line to Pen-y-ghent, is hidden by the edge of Blea Moor itself.

Right of Pen-y-ghent is Ribblesdale, and right again, the low, long hill is Moughton (limestone pavement, pillar right end), with Sulber in front and lower. SSW, Park Fell pillar is tricky to spot because it's set against Simon Fell behind it, and then, finally, Ingleborough is always clear. I could just see the top of the pillar set back on the plateau.

Blea? It's a common name in the area, for hills, tarns and moors, but I couldn't find the origin. Blea is sapwood, under the bark of a tree, but that doesn't help. Maybe it means 'bleak'.

From the pillar, walk north and pick up the county boundary fence (SD 7729 8276). Then follow it NW downhill for 1km to the plantation. As the fence begins to turn more NNW, at SD 7661 8350, you are faced with a very wet, peaty area. Leave the fence there and strike off WNW across the valley – it's much easier than trying to follow the fence. There are two buried streams to hop over, and after about 850m you can rejoin the fence in the corner, where it turns from west to south (SD 7580 8368), with a broken wall alongside.

Climb the fence in that corner (there's a stile of sorts) and continue along it on the west side, now going south, with a view back east to the Blea Moor spoil heaps. It's likely to be wet, but easier than walking on the east side. At SD 7578 8279 the fence turns west – keep to the north side and continue for another 500m (crossing a path) until you can see the wide path coming up from Little Dale on the other side (SD 7530 8280). Step over the fence there (easy) and you can then follow that path all the way to the Whernside ridge and pillar. I was blessed with a fabulous day, but the SW wind was howling up the slope, blowing my favourite hat into the middle of a large stretch of water. I fell in trying to retrieve it, and later I got stuck in the narrow wall-stile that gives access to the pillar on the west side. So it was not a good day.

Whernside (meaning 'The hill where querns – i.e. millstones – are found') is a Primary pillar, one of the first group to be erected. Now it is a 'Passive Station', accurately surveyed by GPS and maintained as one of a nationwide network. In 1999, the OS recorded its height above the Newlyn datum as 736.212m, that's a measurement taken on the flush-bracket, on the top rim of the slot above the arrow. It was due to be surveyed again in 2009.

The nearest other Primaries are shown in the diagram, each of which would have been triangulated at night, using a light on top of the pillar. (From a height of 736m, the horizon – i.e., as dictated by the earth's curvature – is 100km. So looking 40km is not a problem, provided there are no other high points in the way.)

The Whernside pillar is in a poor condition (flush-bracket faces SW), so maybe its days as Passive Station are numbered. And its position by the wall

Pillar details for Whernside	
Name:	Whernside
Position:	SD 73849 81414
Flush-Bracket No:	2982
Height:	736m (2415 ft)
Built:	April 1936
Historic use:	Primary
Current use:	Passive Station
Condition:	Slightly damaged

Whernside pillar – looking NNW to the Howgills

restricts the views a little, particularly north. Round north, east and south, the landscape is similar to that as seen from Blea Moor, except that Blea Moor itself is now clear. Pen-y-ghent is lower as seen from the higher perspective at Whernside, and both the Park Fell and Ingleborough pillars are easy to locate.

The new views are around the west, with Tow Scar low at the end of the Gragareth ridge (SW), right of the left-hand bend in the lane. WSW, Gragareth pillar is easy to find, but coming WNW, the Crag Hill pillar is behind the wall. (Find Great Coum, which is the 'bite' scalloped out of the right side of the hill, then go left to the peak further back.) I think I could just see the top of it. Right of and behind Great Coum is the Calf Top ridge, but the pillar is just

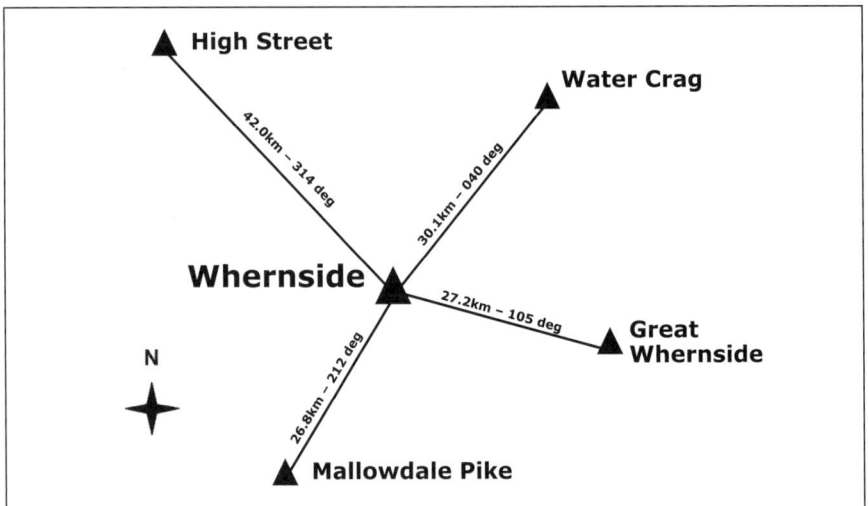

High Street

Water Crag

42.0km ~ 314 deg

30.1km ~ 040 deg

Whernside

27.2km ~ 105 deg

Great Whernside

N

212 deg

26.8km ~ 212 deg

Mallowdale Pike

Primary pillars in view from Whernside

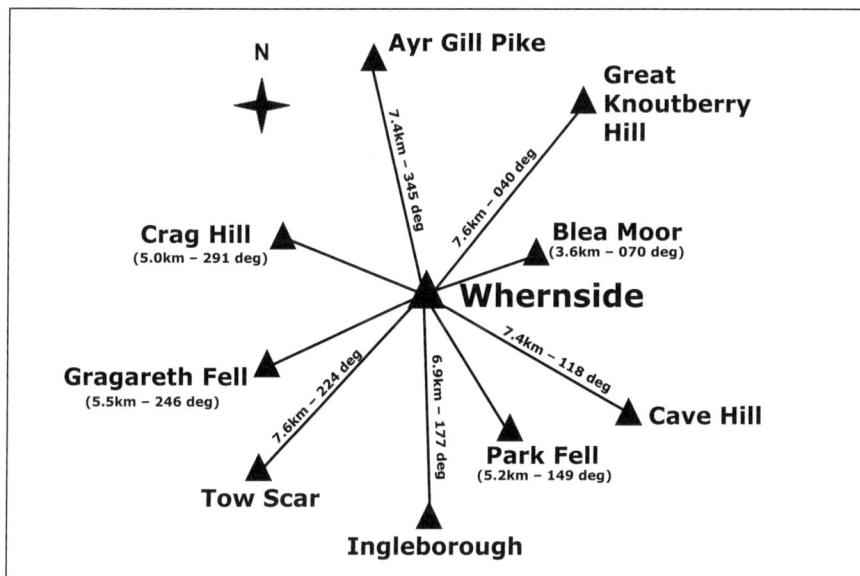

Nearby pillars in view from Whernside

hidden behind Great Coum itself. Finally, as shown in the picture, NNW is towards the Howgills, including Winder and The Calf.

From the pillar, squeeze back through the stile and continue south along the ridge for 250m, down to the boundary fence (SD 7380 8118). Go left there, down the steep slope. Either side will do, but I used the grass areas on the SW side. The first bit is a 1 in 2 descent, needing great care – it would be impossible in snow. Lower down, having crossed back over the fence and wall to the NE side, the path follows a stream gully SE. It becomes vague, crossing a wet area by a stile, and then follows the right of a wall to a stile on to the lane (SD 7510 7999). Go left there, and then right after 100m, following the lane along a stream and up to Gunnerfleet Farm. BM No 3 (cut-mark) is on the angle of the building across the stream – but I didn't find it until I downloaded my pictures back at home.

Finally, go left round the farm, across the bridge signposted to Ribblehead, and follow the track back under the viaduct, watching for falling limestone as you go!

Route summary for Walk 19

Your present location	Your next objective	Waypoint at next objective	Directions and distance
Roadside lay-by, B6255 SD 7662 7932	Point to leave track	SD 7607 7951	West on path from lane junction to join tack going NW – 620m (Two BMs)
SD 7607 7951	Point to leave track on to moor path	SD 7609 8137	NW, turning north on track following railway – 2km
SD 7609 8137	Beyond third spoil heap	SD 7678 8283	NNE on moor path – 1.7km
SD 7678 8283	Blea Moor pillar	SD 7726 8258	ENE across moor – 600m
SD 7726 8258	Fence, north of pillar	SD 7729 8276	North across moor – 200m
SD 7729 8276	Before wet area, go WNW	SD 7661 8350	NW along fence – 1km
SD 7661 8350	Corner where fence turns south	SD 7580 8368	WNW across moor valley – 850m
SD 7580 8368	Fence turns west	SD 7578 8279	South along fence – 900m
SD 7578 8279	Path on other side of fence	SD 7530 8280	West along fence – 500m
SD 7530 8280	Whernside pillar	SD 7385 8141	West, SW, then south on made path – 2.3km
SD 7385 8141	Path for descent	SD 7380 8118	South on track to county boundary fence – 240m
SD 7380 8118	Lane, go left (NE)	SD 7510 7999	SE down steep hillside – 1.8km
SD 7510 7999	Go right (SE)	SD 7519 8007	NE on lane – 120m
SD 7519 8007	Left by farm	SD 7530 7963	SE, turning south on lane – 500m (One BM)
SD 7530 7963	Car, lay-by	SD 7662 7932	SSE on track – 1.4km

Benchmark summary for Walk 19

BM No	Type of benchmark and location	Grid reference
1	Bolt – Culvert over stream, SE side of road	SD 7655 7928
2	Rivet – Boulder, 35m SW centre of stream, 6.4m NW of the road	SD 7650 7926
3	Cut-mark – West angle of building, Gunnerfleet Farm, east side of road	SD 7536 7972

Walk 20. Great Knoutberry Hill

Start:	Roadside, Stone House Bridge
Map reference:	SD 7704 8587
Distance:	9.7km (6.1 miles)
Total ascent:	470m (1540 ft) – average climbing gradient 1 in 10
Estimated time:	4 hours
Walk grading:	Moderate
OS map:	Landranger 98

Walk summary

The route begins along the lane from Stone House to Lea Yeat and on towards Galloway Gate, before using a track and moor path to cross Great Knoutberry Hill. Return is via the Arten Gill lane. Weather should not be an issue. There are ten benchmarks to find.

Parking and access

From Ingleton, take the B6255 NE for 11km (7 miles), through Chapel-le-Dale and Ribblehead; then turn left down the lane signposted to Dent and Sedbergh. 4km on (2.5 miles), there's roadside parking after crossing the narrow Stone House Bridge.

The walk

There's a seat by the parking area. When I arrived, half a dozen hens, well organised by a cockerel, were perched along it in a neat line. They hopped off as I drew up, so I missed a great picture. A pity. I tried to persuade them back on, but they wouldn't co-operate!

Before you set off, look for the cut-mark on the bridge (BM No 1) – it's easy. Then walk NE for 1.6km along the lane to Lea Yeat, following the river. In fact, you might even be able to walk in the river, if it's dry enough. In April, it was very low, and in summer it might be one of those limestone streams that disappears. It's pleasant, quiet walking, with some curious milestones by the roadside, and you have three more cut-marks to find on the way – one on a pub (BM No 2, faint), one on a gatepost (BM No 3, left side of the lane) and the third on the bridge at Lea Yeat (BM No 4).

Go right after the bridge and phone box (SD 7604 8694), into Coal Road (it goes to some old mine workings) and follow it for 2.6km, past Dent Station to a limestone track (SD 7797 8806) that leaves back right, 600m beyond the Dodderham Moss plantation.

As you walk north up the steep lane there's a cut-mark on a barn (BM No 5) that's easy to spot. Next, as you turn NE, the distinctive stationmaster's house

Dodderham Moss

N

Dent Station

Monkeybeck Grains

Fence

Great Knoutberry Hill

1km

Lea Yeat

Cairns

PH

Start

Stone House

Artengill Beck

Wall

Great Knoutberry Hill

600m

400m

Start

9.7km

Route and height profile for Great Knoutberry Hill

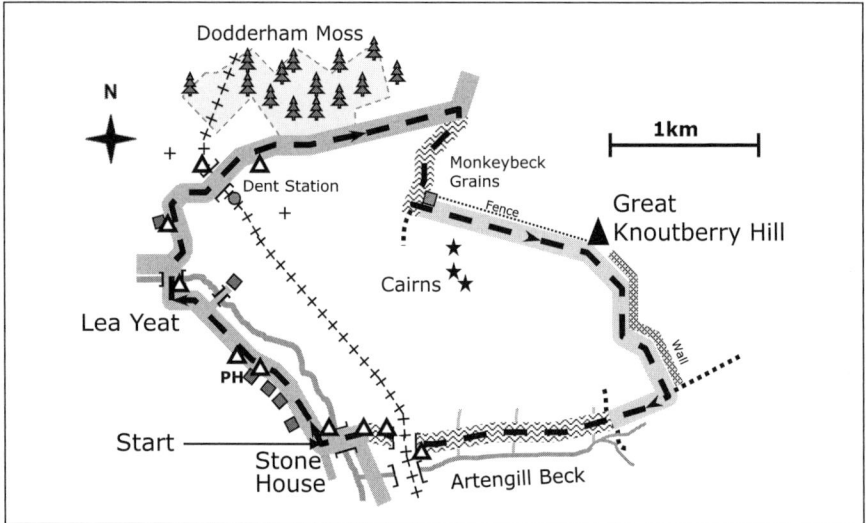

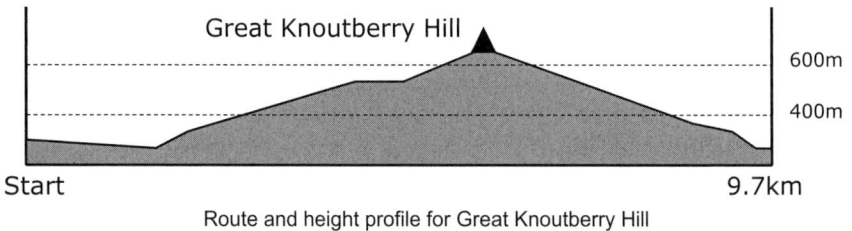

comes into view, high on the skyline. They're always the same design. Then, as you cross the railway bridge, look for the cut-mark on the NW parapet (BM No 6, faint). After that, there's a cut-mark on a gatepost (BM No 7, with a 'private' sign), before you pass alongside the plantation and reach the limestone track, marked 'Public Bridleway'.

Go right there and follow it SW for 700m, with Whernside dominating your view to the fore. At SD 7768 8744 there's a gate on the left, with a sheepfold and a notice welcoming you on to the hill. Use the gates and follow the right-hand side of the fence for 1.3km up to the pillar. On the way up there's a group of tall, nicely built cairns nearby. What are they for? Cairns are used to mark

Cairns – what are they for?

difficult trails for navigation during bad weather, or to celebrate hill summits. These don't seem to serve either. Imagine building one of them, given the rock supply around you at the site. How long would it take? A very long time was my conclusion. Some mark burial sites, or are memorials, but I wonder if these are a case of, 'I was 'ere – I built this – Jonas Arkwright – 1746'? Ego comes in many forms! Perhaps I'll start one myself, adding new rocks each time I pass.

The pillar is one of the later designs, 1955, with a squat, stone-built construction. It's sound, but missing its plug, and the flush-bracket faces SW. The views are splendid, except for the wall and fence getting in the way to the NE, and I was blessed with a superb day.

Pillar details for Great Knoutberry Hill	
Name:	Great Knoutberry Hill
Position:	SD 78860 87157
Flush-Bracket No:	S8285
Height:	672m (2205 ft)
Built:	April 1955
Historic use:	Secondary
Current use:	None
Condition:	Good

Great Knoutberry Hill pillar – Looking WNW to Ayr Gill Pike

Start your observations to the WNW; looking along the fence you walked up, to Aye Gill Pike. The white pillar is easy to spot. Turning NW, East Baugh Fell is on the other side of Garsdale (pillar behind a wall), and between them, Winder is at the end of the valley, overlooking Sedbergh.

NNW, Wild Boar Fell (12km distant, pillar well back and out of sight) is the flat-topped feature, with Swarth Fell blending in, 2km nearer. Going right, NNE, Great Shunner Fell is the rounded hill with the plantation to the fore, 12km away. I could just see the shelter on the top (pillar attached). Right of that (NE), the next hill is Staggs Fell, with (I think) a beacon visible.

ENE, along the other fence, is towards Hawes, and to the ESE the immediate hill is Snaizeholm Fell, with Dodd Fell behind it. I couldn't find the pillar. SSE is the line to Pen-y-ghent (12km away), so that Cosh Outside is in line with Plover Hill, which is left of Pen-y-ghent. It's too far away to see the Cosh pillar. (It's probably obscured by a wall anyway.) Looking SSW is more straightforward, towards Ingleborough (I could see the shelter and the pillar), with Park Fell to its left, the pillar just visible. Then, in the foreground and lower, the Blea Moor pillar is exactly in line with the left edge of the

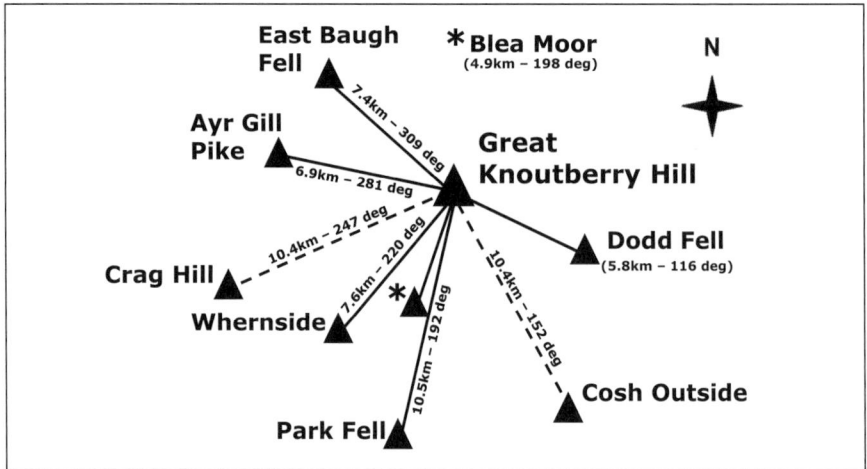

Nearby pillars in view from Great Knoutberry Hill

Ingleborough plateau. (There's a plantation on the facing side of Blea Moor.)

SW, Whernside is dominant, with its axis going away from you, with the Gragareth ridge visible over the other side, coming back to Crag Hill at its northern end. That pillar is only just out of sight, at the back, with the higher (by 5 metres) Great Coum in the way. Last of all, 12km away near due west, Calf Top is the high ridge the other side of Barbondale. I could just see the pillar with my monocular.

To continue the walk, go SSE down the other side, following the wall 1.2km to the track at the bottom (SD 7946 8624). Turn right there and follow the Arten Gill lane for 2.5km down to the car. Once an ancient drovers' route that had fallen into disrepair, it's now been nicely restored. There are two useful information boards, one at each end, and on the way down pause to admire the viaduct, made in Dent Marble, a unique dark limestone. See if you can spot the cut-mark (BM No 8) while you are there, and then look for two more before the car, one on a gatepost (BM No 9, on the right, well hidden) and the second on a house (BM No 10, after the gate at the end of the track).

Route summary for Walk 20

Your present location	Your next objective	Waypoint at next objective	Directions and distance
Roadside, Stone House SD 7704 8587	Right into Coal Road at Lea Yeat	SD 7604 8694	NW, along the lane – 1.6km (Four BMs to find)
SD 7604 8694	Right on to track	SD 7797 8806	North, turning NE on Coal Road – 2.6km (Three BMs to find)
SD 7797 8806	Point to leave track, by fold	SD 7768 8744	SW on track – 600m
SD 7768 8744	Gr. Knoutberry Hill pillar	SD 7886 8716	East on moor path along fence – 1.3km
SD 7886 8716	Track, go right (SW)	SD 7946 8624	SSE on moor path along wall – 1.2km
SD 7946 8624	Car, roadside	SD 7704 8587	West down Arten Gill lane – 2.5km (Three BMS to find)

Benchmark summary for Walk 20

BM No	Type of benchmark and location	Grid reference
Out 1	Cut-mark – SW face, west end of NE parapet of Stone House Bridge	SD 7706 8590
2	Cut-mark – N angle of Sportsmans inn, SW side of road, by some steps	SD 7681 8633
3	Cut-mark – Gatepost, 37.2m NW of a wall junction, SW side of lane	SD 7665 8644
4	Cut-mark – Centre of east parapet of Lea Yeat Bridge	SD 7608 8687
5	Cut-mark – NE angle of building, west side of Lea Yeat Brow	SD 7611 8723
6	Cut-mark – Centre of NW parapet of bridge over railway	SD 7639 8759
7	Cut-mark – Gatepost, 28.4m east of wall junction on south side of Coal Road	SD 7667 8775
Return 8	Cut-mark – East face of viaduct support, south side of track	SD 7761 8592
9	Cut-mark – Gatepost, 48.8m west of wall junction, north side of track	SD 7743 8598
10	Cut-mark – East angle of house, north side of lane	SD 7723 8590

Part D
Walks based from Sedbergh

Sedbergh (pronounced 'Sed-Ber', and meaning 'a hill with a flat top') is distinguished as being England's 'book town', with numerous bookshops that cater for a range of interests – not just the walking and recreation that would be expected. The town is 8km (5 miles) east along the A684 from junction 37 on the M6, so is easy to reach. For campsites, hotels and B&B, consult the town website at www.sedbergh.org.uk.

Although there are the usual attractions – fishing, golf, walking, etc., it is for the books that the centre is worth exploring. The book town initiative, started in 2001, brought together businesses from across the literary spectrum, with writing and publishing establishments as well as the bookshops. An enthusiast can pick up rare and out-of-print volumes, and enjoy hours of relaxed browsing.

There are five walks centred on Sedbergh, visiting seven pillars:

Walk No 21	Crag Hill
Walk No 22	Holme Knott and Calf Top
Walk No 23	Winder and The Calf
Walk No 24	Aye Gill Pike
Walk No 25	East Baugh Fell

There are a number of OS benchmarks listed in the old records, going through the town west to east. Some belonged to a primary levelling line (Kirkby Kendal to Thirsk) from the First Primary Levelling exercise between 1840 and 1860. Most will have gone, but one was indicated on the church – see if you can find it. Another was quoted as 'South pier of Bonnet Bar Toll Bar'. It was located at what is now the junction of the A684 and A683, where a house still has the title 'Tollbar', but the barrier and its piers has obviously long gone. It was where the coachmen and passengers were regularly fleeced for a road toll; perhaps a foretaste of modern day motorway tolls yet to come!

Walk 21. Crag Hill

Start:	Car park, north side of Main Street, Dent
Map reference:	SD 7042 8708
Distance:	6.8km (4.3 miles)
Total ascent:	570m (1870 ft) – average climbing gradient 1 in 8
Estimated time:	4.5 hours
Walk grading:	Moderate to strenuous
OS map:	Landranger 98

Walk summary

From Dent, the route ascends Crag Hill southwards, via the open moor. Descent is east, by Great Coum, joining Deepdale Lane and returning north-westwards. It's short and sharp, but the mainly grass moor is never too difficult, even after rain. Grouse restrictions are unlikely, and navigation is easy, with walls to follow. There are three benchmarks.

Parking and access

From Main Street in Sedbergh, take Finkle Street south towards Millthrop. Follow the lane as it accompanies the River Dee to Dent (9km from Sedbergh). Parking is north off Main Street, just before the cobbled areas.

Dent is a quaint village, with its cobbled streets and whitewashed houses, and with something of an obsession about Adam Sedgwick, the geologist. There is local information at the car park, and in the 'Discover Dentdale' room in the Church.

The walk

From the car park, cross Main Street to examine the old school for a cut-mark (BM No 1) – it's easy to spot. Then take the road SSW, marked 'Bridleway only' and to Flinter Gill, through the residential area. After 350m it becomes a stony track, rising steeply as it follows the gill. There's an impossibly narrow gate, a sinister wishing tree (which failed to deliver on my request for good

Restored limekiln

weather) and a nicely preserved limekiln, complete with information board. It says that, to produce the quicklime, the limestone rock was heated to 900 degrees for three days. Imagine the cost of that nowadays!

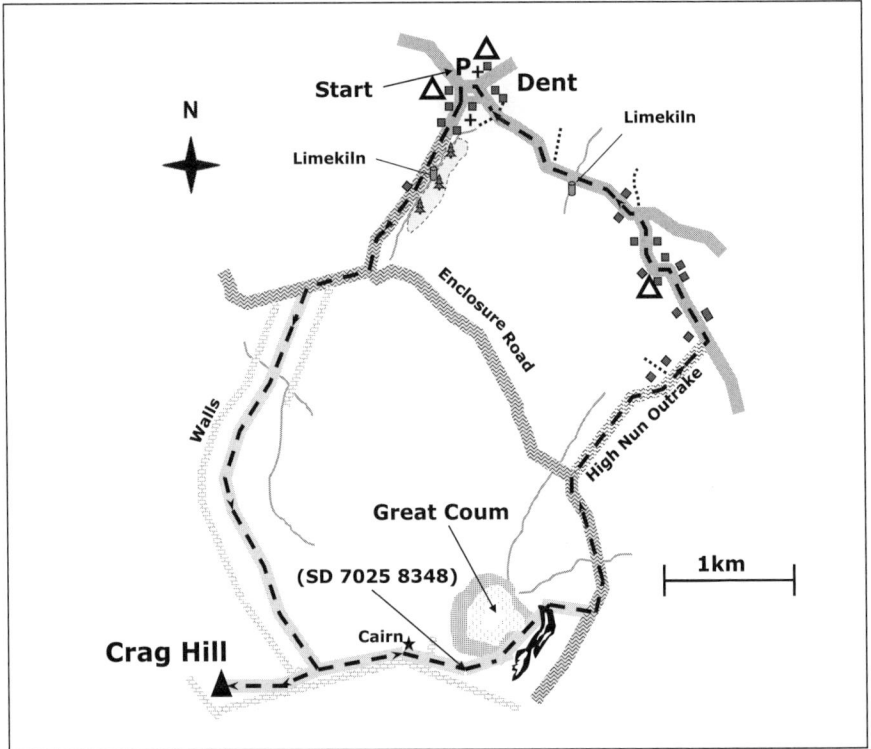

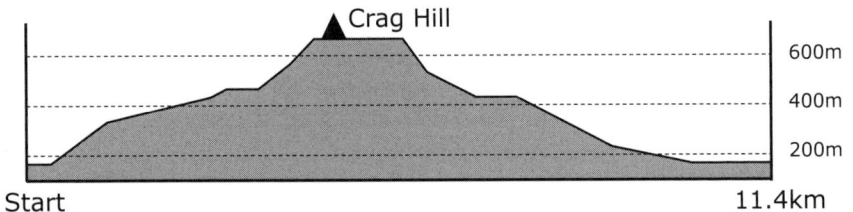

Route and height profile for Crag Hill

At SD 6982 8588 the route joins a walled track, with John McNeil's seat by the gate for your first rest. The track is an 'Enclosure Road' (called 'Green Lane'), giving the farmers of the Middle Ages access to their walled enclosures on the fell-side. It joins Barbondale with Deepdale and, as well as the route up Flinter Gill, there is a second access track, called an 'outrake' ('free passage for sheep'), by High Nun House. It's part of the return leg.

Go right (west) on Green Lane for 450m, to reach a walled track (SD 6940 8578) that leaves to the left (SSW). Follow that track as it meanders SSW for

750m to a gate at SD 6912 8513. From there onwards the route follows the wall 650m SSW to a point where it veers SSE (SD 6884 8458), and then a further steep climb of 1.3km in that direction to a wall junction at the top (SD 6945 8344). It's grass moor all the way, not too wet, the walking area usually obvious, and never more than 30m from the wall.

At the top, go right, using the two stiles to reach the adjacent enclosure. It's then 250m WSW along the wall to the pillar. It's in good condition, with its plug only recently stolen, but everything else intact. Someone has written an 'N' on the flush-bracket face, but it actually faces NW, towards the spectacular Calf Top ridge on the other side of Barbondale, with it's pillar by the small wall cairn.

Pillar details for Crag Hill	
Name:	Crag Hill
Position:	SD 69212 83319
Flush-Bracket No:	S5661
Height:	683m (2241 ft)
Built:	September 1949
Historic use:	Secondary
Current use:	None
Condition:	Good

Crag Hill pillar – looking south

Looking WSW, over the high point of the wall, Brownthwaite is the hill left of the Barbondale valley. I could just see the pillar. SSW, Ireby Hall is low, and (I think) obscured by the wall. South, over the wall corner, Gragareth Fell is close, on the ridge that forms the other side of the Ease Gill valley.

SSE, Ingleborough is unmistakeable over the wall. To its left, along the edge, Park Fell is theoretically visible, but by then it was misty, and I think that the wall gets in the way. ESE, Whernside is close, but might also be obscured by the wall – I was unlucky; the cloud suddenly rolled in, so I couldn't decide. (Looking from Whernside during Walk 19, I thought I could just see the top of the Crag Hill pillar.)

ENE, Great Knoutberry Hill is theoretically (just) in view, but you're looking over Great Coum, which is slightly higher than Crag Hill, so I couldn't be sure in the poor weather. (Actually, looking the other way on a better day, I couldn't see the Crag Hill pillar from Great Knoutberry Hill.) Finally, NNE, according to my maps, Aye Gill Pike should be just visible over the northern slope of Crag Hill (where you walked up), with East Baugh Fell and (on a good day), Wild Boar Fell both in line behind it. So, except for the north quadrant, Crag Hill does not have the best views in the Dales.

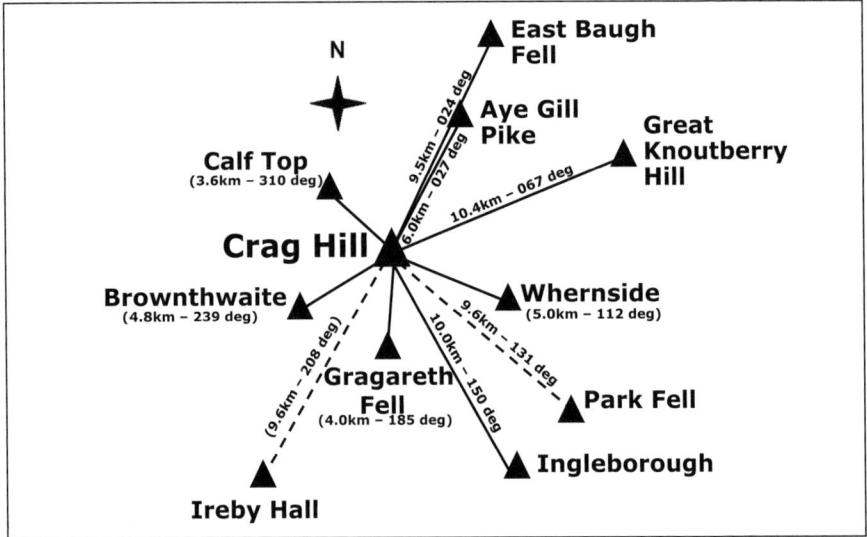

Nearby pillars in view from Crag Hill

From the pillar, retrace your steps along the wall, back over the two stiles, and follow the wall's north side ENE and then ESE for 1.1km. On the way you'll pass a cairn and cross one wall – there's a stile in the corner. At SD 7025 8348, near a triangular patch of water about 10m long, turn ENE and leave the wall. There's no obvious path, but that direction takes you up to, and then down, the steep incline on the SE flank of the Great Coum bowl, so you get a fine appreciation of its shape, with Whernside to your fore across the valley. Below, as you turn more NE, there is a clearer path, crossing the northern edge of a rocky scar and joining a moor track that winds eastwards to rejoin the Enclosure Road (SD 7116 8368).

'Coum' means 'round', and the bowl is typical of a glacial head, the snows of 10,000 years ago accumulating day after day and feeding the creeping sheet of ice that trundled away into the valley. However, there is no U-shaped ravine leading off the coum, which any glacier would have cut on its way into Deepdale, so I have some doubts. I do know that Combe Scar, due west of Gawthrop in Dentdale, is a glacial head, and it has a very similar appearance to Great Coum.

Once on the Enclosure Road, follow it 1.1km generally north, with Aye Gill Pike and Dentdale to the fore, to the point (SD 7109 8460) where it veers NW and a second stony track (outrake) leaves straight on, veering NE. Follow that; it takes you steeply down to Deepdale Lane, past High Nun House where you turn left. (Perhaps nuns once lived there, but 'nun' is also a bird.) 500m on, after a left-hand bend, look for the 'pivot' benchmark (BM No 2) on the house at Slack. It's very difficult, on a moss-covered protruding corner base-stone, a faint cut arrow pointing at the shallow depression (where the surveyor stood the survey pole) on the top face.

Walking on, you join Garlic Lane, going left (signposted to Gawthrop) and soon cross How Gill near a telephone box. The records placed a cut-mark on the north parapet of the bridge (RHS of the lane, SD 7145 8628, 90cm up and on the east end). But I couldn't find it. Yet it should be there, and large, like the one cut on the Dent School. The same applies further on, on the gatepost 15m on and across the road from the lane-side limekiln (SD 7119 8643). That should be 40cm up. Maybe there were once two gateposts, the one with the mark now gone.

As you arrive back at Dent, visit the church. The cut-mark (BM No 3) is easy to spot. Inside, have a look at the 'Discover Dentdale' display. In particular, look at the range of local facilities in the town before the First World War. It defines the time succinctly.

Route summary for Walk 21

Your present location	Your next objective	Waypoint at next objective	Directions and distance
Car park, Dent SD 7042 8708	Junction of tracks, go right	SD 6982 8588	SSW through residential area and on to bridleway – 1.4km. (One BM to find)
SD 6982 8588	Moor track leaving SSW	SD 6940 8578	West along walled track – 450m
SD 6940 8578	End of track – gate	SD 6912 8513	SSW along walled track – 750m
SD 6912 8513	Wall turns SSE	SD 6884 8458	SSW along a wall – 650m
SD 6884 8458	Wall junction, use two stiles	SD 6945 8344	SSE following wall steeply uphill – 1.3km
SD 6945 8344	Crag Hill pillar	SD 6921 8332	SW along the wall – 250m
SD 6921 8332	Point to leave wall	SD 7025 8348	ENE and then ESE along wall – 1.1km
SD 7025 8348	Rejoin the Enclosure Road	SD 7116 8368	ENE, NE, then east on flank of Great Coum, joining moor track – 1.1km
SD 7116 8368	Walled track leaving NE off sharp bend	SD 7109 8460	NE, veering NW on walled track – 1.1km
SD 7109 8460	Deepdale Lane	SD 7198 8545	NE on walled track – 1.3km
SD 7198 8545	Join Garlic Lane	SD 7153 8627	NNW on lane – 1km, with (One BM to find)
SD 7153 8627	Car park, Dent	SD 7042 8708	NW on Garlic Lane – 1.4km (One BM on church)

Benchmark summary for Walk 21

BM No	Type of benchmark and location	Grid reference
1	Cut-mark – North angle of school, SW side of road	SD 7042 8704
2	Pivot – North angle of building, Slack, SW side lane	SD 7166 8591
3	Cut-mark – West face of St Andrew's Church	SD 7051 8704

Walk 22. Holme Knott and Calf Top

Start:	Lay-by, A683, 2.5km north of Middleton
Map reference:	SD 6295 8869
Distance:	16.1km (10.1 miles)
Total ascent:	640m (2100 ft) – average climbing gradient 1 in 12
Estimated time:	6 hours
Walk grading:	Moderate to strenuous
OS maps:	Landranger 97 and Landranger 98

Walk summary

The walk begins from Middleton, traversing open-access moor to Holme Knott, before following established paths across Brown Knott, Long Bank and Green Maws to Calf Top. The return leg is across Middleton Fell. The route is not particularly wet, even after heavy rain, but walking when there is significant snow cover makes navigation difficult. Also, the area is used for shooting, so vigilance is required. There is only one benchmark to find.

Parking and access

From Sedbergh, take the A683 to the SW. After 5km (3 miles), parking is on the lay-by before 'The Head' public house. Coming east from the M6 (J37), turn right off the A684 after 3km (2 miles), down the B6256, joining the A683.

The walk

From the lay-by, walk south and then turn back up the green lane indicated to Hollins, just before the pub. It's open-access, and after 400m it joins a tarmac lane and then a track that takes the route past the 'Fellside' property, with its two wind turbines, to a gate at SD 6386 8886. This marks the boundary to the broader open-access land, where any caution notices will be posted.

Beyond the gate, go left (NNE), up the wide grassy path. It's not marked on the OS maps, but it meanders steeply NE towards the Holme Knott summit. At SD 6439 8929 it crosses a path going NW-SE. Mark it; it's a point you'll return to after visiting the pillar. Continuing NE, the path reaches the crest of the Holme Knott hill at SD 6450 8951, to reveal a splendid view north to the Howgills. The pillar is then 100m to the east, via a narrow path.

It's in good condition, except that it has no plug, and the flush-bracket faces exactly south. Opposite that, just east of north, Winder is on the other side of the Sedbergh valley, with the Howgills behind. The white pillar is unmistakable. Either side of east, East Baugh Fell and Ayr Gill Pike embrace the Garsdale Valley. Both pillars are by walls, and near impossible to spot, but the Ayr Gill Pike pillar is painted white, so it's visible later in the walk. SE, the other pillar on this walk, Calf Top, is on the horizon, on the right of the two summits. (The left one is Green Maws.) I could see the pillar with my monocular, even looking towards the sun.

SW, Scout Hill is difficult to resolve, but High Audland is the hill forming the horizon directly in line with a farmhouse, looking just left of the western peak of the Holme Knott summit. Finally, to the WNW, Millrigg Moor is the green hill left of the windmills, the pillar right of the wall. And, as ever, beyond the wind-farm, the distant Lake District fells dominate the horizon.

Looking around you from the pillar, there are marshy areas and pools to both the north and south. So Holme Knott is a sort of island, which is the usual meaning of 'Holme', the 'Knott' suggesting it is 'gnarled' – perhaps 'lumpy and rocky'. Before I got there, I couldn't see how the name would fit, but it clearly does.

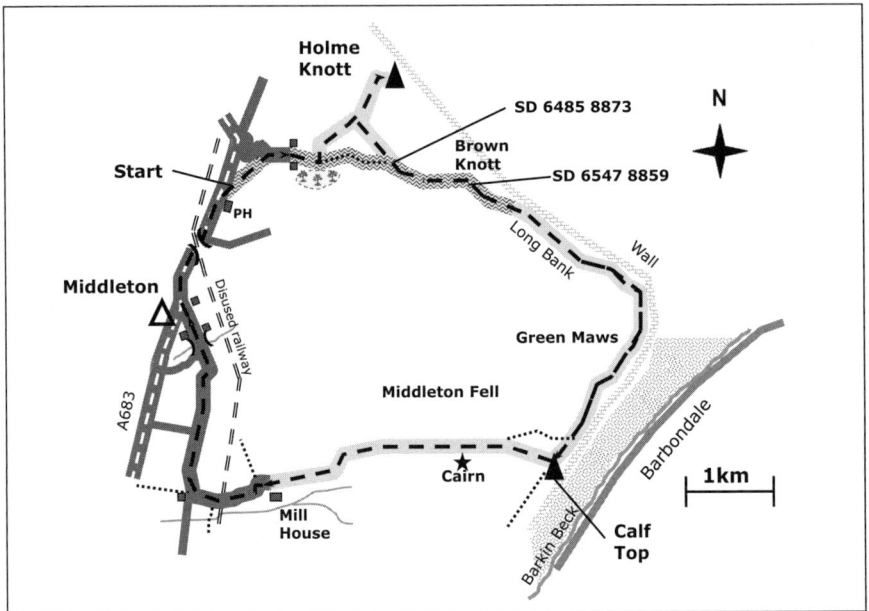

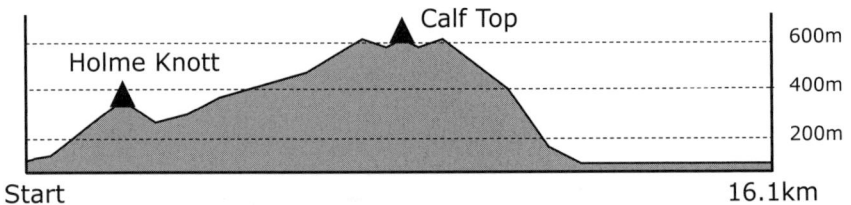

Route and height profile for Holme Knott and Calf Top

Pillar details for Holme Knott	
Name:	Holme Knott
Position:	SD 64601 89530
Flush-Bracket No:	S5518
Height:	350m 1148 ft)
Built:	June 1949
Historic use:	Secondary
Current use:	None
Condition:	Good

Holme Knott pillar – looking NE

East from the pillar, a path goes towards a wall, one that snakes SE into the distance. It's the county boundary, and the route eventually follows it all the way to Calf Top. You could walk to it from the pillar and follow it, but you'd be condemning yourself to some difficult terrain. Better is to retrace your steps to the path crossing point at SD 6439 8929 and then go left (SE).

After 300m from the crossing, the route zigzags across a stream, then turns south for 200m to another stream. Cross that, turning SE again, and continue for about 200m. The area is a jumble of tracks, and at that point the main one (as marked by the double dotted line on the OS maps), is 150m SSE. Aim for that, the key waypoint being SD 6485 8873. Even then, as you follow it ESE again, it's easy to stray off it. Another key waypoint is SD 6547 8859,

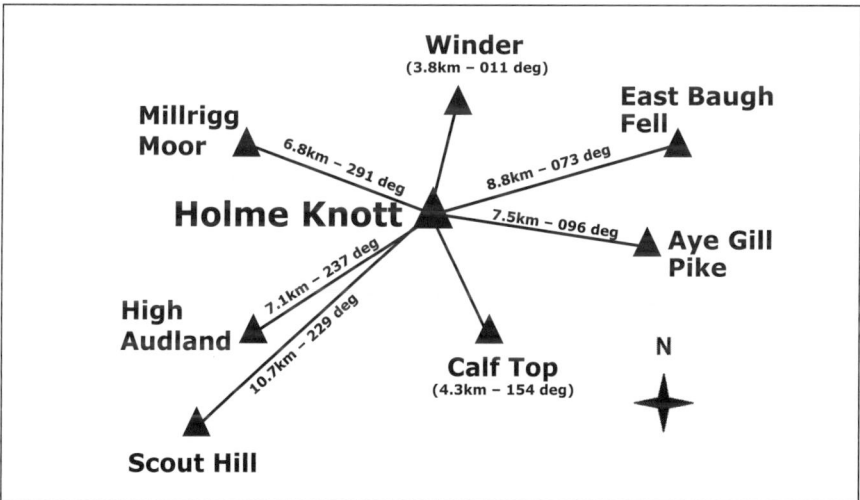

Nearby pillars in view from Holme Knott

700m on, where there are tracks in all directions. Keep ESE, and avoid any that go more east or ENE.

However, whichever way you go around east, you will eventually reach the country boundary wall, and you can follow it from then on. It takes you all the way (4.5km) to the Calf Top pillar. On the way, as you gain height, take time to look at the unfolding views to the NE and east. The white pillar on Ayr Gill Pike is now clear, right of the fourth wall eastwards in the evenly spaced sequence. And over the south flank of that hill, looking along the Dentdale valley, the long flat top of Widdale Fell forms the horizon. Its southern end is Great Knoutberry Hill, but you've no chance of spotting the pillar – it's a squat, stone construction by a wall.

The Calf Top pillar is on an undistinguished spot by a fence and dilapidated wall. It's in good condition, but again without a plug. I climbed the fence to shelter behind the small wall cairn, as well as edging eastwards to get a great view into the Barbondale valley (possibly 'The beaver valley', or 'Where barley is grown'), with Barkin Beck glinting in the sun about 400m (1250 ft) below. On the opposite side, Towns Fell reveals how rainwater cuts its intricate gullies as it drains towards the beck. The valley marks the line of the Dent geological fault, stretching from Kirkby Stephen to Kirkby Longsdale, where the sandstone that characterises the NW area of the Dales separates from the horizontal strata of limestone and gritstone of the classic Dales to the SE.

Widdale Fell – with a splendid lenticular cloud

Looking just west of north, Winder is still visible, with the Howgills behind, and in the foreground, Holme Knott is the light-coloured hill below you, with the Howgill valley beyond. Turning NE, Aye Gill Pike is now more in front of East Baugh Fell. Due east, there is a direct view down Dentdale to Great Knoutberry Hill, and SE, the Crag Hill pillar has come into view. It's left of the wall that runs up the south end of the plateau. To the right of that, 14km away, the distinctive sloping top of Ingleborough is just showing. Then right again, and closer, forming the horizon, is the long sweep of Gragareth Fell. It's another pillar fairly near a wall, so I couldn't make it out.

Near south, looking along the ridge, Brownthwaite is the close, low hill. The pillar is set back, and looking into the sun, I couldn't see it. WSW and west, South Hill and High Audland are too low and indistinct to easily find. Finally, NW, Millrigg Moor is the green hill with a wall, left of the turbines.

Pillar details for Calf Top	
Name:	Calf Top
Position:	SD 66447 85634
Flush-Bracket No:	S5670
Height:	610m (2001 ft)
Built:	July 1949
Historic use:	Secondary
Current use:	None
Condition:	Good

Calf Top pillar – looking east

To start for home, first walk 200m NW (the direction faced by the flush-bracket) across the moor to intercept a grassy path (at SD 6634 8576). Turn left there, following it WNW by an area of water and onwards westerly to pass a tall, narrow cairn at SD 6578 8586. Beyond that, the path remains clear, going west, and passing another small cairn near SD 6468 8591. Then it dives down hill and becomes vague, with a surface stream to follow before you reach a clear grassy path going NE-SW (at SD 6423 8581). Follow that for 900m as it turns WSW until you reach a gate (SD 6350 8552).

There, the landowner has posted a 'Private' notice, advising you to find another way off the fell. He is entitled to do so. The open-access land

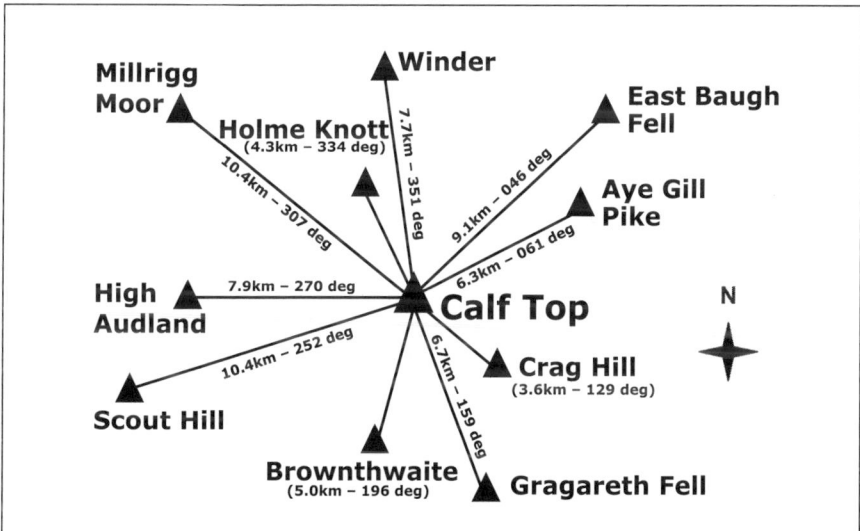

Millrigg Moor ▲

▲Winder

Holme Knott ▲
(4.3km – 334 deg)

East Baugh Fell ▲

10.4km – 307 deg

7.7km – 351 deg

9.1km – 046 deg

Aye Gill Pike ▲

6.3km – 061 deg

High Audland ▲   7.9km – 270 deg

▲ Calf Top

N

10.4km – 252 deg

▲ Scout Hill

6.7km – 159 deg

Crag Hill ▲
(3.6km – 129 deg)

Brownthwaite ▲
(5.0km – 196 deg)

Gragareth Fell ▲

Nearby pillars in view from Calf Top

terminates at the gate, and beyond that there is 30m of private drive before you reach another public right-of-way that passes through the Mill House property. There is no other way off the fell – I checked. So I went through the gate and knocked on the door, ready with an apology for the intrusion and to ask advice on how best to exit the fell. They are holiday cottages, and I was met by bewildered indifference from the occupier. By that point, of course, I was on the public footpath and could proceed onward down the lane. So I will leave it to the reader's discretion as to what to do at the gate.

From Mill House, go west on the lane to the Tee-junction, with 'The Old Smithy' opposite, and then turn right. It's quiet walking, going north, all the way to the main road. I met no traffic, but that lane is narrow and enclosed in places, so vigilance is required. On the OS map you'll see a disused railway. It would have been an ideal route, but it's not a right-of-way.

The main road is quiet, so walking was not a problem, generally on the left. And see if you can spot a very nice OS rivet somewhere between the 'Sharp Bends' sign and the 'Narrow Bridge' sign as you approach the old railway crossing. Then it's the car, but with the pub as a temptation just before you reach it.

Route summary for Walk 22

Your present location	Your next objective	Waypoint at next objective	Directions and distance
Lay-by, A683, Middleton SD 6295 8869	Gate to open-access land	SD 6386 8886	South to green lane, NNE to hard lane, east past farm – 1.3km
SD 6386 8886	Path crosses route from NW	SD 6439 8929	North and NE on grass track – 700m
SD 6439 8929	Holme Knott pillar	SD 6460 8953	NE to 100m west of pillar, then east – 350m
SD 6460 8953	Return to path crossing	SD 6439 8929	West and SW on grass path – 350m
SD 6439 8929	Regain main track	SD 6485 8873 KEY WAYPOINT	Generally SE on track, across two streams – 800m
SD 6485 8873	Many paths, keep SE	SD 6547 8859 KEY WAYPOINT	ESE on track – 700m
SD 6547 8859	Calf Top pillar	SD 6645 8563	SE, then south, then SW by the wall – 4.5km
SD 6645 8563	Join path over Middleton Fell, where you go left	SD 6634 8576	NW across grassy moor – 200m
SD 6634 8576	Near a thin cairn, on left	SD 6578 8586	WNW on grassy moor path – 600m
SD 6578 8586	Near small cairn, on right	SD 6468 8591	West on grassy moor path – 1.3km
SD 6468 8591	Intercept clear grassy path	SD 6423 8581	SSW, steeply down a vague path – 250m
SD 6423 8581	Gate to Mill House	SD 6350 8552	SW, then WSW on grass path and track – 900m
SD 6350 8552	Tee-junction, The Old Smithy, where you go right	SD 6260 8540	West along the lane – 1km
SD 6260 8540	A683	SD 6245 8736	North on narrow lane – 2km
SD 6245 8736	Lay-by, A683	SD 6295 8869	NNE on A683 – 1.5km (One BM to find)

Benchmark summary for Walk 22

BM No	Type of benchmark and location	Grid reference
1	Rivet – Milestone, 'Sedbergh 4 miles', NW side of road (probably 160 years old)	SD 6258 8793

Walk 23. Winder and The Calf

Start:	Church on Ing Lane at Blandsgill, off Howgill Lane, north of Sedbergh
Map reference:	SD 6337 9503
Distance:	13.1km (8.2 miles)
Total ascent:	740m (2430 ft) – average climbing gradient 1 in 9
Estimated time:	5.5 hours
Walk grading:	Strenuous
OS maps:	Landranger 97 and Landranger 98

Walk summary

The route starts south along Howgill Lane, followed by a steep climb over Winder, then around Arant Haw and across Calders to The Calf. Return is down White Fell and around Castley Knott. The going underfoot will be firm, even after heavy rain. There are five benchmarks to look for.

Parking and access

From Sedbergh, take Howgill Lane north off Main Street. It's 4km (2.5 miles) to the church on Ing Lane at Blandsgill where the route starts. (Go left after the telephone box.) Approaching from the M6 (J37), along the A684, Slacks Lane leaves northwards 1km after the junction with the B6257, joining Howgill Lane. It's a more direct route, but is very narrow.

The walk

From the parking spot, walk south along Howgill Lane. But before you start, see if you can spot the cut-mark on the church (BM No 1). Then it's 2.5km of quiet road walking to the bottom of a walled track indicated to Brant Fell (top of a rise, SD 6414 9296), taking care to keep left at the 'Sedbergh 1.5 miles' sign at the junction with Slacks Lane. On the way you should spot four more benchmarks, a cut-mark (BM No 2) on Moss Cottage, a cut-mark (BM No 3) on a gatepost near a bridleway sign for Low Branthwaite, a rivet (BM No 4) on the bridge parapet over Crosdale Beck and a cut-mark (BM No 5) on a gatepost 300 metres up the hill after the 'Sedbergh 1.5 miles' sign. All the cut-marks are unusually large and poorly engraved – probably a short-sighted stonemason.

From the lane, turn ENE up the walled track. After 200m it ends with a gate. Go right, below the park-bench, even though the OS maps show the path going left. It's a pleasant grassy track that veers NE and begins a stiff 1 in 5 climb up to the Winder summit. It gets the heart going, so take a rest now and then and look back NW, beyond the wind farm. The distinctive Lake District hills dominate the skyline some 40km distant.

N

The Calf

White
Fell

Castley
Knotts

Bram Rigg ●

Small cairn
(SD 6707 9600)

★

Calders

Ing Lane

Rowantree
Grains

Arant
Haw ●

Start

Howgill
Lane

Crosdale Beck

1km

Winder

The Calf

600m

Winder

400m

200m

Start

13.1km

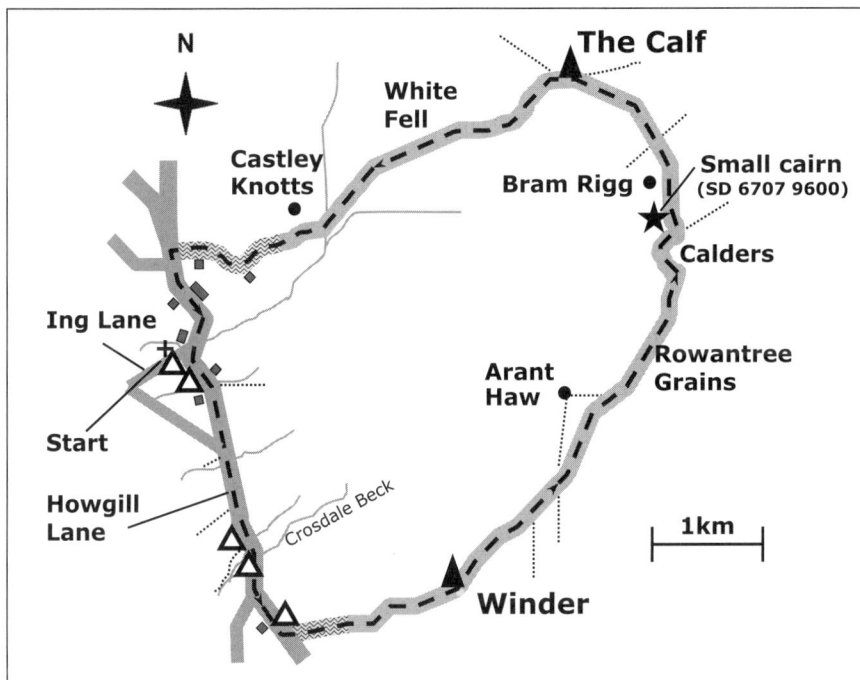

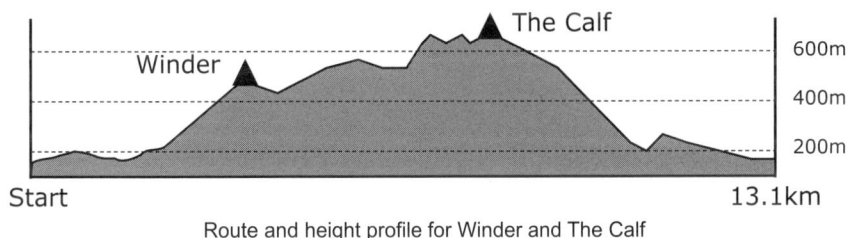

Route and height profile for Winder and The Calf

Winder pillar is in good condition, with its spider and flush-bracket intact, but missing its plug, and the base is exposed. It was white when I got there, but it's been pink some time in the past. 'Winder' is most likely a corruption of 'Winter' or 'Windy', both common hill names.

Direction finding is easy, since the nearby stone topogragh is due east of the pillar. In that direction, Baugh Fell is the long hill across the valley, with its stone-built pillar on the southern end. To the right of that (south), across the Garsdale Valley, is Ayr Gill Pike. Both pillars are by walls, and difficult to see. Between them in the distance (15km) is Great Knoutberry Hill. Then, to the right of Ayr Gill Pike, on the horizon (15km), is the distinctive 'whaleback' shape of Whernside.

Pillar details for Winder	
Name:	Winder
Position:	SD 65393 93272
Flush-Bracket No:	S5659
Height:	474m (1555 ft)
Built:	September 1949
Historic use:	Secondary
Current use:	None
Condition:	Good

Wnder pillar – looking NE to Arant Haw

Due south, below you in the foreground across the valley, is Holme Knott (with its pillar on the left of the two high points), and to the SSE, forming the horizon, is Calf Top. To the right of that, and more distant (11km), with a flat top and steep eastern side, is Crag Hill. To the SW, High Audland is difficult to make out. But Millrigg Moor, just south of west, is the green hill to the left of the wind turbines, with the pillar right of the wall. Just north of west, directly behind the wind-farm, is Benson Knott. Finally, Grayrigg Forest is the green hill across the valley carrying the M6, to the NW. (It has no forest!) The north and NW directions are dominated by the nearby Arant Haw and Brant Fell, so there is no line-of-sight to the second pillar on this walk, The Calf.

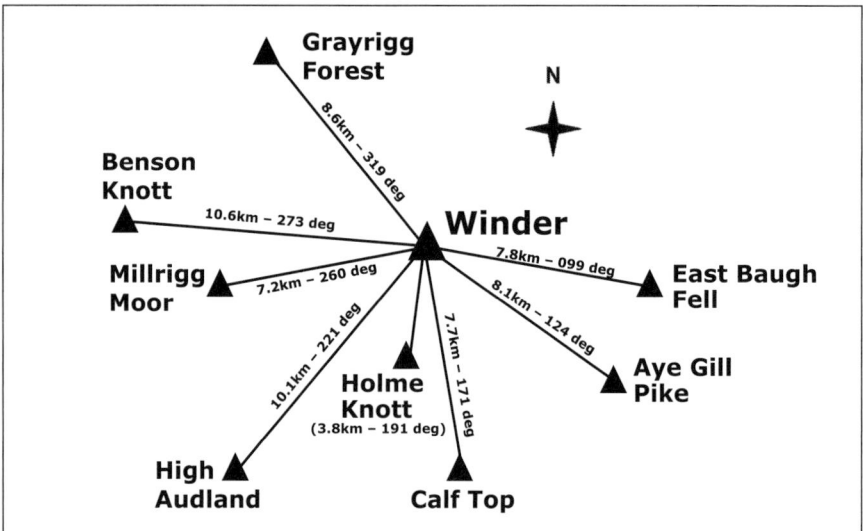

Nearby pillars in view from Winder

From Winder, follow the wide path going NE. Looking ahead, you'll see it divide (at SD 6629 9430), the narrower path going left over Arant Haw. It comes back to the main path on the north side, so I kept to the lower, easier path. Under Arant Haw, as you gain height, look back SSE. Now you can see the distinctive flat top of Ingleborough, behind and to the left of Crag Hill. And to the SE, to the left of and behind Whernside, is Pen-y-ghent, with its steep western edge. If you choose to go over Arant Haw, from where the views are splendid, it adds 100m to the total height climb around the walk.

The main path continues NNE and is easy to follow over Rowantree Grains towards Calders. Rowantree village is near Garsdale Head. 'Grains' means 'tree branches', so I'd guess that, to someone back in the dark ages, from a distance the area looked like branches of a Rowan tree, with it's many dividing streams. As you approach Calders (probably meaning 'the cold place'), the path drops down, rising steeply again NW, with a county boundary fence close by. At the top it swings NE, reaching a small cairn at SD 6707 9600. Keep left there and continue across Bram Rigg Top to The Calf summit.

Pillar details for The Calf	
Name:	The Calf
Position:	SD 66733 97055
Flush-Bracket No:	S5676
Height:	677m (2221 ft)
Built:	August 1949
Historic use:	Secondary
Current use:	None
Condition:	Good

The Calf pillar – looking NW

The pillar is in sound condition, with the flush-bracket and spider intact, and with a stone plug. The flush-bracket points north, but the easiest point to start your observations is ENE, across the right hand edge of the pool. The flat-top hill across the valley is Wild Boar Fell, with the pillar inside the cairn on the north end. SE, in the foreground, East Baugh Fell is the flat hill with a steep southern edge, with Widdale Fell behind it. Looking down the path along which you approached (SSE), with Ingleborough showing over the top of Brant Fell, Aye Gill Pike is to its left and Calf Top to its right. ('Calf' probably means 'The top of a ridge'.)

To the SW, the small, green Millrigg Moor hill is just right of the Killington reservoir, and beyond that is Morecambe Bay, with the Kent Viaduct at Arnside crossing the inlet. NW, Grayrigg Forest is indistinct, low and in the foreground on the west side of the M6 valley, and NNW, Middleton is just visible, close

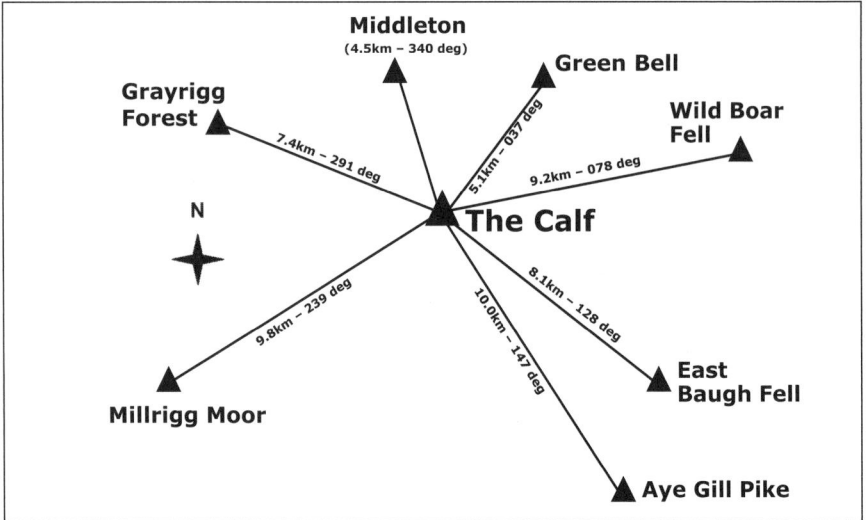

Nearby pillars in view from The Calf

and lower, through the gap between Bush Howe and Cobles. (Look at your OS map.) Finally, exactly in line with the path that leaves past the pool, Green Bell is just peeping above the high ground in the foreground.

Before leaving the pillar, look NW at the onward path. It joins a narrow path coming from the east, with two paths then continuing NW. You take the left one (west), and it quickly bends to the SW as it descends White Fell (SD 6580 9688). It's a nice grassy path, and you should take time to admire the scenery around you as the panorama unfolds. It is classic Howgill Fells. The reason for their even, rounded shape lies in the local geology. It's sandstone, siltstone and mudstone, with all the rocks possessing a similar resistance to erosion, so that wind, rain and glaciers have produced smooth-sided mounds. It contrasts significantly with the rugged igneous rocks of the fells to the north, as well as with the cave-riddled limestone to the southeast.

As the path turns west, the route below comes into view, with the two streams (Calf Beck and Bram Rigg Beck) joining under Castley Knotts hill.

A classic Howgill Fells panorama

('Castle' or 'Castley' normally implies a fort.) It's a knee-jarring descent, and if the streams are in flood at the bottom (SD 6456 9631) you need to choose your crossing with care. I certainly got my feet wet. From there, the path goes round the south of Castley Knotts and joins a walled track by some sheep pens. As it goes west, the track becomes a concrete drive and eventually emerges on to Howgill Lane. It's then 1km south (left) along the lane back to the car.

Route summary for Walk 23

Your present location	Your next objective	Waypoint at next objective	Directions and distance
Church on Ing Lane SD 6337 9503	Walled track leaving ENE	SD 6414 9296	South along Howgill Lane, keeping left at Slacks Lane – 3.5km, with five BMs to find
SD 6414 9296	Winder pillar	SD 6539 9327	NNE along track, then steep grassy path – 1.5km
SD 6539 9327	Path leaves left over Arant Haw	SD 6629 9430	NE on grass track – 1.4km
SD 6629 9430	Cairn at Calders	SD 6707 9600	NNE over Rowantree Grains – 2km
SD 6707 9600	The Calf pillar	SD 6673 9706	NNW over Bram Rigg Top – 1.1km
SD 6673 9706	White Fell	SD 6580 9688	NW, veering to SW on grassy track – 1.1km
SD 6580 9688	Where streams join	SD 6456 9631	SW down steep grassy path – 1.5km
SD 6456 9631	Howgill Lane	SD 6324 9589	SW on path, then west on to walled track – 1.7km
SD 6324 9589	Car park, Ing Lane	SD 6337 9503	South along Howgill Lane – 1km

Benchmark summary for Walk 23

BM No	Type of benchmark and location	Grid reference
1	Cut-mark – Buttress, east angle of Holy Trinity Church, NW side of Ing Lane	SD 6337 9503
2	Cut-mark – SE angle of Moss Cottage, west side of Howgill Lane	SD 6354 9484
3	Cut-mark – Gatepost, south side of track leading off west side of Howgill Lane	SD 6374 9387
4	Rivet – North end of parapet of Huds Bridge, west side of Howgill Lane	SD 6386 9365
5	Cut-mark – Gatepost at wall junction, NE side of Howgill Lane	SD 6403 9303

Walk 24. Ayr Gill Pike

Start:	Car park, A684 east of Sedbergh
Map reference:	SD 6945 9122
Distance:	10.4km (6.5 miles)
Total ascent:	475m (1560 ft) – average climbing gradient 1 in 8
Estimated time:	4 hours
Walk grading:	Moderate
OS map:	Landranger 98

Walk summary

The route uses the open moor around the Whitbeck Plantation, approaching the pillar from the NW. Return is steeply down the Copplethwaite moor to the main road, and west along the lane from Bellow End. There is one benchmark. It could be very wet, and would be unsuitable with lying snow.

For fit walkers, it might be paired with Walk 25 to East Baugh Fell, the latter being done in reverse, picking up the route at Bellow End. A reversed route table is added to the Walk 25 write-up for that eventuality, and assumes that you've read up on the forward route.

If the two walks were combined in one stint, the resultant walk would be strenuous – 14.5km (9.1 miles), with a 900m ascent and an average climbing gradient of 1 in 6. It would take you six hours.

Parking and access

From Sedbergh, take the A684 east for 4km (2.5 miles). The car park is on the left, where the lane branches off for Garside Foot.

The walk

Before you start, cross the main road and see if you can find the rivet on a rock – it's the only BM you're looking for. And have a look at the information board – it provides a useful write-up on the Howgills.

Walk 250m ENE down the main road to a grass moor track (SD 6970 9113) leaving from the right, just before the cattle-grid. On the 1852 OS map, the area to the left of the main road along that stretch is dotted with limekilns and quarries. There's still evidence of working, with mounds and the remains of access tracks, but the only kiln I saw was by the return lane, up the hill on the other side of the river. It's on the south side; set in the embankment below the road level. You'll pass it on the way back.

The open-access moor track goes south, steeply uphill, eventually joining a wall and turning SE. It is likely to be very wet, so keep close to the wall, even when it makes a short detour. The wall is with you all the way to the

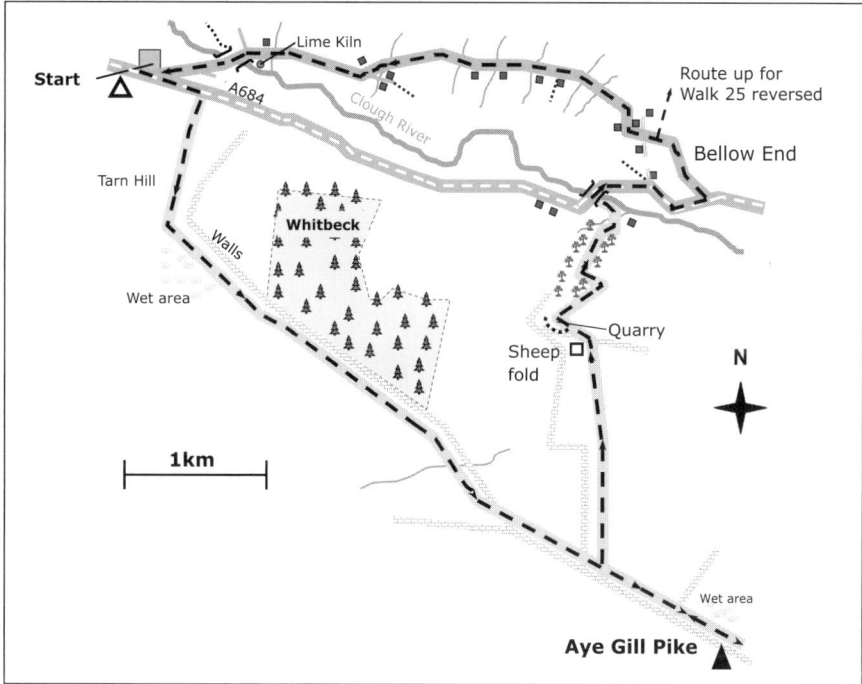

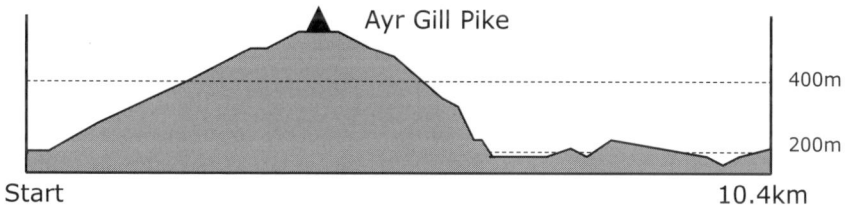

Route and height profile for Ayr Gill Pike

pillar, except for one stretch of fence after the plantation. At that point the view NE to East Baugh Fell has expanded, as well as the outlook behind to the Howgills and Holme Knott. (Always pause to look back now and again, on any walk.)

The Howgills look good from any angle

At SD 7096 8923, 2.6km on from the road, at the corner of two walls, take the wall stile to the left and then continue SE, now left of the wall. After 500m, at SD 7141 8898, you cross a wall that goes back north – it's your way back after visiting the pillar. 300m further on there's a broken wall, with a fence then running parallel to the wall you're following. Keep left of that fence, with 450m of more boggy ground between you and the pillar. Then you'll find a stile and a gap in the wall for your easy access.

Pillar details for Ayr Gill Pike	
Name:	Ayr Gill Pike
Position:	SD 72067 88613
Flush-Bracket No:	S5665
Height:	557m (1827 ft)
Built:	September 1949
Historic use:	Secondary
Current use:	None
Condition:	Good

Ayr Gill Pike pillar – looking SSW to Grag Hill

The pillar is well kept, painted white, and has probably been adopted by a local. It has all its bits, except for a plastic plug. The flush-bracket faces slightly west of due south. (It surprises me that Hotine, such a perfectionist, didn't specify that the pillar faces should always point N, E, S and W, with the flush-bracket facing, say, north.)

Opposite the flush-bracket, East Baugh Fell is NNE across the valley. The pillar is behind the wall at the highest point, with a wall coming down from the location. NE, the rounded hill on the horizon is Great Shunner Fell (16km distant). The structure you can see on the top (with binoculars) is a shelter, with the pillar attached to one end. ENE, the next hill on the skyline is Stags Fell, which is a weird place with several beacons. I'm sure I could make one out.

ESE, directly along the wall, Great Knoutberry Hill has a wall and fence on the top, as well as a squat pillar that is difficult to see. Behind its right flank is Dodd Fell, and coming round SE, Pen-y-ghent dominates the horizon (20km distant), with Blea Moor closer and just left of the same bearing. SSE, Whernside is unmistakable, its axis going away from you. Its pillar merges into a wall. Behind its right flank, the north side of Ingleborough is just visible.

SSW is Crag Hill, with Gragareth showing behind Great Coum on its left flank. The pillar is on the right side of Crag Hill, and visible, so that confirms that I should have been able to see the other way when I'd stood in the murk on Crag Hill. Looking SW, Barbondale is flanked on its right by Calf Top, with Brownthwaite at the far end of the valley. There's a wall going up Calf Top, with its pillar alongside. West, Holme Knott is cut-off by the nearby moor and wall, but WNW, overlooking Sedbergh, the white pillar on Winder stands out nicely. Finally, NW, Bram Rigg Top gets in the way of The Calf on top of the Howgills.

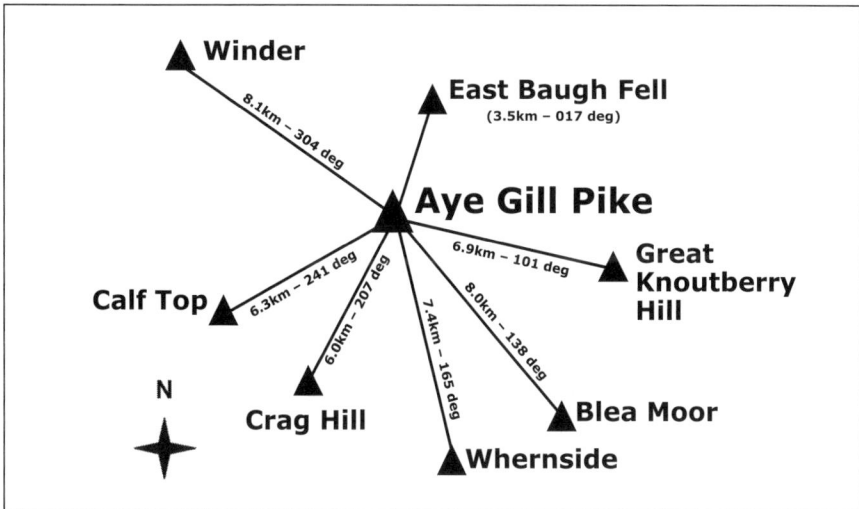

Nearby pillars in view from Aye Gill Pike

And Aye Gill Pike? 'Aygill' means 'The river in the ravine.' But which river? And 'Pike' means 'Pointed hill'. But it doesn't look that pointed to me. However, when you look back from Great Knoutberry Hill, looking down the axis of Ayr Gill Pike, it is quite sharp by Yorkshire Dales' standards, so I guess that's enough.

From the pillar, retrace your steps 750m to the wall that leaves due north. There, you have a choice. A short section of this walk (to reach the main road) encroaches on private land, albeit rough. It's often the case that open-access land is all very well, but there are few legitimate ways to get on and off. If your principles discourage even a modest trespass, then you could simply retrace your steps to the car park. Otherwise, follow the right-hand side of the wall north down the hill. The grass moor is not too difficult, and there's clear evidence that it's walked.

After 570m, at SD 7140 8954, the wall turns west. But you can carry on due north, through the reedy grass (watch out for streams and bogs), aiming for a NW corner of walls (SD 7137 9003), with a sheepfold and gate, 500m down the slope. It's from there that you have the best view of the southern slope of East Baugh Fell. Take time to look at the wall map in Walk 25 and see if you can match it to the real thing. It will help when you come to do that walk.

On the other side of the gate, go left (NW), edging away from the wall that goes west. About 180m on (SD 7122 9012), before a wall and fence going

Looking back from Great Knoutberry Hill

down the slope northwards, you'll find an old quarry. Pick your way down that and look for a track that joins from the right. Follow that as it zigzags down, reaching a fence and a gate, the limit of open-access land.

You emerge into an avenue of trees. Follow it down, ford the stream at the bottom and then go right on a wooden bridge over a joining stream. Keep north, by the right of that stream, up to the fallen wall. There is then a little stone bridge back across the stream (left), with a fence stile into the rough pasture on the other side. Across that pasture is a set of steps (SD 7136 9064) going up to the main road.

I was a little nervous of this section on private land (I could not establish the owner), but the presence of the stile and steps was reassuring, even if their main use might be for fishermen. As always, if challenged, a profuse apology will usually suffice. But a landowner can ask you to leave his land by the quickest possible route. That you should do with good grace (to the road, in this case). Trespassing is a civil offence, and is not open to criminal prosecution. A civil suit is possible, but would probably require demonstrable nuisance or damage, and no walker should cause either.

Walk east along the main road for 600m, to the lane that goes back left, then follow that west through Bellow End. After 350m, at SD 7166 9093, a gated rough lane leaves north. If you're doing Walk 25 as well, that is the point to turn up the hill and use the reverse route summary for that walk.

If not, then you have 2.5km west along the lane, with four gates, a ford and the limekiln as the only attractions. However, I did get one nice surprise – a red squirrel hopping across my path, pausing to look on disdainfully, then disappearing up a tree.

Route summary for Walk 24

Your present location	Your next objective	Waypoint at next objective	Directions and distance
Car park, A684 SD 6945 9122	Right (SW) up moor track	SD 6970 9113	ESE down the main road – 250m
SD 6970 9113	Wall stile	SD 7096 8923	South and SE on grass moor path by wall and plantation – 2.6km
SD 7096 8923	Wall stile (return point)	SD 7141 8898	SE along wall – 500m
SD 7141 8898	Ayr Gill Pike pillar	SD 7207 8861	SE along wall and fence – 750m
SD 7207 8861	Wall stile, to turn north	SD 7141 8898	Retrace your steps NW – 750m
SD 7141 8898	Wall turns west	SD 7140 8954	North along the wall – 570m
SD 7140 8954	Sheep fold with gate	SD 7137 9003	North on moor – 600m
SD 7137 9003	Above quarry	SD 7122 9012	NW towards wall and fence – 180m
SD 7122 9012	Stream at bottom of tree avenue	SD 7143 9049	NNE down quarry, then on track, and then down tree avenue – 650m
SD 7143 9049	Steps to road	SD 7136 9064	Wooden bridge east, north along stream, stone bridge and stile back west, then west – 250m
SD 7136 9064	Left into lane	SD 7187 9066	East along main road – 600m
SD 7187 9066	Gate to rough lane – Walk 25	SD 7166 9093	NW on lane – 380m (Go past if not adding Walk 25)
SD 7166 9093	Car park, A684	SD 6945 9122	West on lane – 2.5km

Benchmark summary for Walk 24

BM No	Type of benchmark and location	Grid reference
1	Rivet – On rock, 17.7m south of south side of A684. (Opposite west end of car park.)	SD 6937 9121

Walk 25. East Baugh Fell

Start:	Car park, A684 east of Sedbergh
Map reference:	SD 6938 9124
Distance:	9.0km (5.6 miles)
Total ascent:	590m (1940 ft) – average climbing gradient 1 in 7
Estimated time:	3.5 hours
Walk grading:	Moderate to strenuous
OS map:	Landranger 98

Walk summary

The outward route is via Garside Foot and the Ringing Keld Gutter. Return is a steep descent down the open-access moor, joining the lane back to Garside Foot at Bellow End. It's likely to be wet, and is not recommended when there is lying snow. For fit walkers, it might be paired on the same day with Walk 24 to Ayr Gill Pike, doing Walk 24 first and tagging on this Walk 25, but reversed. For that eventuality, a reversed route table is included, from Bellow End, where Walk 24 intersects the route.

Parking and access

From Sedbergh, take the A684 east for 4km (2.5 miles). The car park is on the left, where the lane branches off for Garside Foot.

The walk

From the car park, take the lane that leaves NNE, downhill and across Clough River, with East Baugh Fell to the fore, and by the area of the old limekilns described in Walk 24. You'll see the single limekiln to the right of the lane, after you've crossed the river. Why so many kilns? The locals used them to produce large amounts of quicklime, spreading it on the moorland to sweeten the ground, reclaiming it for farming and grazing.

At the Tee-junction (SD 6999 9130), go left (NNW) and follow the lane to Garsdale Foot Farm. There, use the gate (SD 6991 9156) and take the stony moor track that winds up the hill (not the grassy track that follows the wall). The stony track goes NW and then ENE, and you leave it after 250m, just before a stream, to take another moor track (at SD 6997 9172) to the left (NNE).

This track quickly becomes vague amongst the reedy grass. Keep going north, with a fence in view to your right, and the track becomes clearer again. It eventually converges on the fence, to a corner and a gate at SD 7009 9202. Don't go through the gate; follow the north side of the fence, climbing along a vague grass moor path, until you reach the corner of a wall and the Ringing Keld Gutter at SD 7061 9212.

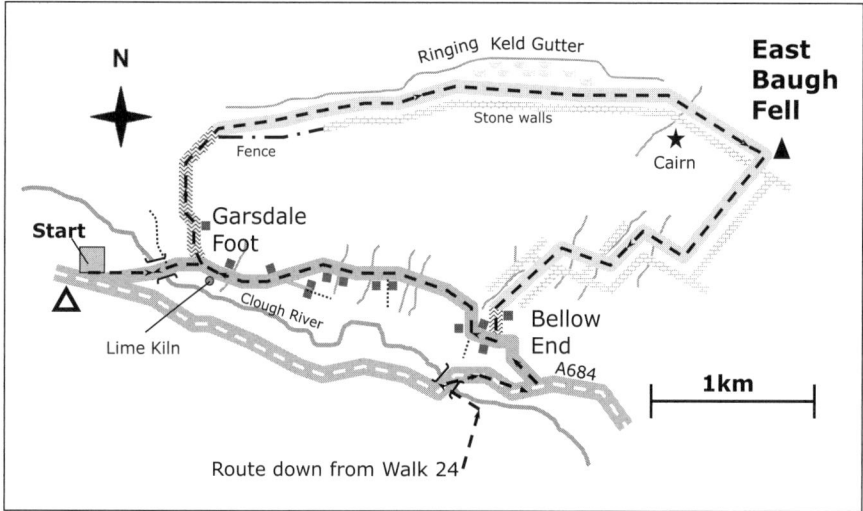

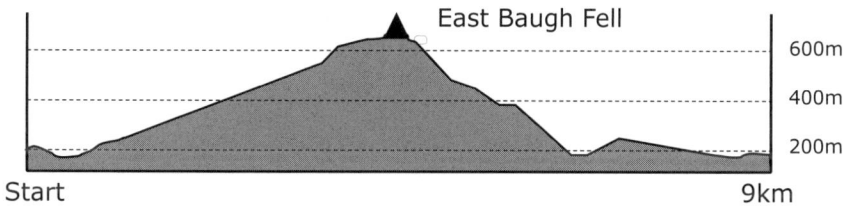

Route and height profile for East Baugh Fell

You now follow the north side of the wall for 2.6km, all the way to the pillar. As you gain height, on the skyline to the fore you'll see a large cairn looking out over the Garsdale valley – it's not the pillar!

For much of the time you can walk by the stream, but there are some very wet bits to negotiate. It would be difficult with lying snow – you need to see where you're putting your feet. The 'Keld' (meaning 'spring') tinkles and rings, but why is it called a 'gutter' rather than a 'gill' or a 'beck'? I can't imagine.

The pillar is actually on Knoutberry Haw, rather than East Baugh Fell itself. It's stone-built and covered in moss, but sound, with a stone plug. 'Baugh' means 'rounded' and 'Haw' means 'view', but 'Knoutberry' is a mystery. There's a 'knotberry' fruit, or a 'knout' is a 'whip'. That's as far as I can go. (I found six other 'Knoutberry' named hills in the region, so it obviously conveyed something to someone back in the dark ages.)

If you've just come from Aye Gill Pike, you'll find that the panorama has changed only slightly. The flush-bracket faces ESE, along the wall, so that SE, diagonally across that wall, is towards the namesake at Great Knoutberry Hill. With my monocular, I could make out the various features on the summit, but

Pillar details for East Baugh Fell	
Name:	East Baugh Fell
Position:	SD 73133 91938
Flush-Bracket No:	S5662
Height:	676m (2218 ft)
Built:	September 1949
Historic use:	Secondary
Current use:	None
Condition:	Good

East Baugh Fell pillar – Howgills behind

not the squat pillar. South, Whernside still dominates, the long SSW axis going away from you. The pillar blends with a wall. Behind its left (east) flank, Simon Fell is showing (so that Ingleborough is now hidden behind Whernside), and left of that, across the shallow Little Dale valley, Blea Moor is the low, rounded hill.

To the right of Whernside is Deepdale, with Crag Hill to the right of that (SSW). I could still see the pillar on its right-hand end. Then, close in the foreground, the long Aye Gill Pike is below you, across Garsdale. Its pillar is in line with the left end (Great Coum) of Crag Hill – I could just see its white top.

Right of Crag Hill is Barbondale, with the steep-sided Calf Top unmistakeable (SW). Right again and lower (WSW), overlooking Sedbergh, the 'Knotty' hillocks of Holm Knot are now visible, pillar on the left hillock. In line

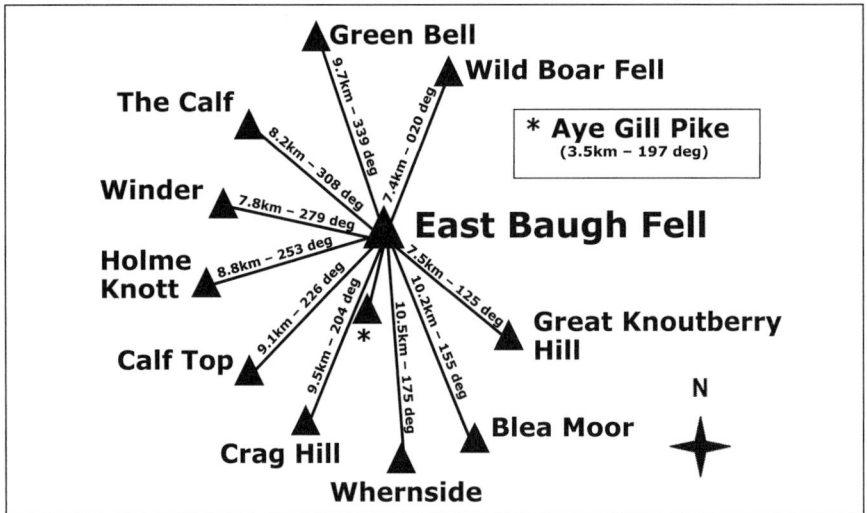

Nearby pillars in view from East Baugh Fell

with Sedbergh, only 500m from you, the large cairn is now very clear. All I know about it is that is was rebuilt to look nice for the millennium. North of Sedbergh, Winder overlooks the town (NNW, white pillar) and then The Calf (NW) is the highest point of the flat profile area of the Howgills. Green Bell is NNW – the high peak at the end of the range. Clearest of all, Wild Boar Fell is the flat-topped hill to the NNE. I could see the cairn with the pillar inside it. (From Aye Gill Pike, Wild Boar Fell was hidden behind the point you're standing on.) Finally, ENE, the distant rounded hill is Great Shunner Fell.

To head for home you need to climb over the wall by the pillar. The rules of open-access land allow it, but without causing damage. In fact, it's easy. Then you follow the NW side of the joining wall steeply down the hill. It's grass moor, with some rocky areas, and a splendid view into Garsdale and across to Ayr Gill Pike. At SD 7272 9138, turn right (WNW) along a new wall, to a point (SD 7243 9148) where it turns SSW.

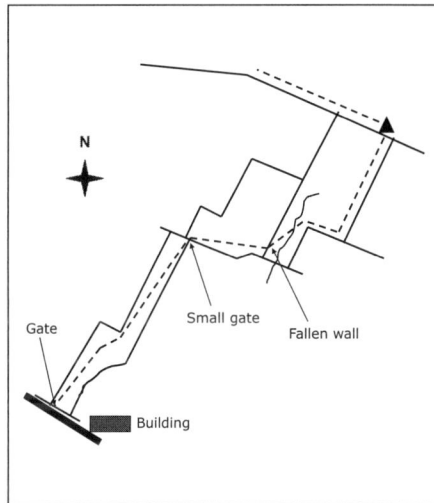
The way down around the walls

Go down the hill again, but veer more SW to cross the enclosure diagonally (jumping a stream gully) towards another wall junction in the SW corner (SD 7224 9133). There, in the NE-SW wall, you'll find a section that has fallen, so you can turn WNW again on the other side. There's a faint path, and it leads (with some wet bits) to another SW wall corner, with a small gate (SD 7201 9141). It's the limit of open-access land, but clearly walked.

Climb that gate, and go SSW down the narrow enclosure. There's a path of sorts, a more open area of gorse, and then the route narrows again at the bottom as you reach a gate on to a rough lane (SD 7163 9107). The area is private. But I could see no residents, and I can't imagine that there would be any problems. As before, a polite apology works miracles if anyone grumbles. Follow the lane south, down to rejoin Danny Brow Lane at the bottom. (It is this point that you would begin a reverse of this walk if you were combining it with Walk 24, having come down the steep slope from Ayr Gill Pike and along the main road.) The final leg is then 2.5km west along the lane, but this time I was not blessed by a red squirrel.

Route summary for Walk 25

Your present location	Your next objective	Waypoint at next objective	Directions and distance
Car park, A684 SD 6938 9124	Left (north) at Tee-junction	SD 6999 9130	ENE down the lane and across the river – 650m
SD 6999 9130	Gate to moor track	SD 6991 9156	NNW on lane to Garsdale Foot Farm – 300m
SD 6991 9156	Another track leaving NNE	SD 6997 9172	NW, NE and then ENE on track – 250m
SD 6997 9172	Fence corner, with gate	SD 7009 9202	North and then NE on moor track – 500m
SD 7009 9202	Wall, by Ringing Keld Gutter	SD 7061 9212	ENE on moor path along fence – 350m
SD 7061 9212	East Baugh Fell pillar	SD 7313 9194	Generally east, follow the wall and Gutter – 2.6km
SD 7313 9194	Corner of walls	SD 7272 9138	SSW along a wall, steeply down hill – 700m
SD 7272 9138	Wall turns SSW	SD 7243 9148	WNW along the wall to the corner – 300m
SD 7243 9148	Fallen wall	SD 7224 9133	SW to corner – 280m
SD 7224 9133	Wall gate	SD 7201 9141	WNW on faint path – 330m
SD 7201 9141	Drive to lane	SD 7163 9107	SW on moor path – 500m
SD 7163 9107	Lane	SD 7166 9093	South on drive – 160m
SD 7166 9093	Car park, A684	SD 6938 9124	West on lane – 2.5km

Reversed, if joining off Walk 24 from Ayr Gill Pike

Your present location	Your next objective	Waypoint at next objective	Directions and distance
Lane, gate SD 7166 9093	Gate to pasture	SD 7163 9107	North on rough drive – 160m
SD 7163 9107	Four walls junction, gate	SD 7201 9141	NE up moor path – 500m
SD 7201 9141	Fallen wall	SD 7224 9133	ESE on faint path – 330m
SD 7224 9133	Wall turns ESE	SD 7243 9148	NE to wall corner – 280m
SD 7243 9148	Corner of walls	SD 7272 9138	ESE along the wall to the corner – 300m
SD 7272 9138	East Baugh Fell pillar	SD 7313 9194	NNE along the wall, steeply up hill – 700m
SD 7313 9194	Wall, by Ringing Keld Gutter	SD 7061 9212	Generally west, follow the wall and gutter – 2.6km
SD 7061 9212	Fence corner, with gate	SD 7009 9202	WSW on moor path along fence – 350m
SD 7009 9202	Join another track	SD 6997 9172	South and then SW on moor track – 500m
SD 6997 9172	Gate to lane	SD 6991 9156	South on track – 250m
SD 6991 9156	Lane to south	SD 6999 9130	SSE to lane junction – 300m
SD 6999 9130	Car park	SD 6938 9124	WSW down the lane and across the river – 650m

Trigpointer's visit log

Pillars	Date	Benchmarks	Remarks
1 Haw Crag		Out of 9	
2 Sharp Haw		None	
3 Crookrise and Halton Height		Out of 12	
4 Beamsley Beacon		Out of 7	
5 Calton and The Weets		None	
6 North Nab and Simon's Seat		Out of 3	
7 Thorpe Fell and Langerton Hill		Out of 11	
8 New Pasture Edge		Out of 6	
9 Kilnsey Moor		Out of 13	
10 Newton Moor and Hunter Bark		Out of 6	
11 Langcliffe and Rye Loaf		Out of 9	
12 Smearsett Scar and Moughton		Only one	
13 Pen-y-ghent		Out of 2	
14 Sulber		One FBM	
15 Knowe Fell and Cow Close Fell		Out of 2	
16 Cave Hill and Low Green Field Lings		Out of 2	
17 Park Fell and Ingleborough		None	
18 Gragareth Fell and Tow Scar		Out of 6	
19 Blea Moor and Whernside		Out of 3	
20 Great Knoutberry Hill		Out of 10	
21 Crag Hill		Out of 3	
22 Holme Knott and Calf Top		One only	
23 Winder and The Calf		Out of 5	
24 Aye Gill Pike		One only	
25 East Baugh Fell		None	
Swinden site		None	
Parson's Pulpit site		None	

Also from Sigma Leisure:

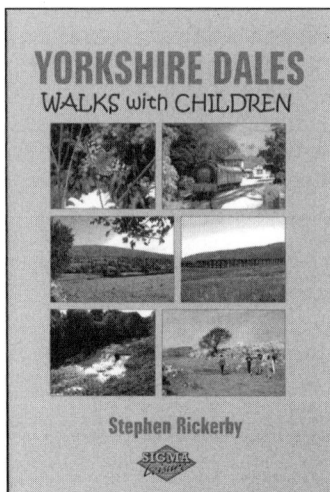

Yorkshire Dales Walks with Children
Stephen Rickerby

There are 21 circular walks — all less than 5 miles long across the Dales from Swaledale in the north to Bolton Abbey in the south, and from Dentdale in the west to Nidderdale in the east.

Directions are clear and easy to follow, and the facilities available, points of interest, and places to visit on each walk are listed. You can see at a glance if a particular walk is suitable for pushchairs and where refreshments and toilets are located. There are even suggestions for alternative entertainments if it rains — every parent's nightmare when a walk has been planned!

£8.95

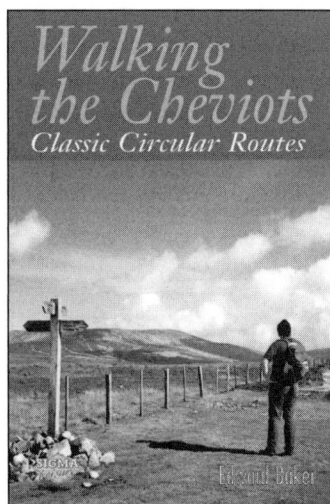

Walking the Cheviots Classic Circular Walks
Edward Baker

The walks in this book provide an excellent introduction to this lonely, wild countryside — a true wilderness area. Everyone is catered for — from weekend family groups to the experienced hill walker. Each route is full of interest, with details of the natural history, geology and archaeology of the area.

In the northern area of the Cheviots, five main valleys cut deeply into the heart of the range. These provide quick and easy access to the wild upland regions. The southern area is explored with walks radiating from the Coquet Valley. These introduce you to a gentler terrain. Many of the walks follow old drove roads, smuggling routes and Roman roads which cross the hills and have been used for centuries.

£9.99